Off Key

Off Key

When Film and Music Won't Work Together

KAY DICKINSON

OXFORD

UNIVERSITY PRESS

2008

OXFORD
UNIVERSITY PRESS

Oxford University Press, Inc., publishes works that further
Oxford University's objective of excellence
in research, scholarship, and education.

Oxford   New York
Auckland   Cape Town   Dar es Salaam   Hong Kong   Karachi
Kuala Lumpur   Madrid   Melbourne   Mexico City   Nairobi
New Delhi   Shanghai   Taipei   Toronto

With offices in
Argentina   Austria   Brazil   Chile   Czech Republic   France   Greece
Guatemala   Hungary   Italy   Japan   Poland   Portugal   Singapore
South Korea   Switzerland   Thailand   Turkey   Ukraine   Vietnam

Published by Oxford University Press, Inc.
198 Madison Avenue, New York, New York 10016

www.oup.com

Oxford is a registered trademark of Oxford University Press

Publication of this book was supported by the Gustave Reese Publication
Endowment Fund of the American Musicological Society.

Library of Congress Cataloging-in-Publication Data
Dickinson, Kay, 1972–
Off key : when film and music won't work together / Kay Dickinson.
    p.   cm.
Includes bibliographical references and index.
ISBN 978-0-19-532663-5; 978-0-19-532664-2 (pbk.)
1. Motion pictures and music.   2. Motion picture music—History and
criticism.   3. Culture in motion pictures.   I. Title.
ML2075.D59 2008
781.5'42—dc22   2007024845

1   3   5   7   9   8   6   4   2

Printed in the United States of America
on acid-free paper

This book is dedicated to all the workers who have contributed to it,
but whose names I do not know.

Acknowledgments

One of the most torturous paradoxes of writing a critique of the inequality of recent labor relations is that it is nearly impossible, once such a book is completed, to acknowledge everyone who has contributed it—particularly those involved in its physical production as printed, bound paper. The following acknowledgments are frustratingly deficient, but still heartfelt.

My first debt goes to everyone at Oxford University Press, particularly Norm Hirschy, whose indefatigable spirit, patience, humor, trust, and good judgment have been invaluable since first we began corresponding. It would be hard to imagine a more perfect commissioning editor. I would also like to express my appreciation to the various readers contracted to comment upon this book—Tim Anderson, Andrew Blake, Corey Creekmur, Jamie Sexton, and Carol Vernallis—whose suggestions I hope I have honored.

A veritable crowd of people were imposed upon to read this project before its submission. Lee Grieveson, as ever, has remained both a great friend and an engaged, astute commentator on my ideas—my often unfathomable ways of structuring and clarifying them, in particular. Glyn Davis lent a welcome fastidiousness to the preparation of this manuscript, despite having one of his own to complete by a similar deadline to my own. Janet Harbord's rigorous and inquisitive thinking has been an inspiration throughout, and I am much obliged to her for encouraging me to not hurry onward, but to stop and contemplate certain larger questions. Rachel Moore intervened at a crucial stage and gave me the confidence to head directly to the heart of the matter, although whether I have accomplished this with the wit and grace of her writing is another matter. Raiford Guins proved a careful reader whom I have to thank for leaving no stone unturned. Amelie Hastie assisted in the early stages, offering erudite advice and much-valued belief in my arguments. More important, all of these people have been extraordinary company during the writing process; they have been generous, supportive, and a great diversion, the kind that leads a project onward in surprising directions rather than leaving it temporarily by the wayside.

The following individuals have been directly influential and helpful in how I have formulated my ideas, and a good number of them have offered extremely constructive guidance on small snippets of the book: Paul Antick, Chris Berry, Mark Betz, Iman Hamam, Dave Hesmondhalgh, Michael Lawrence (thanks too for an imaginative index), Jo Littler, Anna Lora, Aoife Mac Namara, Suhail Malik, Angela McRobbie, Andy Medhurst, Laura Mulvey, Golda Quimwinner, Adrian Rifkin, David Rodowick, Jeffrey Sconce, and Leon Wainwright. Among this group, there are many colleagues, past and present. *Off Key*'s production has spanned three different academic posts, at Middlesex University, King's College, and Goldsmiths College (both in the University of London). At moments when I have felt utterly captive to the isolating and disruptive tides of current labor structures, the lecturers and students of these institutions have reminded me how precious, worthwhile, and fruitfully challenging academic work can be and how lucky I am to have such a job. The same goes for the various research groups that invited me to discuss my ideas with them at the Universities of Glasgow, Aberystwyth, and London (University College and the Institute of Education), as well as the staff of the British Film Institute library, who provided such a hospitable space in which to study.

As is typical nowadays, my work on this venture has spilled over into my home life. I cannot register my gratitude or apologize enough to Abdulhadi Ayyad, who frequently took second place to my research, providing insight, reassurance, friendship, and numerous especially creative cups of tea. My parents, Christine and Bill Dickinson, have provided me with the backbone to work under pressure and the compulsion to politicize culture. In appreciation of their immeasurable helpfulness, I would like to promise my father that I will never wheedle proofreading out of him on holiday again, although I am sure he is as doubtful of this declaration as I ultimately am.

Last, I would like to thank Michele Occelli, Rafa Perez Evans, and Jaime Gil Larios for the parts they played in creating this book's cover art and for their companionship during my journey away from the manuscript, exquisitely maintaining all of its most important convictions and expanding them outward.

Earlier versions of chapters 4 and 5 can be found in the following articles, and I am obliged to those involved for permitting me to republish sections here:

"Troubling Synthesis: The Horrific Sights and Incompatible Sounds of 'Video Nasties.'" In *Sleaze Artists: Cinema at the Margins of Taste, Style and Politics,* ed. Jeffrey Sconce (167–188). Durham, N.C.: Duke University Press, 2008.

"The Limits of Celebrity 'Multi-Tasking': Pop Stars Who Can't Act." *Mediactive* 2 (January 2004): 74–85.

Contents

Illustrations

Frontispiece: Vintage synthesizer. Copyright © Rafael Perez Evans.

Overture: Elvis Presley as Johnny in *Harum Scarum* (Gene Nelson, 1965). Copyright © MGM Pictures.

Chapter 1: Elvis Presley as Vince in *Jailhouse Rock* (Richard Thorpe, 1957). Copyright © MGM Pictures.

Chapter 2: Mamie Van Doren as Penny in *Untamed Youth* (Howard W. Koch, 1957). Copyright © A Devonshire Pictures Production for Warner Brothers.

Chapter 3: Ringo Starr as the pope in *Lisztomania* (Ken Russell, 1975). Copyright © Warner Brothers.

Chapter 4: *Inferno* (Dario Argento, 1980). Copyright © Produzione Intersound S.p.a.

Chapter 5: Madonna as Amber in *Swept Away* (Guy Ritchie, 2002). Copyright © Columbia Pictures.

Conclusion: Fats Domino in *The Girl Can't Help It* (Frank Tashlin, 1956). Copyright © Twentieth Century Fox.

Off Key

An Overture

Harum Scarum (Gene Nelson, 1965) is widely damned as the worst movie in which Elvis Presley ever starred.[1] There are no prizes for deducing that this is a step eastward for the Presley franchise, the "Arabian" take being one of the few factors that distinguish the movie from the other formula quickies he completed during his MGM contract.[2] Presley plays a successful screen actor, Johnny Tyronne, who is kidnapped by a band of Middle Eastern assassins. Awed by his latest picture (in which Tyronne karate chops a leopard) and unable to distinguish between cinematic fantasy and reality, they press-gang him into their plot to murder King Toranshah of Lunacan (Philip Reed), the ruler of a country effectively cut off from "civilization." Naturally, thanks to Tyronne, the kindly monarch escapes his fate and we learn that the whole dastardly connivance has been masterminded by the king's younger brother, Prince Dragna (Michael Ansara), and Sinan (Theo Marcuse), lord of the assassins, who are both eager to get their hands on Lunacan's oil reserves. Every twist of the plot turns upon a worn-out cliché of the Arab world, be it benign or more stinging, including references to ongoing slavery, lawless brigands, greed, and corruption when it comes to vying for American foreign aid. Along the way, Presley chips in at least one song every ten minutes to this bundle of stereotypes through gimmicky numbers like "Go East, Young Man," "Harem Holiday," "Desert Serenade," "Mirage," and "Kismet," songs that, perhaps rather distressingly to many viewers, fit the narrative more than the star of the vehicle himself.

What would it mean to pick up this piece of cinematic detritus, washed ashore in the lands of critical dismissal, and to get to know it for reasons other than to pass judgment upon it once more, either positive or negative? This is one of the questions that launches *Off Key*. Throughout this book, material like *Harum Scarum* will allow me to assert that there is a strong but underresearched connection between the public treatment of media industry synergies that run aground and much broader anxieties about how we have earned our livings over the past fifty or so years. The more such "failures" are examined, the more what "doesn't work" on the aesthetic level appears to be intimately related to the organizational and semantic systems of *work itself*. By this, I mean not only that we should interrogate the labor expended on maintaining horizontal integration across entertainment industries like music and cinema, not only that leisure commodities might somehow speak to and of greater fractures in how more everyday employment functions, but also that the *work* of the media, in all sorts of senses, should feature more prominently in academic inquiry. Even the briefest inspection of *Harum Scarum* alerts us to how these issues interlock. And Presley will stage numerous comebacks in the following chapters, where more prolonged debates about the historical and political consequences of film and music "not working" together are set in motion.

Presley's later movies are often summarily discredited, mocked, or, more often, shrugged off melancholically as products redolent of his exploitation and willful distraction. From the very outset, the language of work, its destructiveness and its avoidance, bubble through the popular discourse. Despite being among MGM's highest paid and most successful performers at one point (although his appeal was on the decline by *Harum Scarum*'s release), regardless of the evident financial rewards of his labor, Presley is rarely thought of as a Hollywood icon.[3] What marks out this detachment of music and film cultures, doubtless founded on a mutual distrust of and unfamiliarity with the work that could and "should" be achieved in either sector?

Considering how much cash the Presley fans were laying out for movies like *Viva Las Vegas* (George Sidney, 1964) throughout the 1960s, and bearing in mind MGM's reputation as a "prestige" picture studio, it is initially quite startling to witness how cheap and shoddy this series of films was and how geared production was toward profit rather than quality. The producer Sam Katzman was hired for *Harum Scarum*'s fleeting shoot (a mere fifteen days) because, in the eyes of Presley's manager, "Colonel" Tom Parker, Katzman's notorious status as the "King of Exploitation" meant that net profits would be augmented if Presley simply churned out a greater quantity of movies per year. In their biography of the relationship between Presley and Parker, Dirk Vellenga and Mick Farren convey the lack of regard for Presley's audiences by those compiling his image:

> An MGM employee was moved to remark that the Elvis movies didn't even need titles. "They could be numbered. They'd still sell." For a while it looked as though the Colonel's crudity and cheapness were actually what was needed. The Elvis fans were proving themselves to be completely indiscriminating.[4]

This seemingly being the case (with all involved happy not to up the ante), *Harum Scarum*'s sets were recycled from Cecil B. DeMille's *The King of Kings* (1927), while the mothball-reeking costumes had seen better days on the cast of *Kismet* (William Dieterle, 1944). The quality of "the film itself" appears to have assumed a secondary position in the greater plot to enlarge the range of Presley commodities.

Understanding the decisions behind this corner cutting is reliant upon us weighing up the contemporary attitudes of and dealings between the film and music industries. Although everyone concerned happily profited from the movies and their soundtracks, minimal investments were made, especially at the level of human labor, and one has to look to labor history, I contend, in order to grasp why.[5] Might the shocking incoherence of the movie derive not only from the lack of effort in smoothing its rough edges, but also from the incompatible occupational traditions that *Harum Scarum* awkwardly draws together and fails to coalesce? How were the two sectors *working* at that particular moment? Can we comprehend the film more fully if we relate it to certain seismic historical shifts? The material in which *Off Key* involves itself, including *Harum Scarum,* all benefit, I feel, from an inscription within "post-Fordist" rubrics. Briefly stated, "post-Fordism" is a mode of production that favors increased decentralization and fragmentation; it took hold on the media businesses fairly early on and directly impacted upon how *Harum Scarum* was assembled, most centrally in that it stars a musical celebrity, rather than a trained actor. This was not, strictly speaking, an unheard-of proposition in the history of entertainment, nor did "post-Fordism," as will become clear, amount to a wholly radical break from past traditions (which cannot themselves be argued to have provided unanimously consistent end products). However, "post-Fordism" did instigate dramatic and pervasive changes in how, where, and when people worked, reorganizing the very structures of employment itself. But more of this in the chapters to come.

In the meantime, it is crucial to establish what we might gain by locating *Harum Scarum*'s icon more solidly within the paradigms of labor history. Stars often act as politically crucial bridges which allow greater traffic between opposing public-sphere actions, concepts, and ideals.[6] In Presley's case, critics frequently credit his meteoric rise to his exemplification of a multifarious and warring set of notions of "American-ness."[7] What I wonder at this point is whether we might look upon some of these classic Presley actions and attributes with more of an eye to labor stratification.

Uppermost in Presley's most controversial negotiations was his engagement with "race," a fraught and violent social formation in America prior to civil rights legislation—and after—and one that has everything to do with a legacy of labor divisions derived from slavery. "Race" has enabled a classification of people into "appropriate" working corpuses. In many ways, segregation also culturally paralyzed a broader movement for collectivity among the disenfranchised poor of America, many of whom were being exploited through almost identical capitalist mechanisms. Presley is renowned for incorporating into his musical style not just country and bluegrass, but also more distinctly African American idioms (rock 'n' roll, gospel, and blues in particular); he *worked* across the social divide. Like his music, Presley's appearance was hybrid (although "essentially" "white"): his hip clothes, his dyed black hairstyle that resembled the "process" used for straightening African hair, and his provocative dance moves were all coded, through an often racist and "primitivizing" understanding of sexual charge, as displaying an allegiance to African American fashions. In a time that witnessed an apartheid of even the record charts, this was a vital move toward an integration of sorts, although its politics of appropriation and the commercial gains that followed are not to everyone's tastes or ethics and, for many, are still distinctly contentious.[8] For one, developing the musical style of rock 'n' roll had taken untold African-American time and this effort was now, for many, being buried by the explosive "newness" of stars like Presley to the white mainstream.

Presley's name, then, was made through seemingly groundbreaking and largely flattering requisitions of nonwhite gestures. By contrast, "the worst ever Elvis movie" reveals an arbitration of cultural difference that smacks of a decidedly different flavor. While Presley's character is never outwardly prejudiced toward the Arabs he meets during his adventures, and he does keenly adopt their dress, these interactions are film industry fantasies rather than politically charged communions. They do not really hint at a proximity of labor practices nor seek to inspire class-related solidarity and empathy. If anything, they indulge the very forms of Orientalism that have helped to justify colonial expansion and its concomitant exploitation of resources and workers. Might this significant about-face in a central popular figure's enactment of cultural exchange, understanding, and employment categorization reveal much to us about why *Harum Scarum* is so unpopular? As Allison Graham remarks in *Framing the South: Hollywood, Television, and Race during the Civil Rights Struggle* in relation to his greater body of later films:

> With Elvis's potentially disruptive racial ambiguity undercut and patronized by his narrative alliances with a series of Mexican, Chinese and Polynesian [and, in this movie, Arab] children, Hollywood showcased the castration of the redneck in widescreen Technicolor. Cut loose visually from social reality, set adrift into surreal landscapes of back-projected, perpetually sunny resorts, Elvis became, in effect, an endlessly replicable logo for the commercialization of the exotic.[9]

Earlier, the southern-ness to which Graham refers had worked to the advantage of Presley's career. Born into a much maligned and socially deprived section of society, his heritage conveniently adhered certain long-standing stereotypes of the southerner (especially those of "the rebel") to both the well-loved ideal of "the poor boy made good in the land of opportunity" and the increasingly attractive misfit figure of "the teenager" (interestingly, Presley greatly admired James Dean) and its less preferred variant, "the delinquent." All of these are categories laid out by greater historical patterns of working. His 1950s cinematic oeuvre, particularly films like *Jailhouse Rock* (Richard Thorpe, 1957) and *King Creole* (Michael Curtiz, 1958), compress many of these archetypes into the roles Presley plays, binding rock 'n' roll and blues soundtracks with stories of the redemption and reeducation of the wayward southerner who has found himself circumstantially on the wrong side of the justice system. At this moment in time, Presley's unions of film and music semantics and their connotations within patterns of labor were almost perfectly in tune.

The same cannot be said of *Harum Scarum,* where even his songs consistently eschew the redolence of the rock 'n' roll genre. Instead, "Desert Serenade," "Go East, Young Man," "Mirage," "Kismet," "Golden Coins," and "Paradise" follow the conventions of softer crooner ballads, complete with constrained vocal delivery and luxurious orchestration (atypical of rock 'n' roll) that melts effortlessly into the unchallengingly Hollywood-esque soundtrack. If anything, the musical influences, as is common of mid-twentieth-century balladeering, recall exoticism through Spanish, Latin American, or even Hawaiian references, rather than the worker rhythms and the rebellions against them to be found in earlier rock 'n' roll. Even the jaunty, more rock 'n' roll shuffle rhythms of "Harem Holiday" are offset by brassy, affluent, big band arrangements and lyrics that speak more of vacationing than blue-collar toil. Out of context, "Shake That Tambourine" and "Hey Little Girl" bare the teleological constraints, linguistic obsessions with dance, and instrumental signifiers of rock 'n' roll, but they are flung far from their homelands by the movie, which situates the former amid women dancing in an Arabian souq and the latter as a tribute to a literal "little girl" (Vicki Malkin) of "Arab" descent. The monetary leisure aspirations of Las Vegas rather than the manual labor overtones of the rural South are the true domains of such numbers, and a chasm opens up between the earlier oeuvre and this fare. Las Vegas, it must be mentioned, is where the film deposits us at its denouement. Here, the Arab "good guys" celebrate their newfound openness to intercontinental travel with some mild (un-Islamic) gambling and a Johnny Tyronne concert. Resolution is attained according, most pointedly, to the labor of leisure. An historical analysis of how such sectors of employment and commodification sit within "post-Fordist" economic priorities occupies the next chapter much more thoroughly.

For the moment, though, what we need to think about is how the clash between earlier and later Elvises might be illuminated by a greater concentration on the *ethics* that encircle labor. Whether or not Presley was ever truly an "outlaw" is a moot point,[10] but what is significant are the steps that were taken to dampen these associations as the Presley management attempted to reach a broader audience later on. Here, the economies of the entertainment industries and their harsh inscriptions of their employees' personas come to the fore. Strategies to revamp Presley included not only his enlistment in the U.S. Army and the subsequent shearing of his all-important locks, but also the selection of very specific film roles upon his return from military duty. Just as the literal substitution of Presley's career from renegade singer to soldier points out how crucial the moral integrity of labor can be to consumers, so too does his reconfiguration within the work of entertainment. Even *Harum Scarum*'s plot provides examples and allegories of many of these shifts in "what Elvis means":

Johnny Tyronne is not the struggling loner of yesteryear, he is a well-known screen actor; the theme of rising up against the odds is no longer a desirable or suitable trajectory with which to associate Presley. Although there is much to suggest that Presley's shift from rebel to all-around entertainer was partially of his own design, for those who had fallen for the raucous, hell-raising rock 'n' roller, and still continue to do so, this metamorphosis was tantamount to consciously "selling out." In this condemnation, Presley is converted from worker (or, rather, rebel-as-reworker-of-work) to commodity.

Luckily for his fans, Presley can be rescued from this doomed state by yet another archetypal social myth: the innocent exploited by the system. The fable runs as follows: Elvis, trapped in the clutches of his Svengali manager ("domesticated,"[11] as Allison Graham says, bringing a conspicuously gendered dimension to the transition), was corralled into a torrent of low-grade movies in which his talent and originality were grossly undermined in the scramble for a fast buck in a new marketplace: the cinema. Within this narrative, Presley's 1950s music rises to an almost sacrosanct standing, as if his climb to fame were not partially the result, from the outset, of Sun Records' Sam Phillips's opportunistic search for a profitable white musician who could deliver rock 'n' roll to a greater and richer number of consumers. It is also doubtful that this genre alone would have served him that well during the 1960s; its popularity had been superseded by an appreciation of "poppier" musical styles and its reputation tainted by the misdemeanors of key performers like Chuck Berry and Jerry Lee Lewis.[12]

Nonetheless, and regardless of whether or not Presley's "authentic" connection to rock could have been maintained, a powerful tragedy emerged, accelerated latterly by Presley's premature death. This tragedy is relevant to any of us who notice a patent rift between "who we are" (here symbolized by Presley's musical activities) and what we are forced to do by greater social and economic forces in order to make a living. Cinema, the people who brought Presley to Hollywood, and the rather tame soundtracks that became the bulk of his musical output during this period are all classified as the crass, heartless machinery that crushed raw talent. At times like these, when we shift our attention away from a narrower concern with the formal components of music on screen, of what works in a purely aesthetic sense, a more complex perspective on the mythic function of entertainment culture emerges. In order for us to invest in a more noble fable—and the word "invest" is apt here, because we still continue to purchase from the Presley franchise when we critique his movies—films like *Harum Scarum* must be willfully cast aside by all but the die-hard fanatics who cannot help but love Presley in his entirety.

These negotiations make "failures" worth studying, particularly through the lens of labor relations and, in these cases, with an eye to how work is ordered (or disordered) when entertainment industries hook up. For those wishing to involve themselves in this music-versus-film equation, Presley's complicity in his "exploitation," his dreams of becoming an all-around entertainer, and his tendency to sign Parker's contracts without even reading them must shrink to one side, while his increasing depression, Parker's mercantile voraciousness, and Presley's eventual triumphant return to live performance have to be positioned in the limelight.[13] Presley had previously rebelled against the system as both a disgruntled, white, working-class hero and as a figure refusing to stay within the barriers that enforce a segregated and unjust economy. Consequently, he can only maintain continuity with this status if the cruel, exploitative, and overpowering forces of capitalist productivity are foregrounded.

This stance is easily bolstered by actually watching *Harum Scarum*. While Presley fleshes out the character in a pleasant enough manner, it is not difficult to ascertain his dissatisfaction with the film if one so desires: the electricity of the earlier cinema, stage, and television appearances is all but gone. He almost seems to be yawning through his performance, the lip-synching is often ill matched, and, retrospectively, his blankness can be interpreted as the effect of the drugs he may have been taking to numb his discontent with his Hollywood contract. The tracks he sings are much less memorable than his greatest hits and, as a string of mid-tempo airs and soothing ballads, they are squeezed dry, as has been observed, of the urgency and the generic markers of previously marginalized musical forms that distinguish the Presley canon. There is little to tie him, but for his distinct voice, to his earlier repertoire.

Acknowledging that *Harum Scarum* doesn't work, then, becomes a powerful indicator of cultural capital and all of the social prestige encapsulated within it. Maligned film-music collaborations demand our scholarship, I argue throughout *Off Key*, because certain kinds of fans (or purchasers of the fruits of this labor) are placed lower down the pecking order of who "understands" art "properly." What all these viewing relationships come to represent are the outcomes of an intriguing set of social relationships concerning performance labor and its consumption. Presley is frequently interpreted as being "imprisoned" within certain films by the demands of his audiences. Once, he was incarcerated because his modes of work were considered illegitimate; in *Harum Scarum,* he is hostage to debilitating consumer demand. More "serious" and well-acted movies, such as *Flaming Star* (Don Siegel, 1960), did not fair so well at the box office, prompting Presley's inevitable casting in more straightforward "nice guy" roles, where he sings back-to-back musical numbers throughout a rather predicable plot. Everything that Presley had stood for as a visual icon was blurred by a more vigorous plan to portray him as a broadly acceptable, physically attractive pin-up. Now, he was romantic, affable, and hardly threatening;

he could, at last, be comfortably filmed below the waist. The cutting edge that he once represented to so many had been dulled into a repeatable formula. The question of Presley's "decline" is thus laced with politically determined preferences and prejudices. How did the "purer," earlier Presley differ from this mid-1960s one, and what roles do the industries of music and cinema assume in this journey of clumsy semantics, intolerances, and ensuing cultural penalties? Unraveling these particular networks of power, appeal, and value is one of the core concerns of *Off Key*.

While *Harum Scarum*'s incarnation of Presley might, arguably, have been acceptable to a teen drive-in audience, it was not good enough for those deeming themselves to be more reflective or daring guardians of his inheritance. Respected Presley biographer and cultural critic Peter Guralnick's analysis of the later Elvis movies betrays a common perspective on this development:

> The character that Elvis played [post-army] was at odds not just with the characters that he had played in all of his pre-army films but with the very image of rebellion that had always defined him. Far from being an outcast, this Elvis Presley was safe, "social," and cheerfully domesticated, a conventionally bland Hollywood stick figure.[14]

Once more, the term "domesticated" is employed, as if to negatively insinuate a feminization of Presley by a movie industry catering, perhaps for the most part, to an audience of young women and future workers within the home, who longed to gaze lovingly upon him from the safety of their cinema seats. Here, incompatible notions of distance and immediacy mark out various dimensions of social status and work.

Once an innovator, a resister against the stratifications of American labor, he appears to more "discerning" audiences to be stuck in an ill-placed rut, but a rut whose archaeology discloses layer upon layer of valuable information about the world in which we live: how we erect and maintain social barriers according to foreign-ness, "race," rebellion, class, working practices, contemporaneousness, age, and gender, to name but a few categories brought up by this particular example. The wariness of many viewers/listeners and critics to thrust their hands into what they seem to distinguish as the grime of *Harum Scarum* means that the analytical treasures that lie beneath this top soil or even on its very surface are often left unexamined. This kind of grubbing around and unearthing of more weighty political debates is the central objective of *Off Key*, a book exhilarated, rather than discouraged, by untidy surfaces.

All the slip-ups and disappointments detectable in *Harum Scarum*—ones that could have easily been remedied in production—seem to ooze from a disregard for Presley's *potential* within so many quarters of the entertainment industries. Hierarchies of appreciation according to these "errors" have been established and, as my following chapters contend, the organization of taste and interpretation is an exceedingly potent means of regulating social power. What we are really confronting here is a disjunction that implicates cinema within a brawl over what people might contribute to and draw from the Presley legend. The broader issues of control and regulation that arise from this paradigm are something which I address at greater length as the book unfolds. I have only just begun in this examination of *Harum Scarum*'s working conditions to unpack their relation to the governance of raced and gendered labor and to look at the critical standardization and solidification of the film's significance.

For all of Presley's verve and dynamism as a musician, he struggles to move through this tacky potboiler without becoming mired in a set of cinematic meanings that seem incongruous to the image of our rock 'n' roll hero. The energy and potential productivity of the star is blocked; his work as an entertainer is frustrated. The Presley persona is constituted of a sticky and ill-bonded mixture of music and film at this point in his career, yet an analysis of its composition reveals traces of some particularly forceful social myths that are well worth our examination.[15] If we poke around in this aesthetic jumble, we find all number of pressing dramas taking place within—ones that animatedly debate the way that work embodies and reflects upon significant forms of social organization and the extent to which our command over personal labor is so readily and politically compromised.

◆ 1 ◆

The Status and the Potential
of Film-Music That "Doesn't Work"

Film and music lovers alike cherish those sublime moments when the two art forms commune together so empathetically that each draws out only the best from its partner. On occasion, these media appear almost on the brink of defying their formal boundaries—as "film," as "music"—so perfectly are they in tune with each other's registers. At other times, these raw, previously unrelated elements seem to conjure an alchemical transformation, and a fresh approach to understanding materializes, one that could never have been imagined beforehand. These bonds between film and music are often wrought with such precision that the extrication of any element would amount to an eerie incompleteness for many a viewer/listener. Fans fill up their own private reservoirs with favorite examples of music on screen, be they scores (of whatever musical genre), song and dance numbers, biographical treatments (factual or fictional), pop videos, diegetic characterizations brought to life on screen by musicians, particularly "filmic" features within a recording star's public persona or body of musical output, or musical performances pulled off with aplomb by entertainers better known for their acting. Most books on music and cinema also draw enthusiastically upon these resources. But these exemplary cases, as was evident from the *Harum Scarum* discussion, are not what *Off Key* is about.

There is also a host of similarly breathtaking dialectical plays between the two forms within which the intentional grinding of "inappropriate" music against film images has been an ongoing concern. In these, the supposed unity of music and cinema is unfurled, and we are skillfully asked whether the two media could ever stand in a vacuum ("the music," "the film"). All the while, the collaboration makes explicit the elaborate means by which such mass (re)produced commodities relate with each other and with us, their consumers. Well-known films from *Scorpio Rising* (Kenneth Anger, 1964) to *Goodfellas* (Martin Scorsese, 1990) deliberately and successfully stretch the paradigms of what can make sense; the sparring that they enact is purposefully exploited for its transformative potential. But *Harum Scarum* and its relatives cannot be thought to bear these sentiments either.

Littering the path to perfection and expunged from our canons and "best of" lists are numerous situations where music and cinema misunderstand or embarrass each other, seem utterly clueless about each other's intentions, with one insensitively trampling upon the messages the other has so meticulously tried to articulate. This is the film-music example that "doesn't work," and it may do so according to either aesthetic or ethical sociocultural prerequisites (if the two can be disconnected), as *Harum Scarum* demonstrates.

Granted, such cases might also have been resuscitated in the meantime (even produced there and then) as camp, whose aura offers us an alternative and often politicized critique of conventional organizations of what is valuable. On many occasions, camp's pleasures do overlap with the aims of my research, but I want to stop short of its desire to recast, validate, and enjoy. The potency of this suspension, my examination of *Harum Scarum* postulated, often lies in the breathing space it provides for in-depth analyses of how formal inconsistencies overlap with incompatibilities in the techniques by which labor is carried out in both media production and the wider social context. Camp is regularly used as a *strategy* against some of the resulting injustices that are the more central focus of this book: the apparatuses of critique and their foundations in cultures of work, ones that often successfully prohibit recuperation according to the somewhat exclusive requirements of camp.

None of these notions of competence can truly be understood unless we also peer closely at their techniques of gatekeeping. To this end, I do not make judgments, like camp does, about whether my chosen examples are successes or failures. Each case study is repositioned in front of its own dominant, largely contemporary jury, and I shall pay particular attention to the critical effort—from the trade and consumer presses to audience ratings and censorship procedures—that went into building its gallows. The machinations of public discourse, rather than the veracity of these rulings, are what interest me, along with the pure *extent* of producers', critics', and everyday consumers of entertainment's vulturine desires to discredit these "mistakes." For this reason, I privilege readings of criticism rather than of media examples on many occasions throughout this book. Such responses present a detailed picture of why our investments in entertainment, synergy, work, and aesthetic value (to name but a few significant systems) exist in their current formations. Nor have I forged this correspondence alone; the word "work," along with various other employment-related concepts, pops up with unstinting regularity, as my case-study chapters will expose, in the vocabulary of criticism leveled against movies like *Harum Scarum*. The attacks on film-music collaborations that "don't work" open out onto something bigger, I contend: a pervasive anxiety about the very activities that earn us our livelihoods and, often, our senses of duty and its fulfillment.

What I aim to establish in this chapter is that there is a set of rules in place that arbitrates against and reprimands certain meetings of film and music (proto-camp or otherwise) and that is firmly located in particular traditions of production and consumption. For me, these judgments frequently betray nostalgia for an attitude toward work that has, in many instances, been overtaken by another: something that is variously dubbed "post-Fordism" and "post-industrialism," although both terms bear slightly different connotations. I shall define these concepts, or historical periodizations, in order to stress how the alteration of working methods they prescribe not only regularly brings into being the kinds of "mistakes" that *Harum Scarum* exemplifies, but can also provoke the apprehensions that drive the criticism of film-music alliances that "don't work." "Failures," I conclude, require our attention because they inform us of modes of working that encroach upon our everyday lives in countless ways. If we look at "what doesn't work" from a particular vantage point, its inability to do so can also contain answers about how to realign labor in a more just and egalitarian manner. If "mismatches" like this are so potent, then why, one might wonder, have they rarely been the subject of sustained academic study?

The Allure of Perfection and the Price We Pay for It

Simply put, smart, scintillating, involving, and aesthetically intoxicating film-music alignments are absolutely gripping. This is why they usually sell better than the kinds of vehicles that preoccupy me. It is also why scholars have been more attracted to success stories: how and why do competent film-music concordances captivate us so, they ask.

There is a multitude of persuasive answers to this. Jeff Smith's *The Sounds of Commerce: Marketing Popular Film Music,* for instance, investigates the entertainment industry synergies in order to find out how they bear such fruit.[1] Claudia Gorbman's *Unheard Melodies: Narrative Film Music* delves into the psychoanalytic propositions of figures like Guy Rosolato and Didier Anzieu and, from them, constructs an understanding of music whereby the soundtrack both taps into primal desires and smoothes over the cracks left by the chaotic modes of film assembly.[2]

Then there is the constantly regenerating and boisterous lineage of film-music experts who are dedicated to searching out, from a more practical scorer's perspective, how praiseworthy artistic accomplishment might be achieved. As these books are in the majority, the standards they set are deeply influential and well worth prolonged examination. In them, we repeatedly hear that the purpose of the soundtrack is "to help realize the meaning of a film,"[3] to "make potent through music the film's dramatic and emotional value"[4]; its duty is to "support,"[5] "accentuate,"[6] to be "auxiliary to the visual image."[7] These attitudes cultivate and are nurtured by the suggestion that not only is music a mere accompaniment to cinema, but its producers should undertake a distinctly submissive type of employment. Both readings reposition film-music within the politics of labor and need to be dissected if we are to understand what "doesn't work," according to such pervasive conventions.

Mulling over these assertions, many proffered by leading film composers, it would be easy to come to the conclusion that a soundtrack (at the very least) is simply a formal component at the service of some larger and clearer concept called "cinema." No wonder a movie like *Harum Scarum,* whose whole raison d'être is musical celebrity, rarely receives attention from these kinds of writers: its hierarchies of labor and order of manufacture seem unreservedly distorted.

At first glance, this assertion about the primacy of cinema could possibly appear quite logical given that it overlaps with the order of manufacture of scoring we generally attribute to films of both the silent and the production line eras. If scoring is the most popular topic in film-music literature, then it stands to reason that its modes of production influence how this output is judged. Yet, after closer inspection, and even when we are contemplating classical film scores, these narrow understandings of temporal arrangement are too superficial to encompass the multitudinous negotiations that have taken place between the movie and music industries, which can be either separately owned or portions of a business convergence. Scoring, moreover, has never been the sole mode of integrating music into cinema, nor might it be the dominant one, as the *Harum Scarum* case study testifies. We should also be wary of drawing up a timeline that starts with music acquiescing to film and then graduating onto a more level playing field courtesy of the horizontal integrations of the late twentieth century.[8] To summon up just a few fairly random examples, the opera *Carmen* figured as a plot line in silent movies before the coming of synchronized-sound cinema, and Mozart was the subject of several silent films, including Louis Feuillade's treatment, *La Mort de Mozart* (1909).[9] Both instances demonstrate that music does not politely linger in the background nor wait until the last minute for its entrance into cinematic inspiration, although, on many an occasion, its failure to do so means that the end result "doesn't work."

At this point, we come to a central concern of much entertainment culture: the need to acknowledge the frequent necessity for elements (here, film and music) to part ways and present themselves as singular and thus cumulatively numerous commodities, as well as to hang together as a recognizable whole. The coherent totality is implausible almost from the get-go. Moreover, film-music arrangements that "don't work" muddle any comfortable flux between these states, pointing out how uneasy the strategic insistence that films are both unified and also separated product chains—such as the star-related merchandise and the soundtrack album for *Harum Scarum*—can be. Even with the most "classical" of cinematic texts this is the case, for example, when stars remind us that they are famous people as well as characters. Yet the nagging perseverance of textual coherence obdurately stands its ground in so much of the discourse around the subject, denying the ("post"-)industrial conditions that cruelly and profitably fragment peoples and commodities on a number of levels—and for quite explicable reasons.

Filmmaking may just, every now and then, stick to a particular linear schedule, but reception is certainly not plotted in this way. All manner of sensory experiences are lavished upon us simultaneously, including those specific to the space of exhibition, rather than the "film text" itself, and we then refigure them according to their relationship to our own particular chronologies.[10] As Nicholas Cook's *Analysing Musical Multimedia* highlights, "In reality, music—like any other filmic element— ... participates in the construction, not the reproduction, of all cinematic effects."[11] It is this tangle of different experiences and influences that often determines whether or not film and music can work together, a decision that then, as will become obvious, freezes certain labor-related injustices.

For one, creating a superlative film-music arrangement evidently involves team effort: the emotional and professional subsumption of the self for the greater aesthetic good. The attraction of congruence is evident in all of these discourses, but how might this agenda obscure and replicate models of labor exploitation and preferential treatment that are endemic within both the film and music industries—and elsewhere?

Of all the possible film-music subjects that are deemed worthy of scholarly attention, it is the contract-bound or freelance composition drafted in order to supply something complementary to almost-finished film objects of which we hear the most. It is also constrained by some very stalwart, largely Fordist-Taylorist specifications, as Caryl Flinn's thoughtful *Strains of Utopia* points out, ones that keep a tight rein on working methods, expect conformity to particular traditions, and allow little leeway for dialogue between or reworking of other aspects of the movie.[12] Amid this matrix, the composer is a removed, specialist employee restricted by all manner of predetermined forces exerted by the filmmaking machinery and the Fordist hierarchies of assembly. Given the working conditions of these composers in the movie industry, scoring as a career is chock-full of insecurities; if a soundtrack does not "fit the film," its creator may well struggle to garner future employment and this, in many ways, helps to create a culture of a very particular kind of resentful subservience. It comes as no surprise, then, that few of the books on scoring seem eager to digress from a what-film-music-should-be model, which prepares their readers for conformity (in practice as well as reception) above all else.[13] Writers and scorers share an evident dissatisfaction with the working conditions of the production line system,[14] and yet they often still try their utmost to be dutiful and loyal to the film's aims, rather than corrupting, subverting, or expanding them. Ultimately, a laudable scorer is beholden to "the movie," works within such limitations with panache, grace, and subtlety, and rarely allows her- or himself to question the value systems that render these skills so highly prized above any others.

The following question may very much spoil our fun, but: when practitioners, audience members, and even some writers search so longingly for the ideal match of film and music, are they irresponsibly masking the injustices and incompatibilities of mass entertainment production? In privileging these distinct pleasures, are we also often unwittingly supporting modes of creation that impose particular industry norms and standards, ones that cannot hope to please all workers, or even consumers? Dilemmas like these are central to Theodor Adorno and Hanns Eisler's tirade against industry practice, *Composing for the Films*. What stands out from this work is a commitment not to rebuke music and cinema's stubborn irreconcilability unthinkingly, but to acknowledge it as just one endemic and doomed outcome (to be followed by pervasive alienation) of the capitalist modes of production:

The alienation of the media from each other reflects a society alienated from itself, men whose functions are severed from each other even within each individual. Therefore the aesthetic divergence of the media is potentially a legitimate means of expression, not merely a regrettable deficiency that has to be concealed as well as possible.[15]

Their argument presents a forceful case that a partial or unconvincing sense of clarity and coherence can only be created at the cost of many of those involved in making and receiving such products.

In examining the ensuing estrangements, we also have to take into consideration the degrees of self-sufficiency characteristic of two mature entertainment industries, even when they are working together. At the very least, if we can separate music production from the more recent invention of cinema, then we see a plethora of inconsistencies in creative processes, in constitutions of labor, and in representational politics. It is the negotiations between these factors that this book urges us to consider through a deeply political sensibility. The movement of time, I argue later on, also complicates the rules of film-music unity. As Caryl Flinn points out, "utopian expression is by its nature limited and incomplete since its borders are continually laid down and demarcated by such forces as economics, history and human subjectivity."[16] These are the pressing issues that the film–music example that doesn't work brings up.

Defining and Approaching "the Mismatch"

The desire for perfection has evidently created a hierarchy of skills and of meaning-making that struggles hard to smother troubling oppositions for the sake of peaceful communion. Frankfurt School theorists Theodor Adorno and Max Horkheimer, unlikely as they were to be found in the front row at an Elvis movie, have words of warning about such "harmony": "[f]alse clarity is only another name for myth; and myth has always been obscure and enlightening at one and the same time: always using the devices of familiarity and straight-forward dismissal to avoid the labor of conceptualization."[17] Although the derivations of this argument are far removed from film-music theories, such ideas do much to complicate both the all-too-easy sense of clarity that can emanate from certain propositions about and through "the film" and, in addition, the frequent insistence that there is a natural and clear-cut way for us to identify a clash between the two media. Of course, it can also be argued that the socially instigated dividing lines between "music" and "film" are similarly mythic and, as I will later argue, there are commercial incentives for presenting them as sometimes conjoined and sometimes separated. Myth, or rather, in this case, a somewhat mythical claim of common sense or aesthetic limpidness, demands our scrutiny in order for us to understand what principles are being instated and how we are distracted from alternatives, purely through a feeling that anything that doesn't work is illogical, ineffectual, or unsuitable. These decisive appraisals against film-music collisions let slip a great deal of information about our value systems, our aspirations for the entertainment industries (and their designs upon us), and how we utilize culture to formulate somewhat rigid and self-affirming pictures of the world in which we hope to dwell.

Without doubt, there are whole realms of experimental cinematic practice and art-music performance that directly address Adorno and Horkheimer's concerns, and I want to briefly justify why I do not wish to incorporate them into my own definition of the "mismatch."[18] This is because their license to interrogate aesthetic "clarity" is firmly secured within authorial agendas whereby their overseers (at least partially) intend to unleash the exchanges and transmogrifications taking place within their material.[19] Evidently, there is logic presiding over what more "independent" art can say, perhaps precisely because its discriminating audiences understand that the texts *mean* to say it. This endows such examples with a paradoxical coherence that my own mismatches do not display.

Conversely, "mainstream" mismatches, whose precise coordinates I will plot through recourse to coverage from their own time frames, are almost never considered triumphs of premeditated invention—nor will I argue this by singing the praises of misunderstood genius lying unacknowledged within my case studies. "Mainstream" mismatches are often presumed to dream of consistency and then to jeopardize their chances of attaining it through their supposed lack of dexterity. Critics largely judge them according to conformist aesthetic criteria, and the projected ineptitude of these commodities usually disarms their potential to alert us to, say, societal dislocation and alienation, something a fan would happily accept from, for example, David Lynch, precisely because this would be acceptable according to our expectations of such a director.

Throughout this book, then, my argument lingers very much "within the system" and its stricter understandings of appropriate labor. These topics enable me to comprehend why seemingly acceptable signifying practices become troublesome when they are bolted onto other, perhaps even more benign ones. It is mainly in their off-kilter combination of various normally condoned ideas that these cultural products become disorienting, even, as we shall see, threatening exemplars of work. In these instances, we often notice the incompatibility of overblown systems of creation; the potential instability in modern labor and leisure practices is not being adequately glossed over. Situations like these compel a continuity film system to confront how dispersed its "wholeness" might be, how it works at odds with itself. Often, the clashing elements spring from the wider (and vaguer) formations that make up the working practices, histories, cultures, and perceptions of the two entertainment industries. Some bear longer legacies than those with which they are allied and may have to respect independent rules, conventions, means of compilation, and comprehension which grate against those that then materialize within the collaboration.

In order to make evident these connections, my analyses are fueled by the imperative to take a much closer look at work itself: not just the work of entertainment personnel caught up in the confusing environment of laboring across the boundaries that synergy often tries to smooth away, but also the work that we all must complete both to make sense of the media and, even more crucially, to survive financially at the deeper level. It is not enough to merely involve ourselves in the end products of entertainment from the perspective of representation, nor to focus upon the work that is done through audience decoding. In many ways, this preoccupation with product rather than manufacturing process can become complicit in erasing the working methods themselves and, ultimately, the pain and confusion that they provoke.

Work-as-labor in the grander sense is, after all, often the prerequisite for our engagement with purchasable culture in the first place. In simple terms, it is largely our salaries that make such leisure possible, and it is the current positioning of work in relation to consumption and to the "time off" it grants us that renders the diversification of leisure and the sustainability of commodified film and music possible. On a more fundamental plane, Tony J. Watson's *Sociology, Work and Industry* stresses:

> Work is basic to the ways in which human beings deal with the problems arising from the scarcity of resources available in the environment. The scarcity of resources in the world influences the patterns of conflict and competition which arise between social groups. It follows from this that the social organization of work will reflect the basic power relationships of any particular society. But patterns of social relationships do not relate to power structures alone. They are also closely connected to patterns of meaning. Thus the ways in which people think and feel about work will closely relate to their wider political and religious doctrines and to their general cultural orientations.[20]

By claiming that something doesn't work, even in reference to entertainment culture, we are, in effect, opening a skein of debates about what labor does and what it means to us, materially, politically, and interpersonally.

In one way, the solidification of judgment, the process of outspoken categorization, creates an impression of clarity and stability in what is, as will become increasingly clear, an ever-shifting economic environment. The emphasis is on goods and their worth, the examination of the work of others as finished pieces rather than an inquiry into broader swings in labor practices. Given this tendency, I find it logical to alternate between a verbal focus on "not working" and the term "mismatch," which becomes a shorthand for the *products* resulting from "failed" film-music collaborations. In drawing occasionally on a noun form, I am hoping to point out the perceived fixity and definite commodity object status that can result from, to invoke a play on words, horizontal disintegration. It is the act of deeming these supposed end points unworthy, of labeling them in these ways that embodies a certain relationship of audiences and critics to both creative personnel and the working world at large.

More specifically, current trends in labor have demanded small-batch, quick-change production, an amplified range of commodities, rapid turnover, and strategic obsolescence; strict discernment is a useful skill in navigating this overabundance. What exactly has brought about this restructuring? A dramatic turn in how work is carried out on a global scale, often called "post-Fordism" or "postindustrialism," may well be the reason, I claim, that many of today's mismatches emerge and that they are labeled as such by critics. This is not to say that film music always worked beforehand, nor that labor exploitation cannot bring fabulous harmony into being (think, for example of a Busby Berkeley spectacular or a classic Max Steiner score). Yet "postindustrialism" may well account for the particularities of why mismatches matter to us these days and may enable what doesn't work to articulate the current conscriptions of labor with an enhanced fluency.

Resituating (Entertainment) Labor:
The Impact of So-Called Postindustrialism

Since the 1960s, countries like Britain and the United States (which are the geographical focuses of this book) have been altered immeasurably by various economic developments. In its most succinct form, "postindustrialization" can be characterized as both the transference of production to different (cheaper) parts of the world and a consequent reconfiguration of the temporalities, practices, communities, and expectations of employment, including a growth in media work. The sociologist of work Richard Sennett identifies "new capitalism's" central features as "discontinuous reinvention, flexible production, and concentration of power without centralisation."[21] The accent is on ceaseless, just-in-time trimming, reconfiguration at a moment's notice in order to match market forces and to sustain profit in an increasingly globalized and intricate web of commerce.

In many ways, it would seem prudent to enclose my key vocabulary in scare quotes to stress that old production methods have not been abandoned or wiped away—although in many instances they have been relocated away from these particular regions—but the result would be a cluttered book. As terms, "post-Fordism" and "postindustrialism," like most historical periodizations, bear a sense of irrevocable change that is altogether too sweeping, especially when the majority of the world is still embedded in both Fordism and industrialism. Nor are these eras as strictly "new" as their names might suggest: their roots definitely lie in earlier times and they sustain all manner of capitalist logics that pre-date them, meaning that earlier thinkers have much to contribute to their analysis. Yet post-Fordism and postindustrialization are not entirely fictional either; they serve as (admittedly crude, though distinctly evocative) shorthand for a host of concrete, chartable social changes that shape how "mismatches" are produced and framed. An integration of post-Fordist or postindustrial labor trajectories allows me to scrutinize my material afresh, according to some urgently needed political perspectives, ones that prioritize the huge impact of labor reorganization upon our everyday lives.

It would be hard to contest the postindustrial argument that manufacturing has been on a steady decline for many years in places such as the United Kingdom and the United States. In *An Economic and Social History of Britain, 1790–1990,* a detailed account of that nation's move through industrialization, Trevor May records:

> Britain's reliance on manufacturing has been steadily shrinking since its postwar peak in the early 1950s, when 35 per cent of the national income came from that source. Between 1966 and 1979 the gross domestic product increased by 29 per cent but manufacturing output grew by only 11 per cent. Between 1979 and 1981 production fell by 17 per cent, and the average annual growth rate of manufacturing was less than 1 per cent during the 1980s, a figure much lower than that of the 1960s.[22]

Production, where it does take place in these geographical quarters, is now on a much smaller scale, focusing less on accumulation regimens and more on searching out both smaller, specialized markets and workers and technologies that are flexible (or disposable) enough to deal with variable production.[23] These tactics are a world away from those of the preceding era, when a Keynesian model often predominated, encouraging the state, as the controller of a coherent and more manageable national economy, to scientifically balance supply and demand and stabilize its larger, more long-lived mass markets. These changes have utterly repositioned employment, both politically and spatially, and are part and parcel of, as well as a survival mechanism against, the reorganization of trade that is often termed "globalization." The current decentralization and fragmentation of the media industries is one tiny outcome of this shift but is entirely central to how mismatches often come into being.

The world can now be seen as less divided into spheres of industrial "development" and "underdevelopment" and more as a space witnessing a movement of raw-material provision to peripheral zones that lie geographically (but not necessarily financially) beyond the U.S.–UK axis upon which I am concentrating. The labor force within this picture is globally and even locally dispersed, the goods we receive are now created in much more partial and multiple ways, and these are the production specificities that often give rise to the incoherence embodied within mismatches. The fabric of postindustrialization is thus understandably fashioned according to a new tension between social connectivity (through, say, the latest communications networks) and dispersal (made possible through these very technologies). The potential for destabilizing the balance between proximity and distance is high; it bursts out of, to give one example, the odd references to the Arab world in *Harum Scarum,* a film which ineptly tries to come to terms with unfamiliar transnational relationships. Unsurprisingly, the movie was generated in a climate where such economic agendas, as the next chapter illuminates, were proliferating.

Certainly, cross-border trade and interactions are nothing new. However, the more fluid mobility of capital across the planet, marked by developments in worldwide telecommunications systems along with their expansion of the scope for competition and the subsequent squeezing out of individual governments' fiscal regulation, has rendered previously more protected nation-states increasingly vulnerable. Job security, for one, is less of a guarantee, and there are greater numbers of part-time and short-contract employees working longer hours for fewer benefits and, in some countries during certain periods, mass unemployment. In all sorts of ways, this situation concretely and symbolically plays out in the vicissitudes of entertainment labor; as will become more and more apparent, the media do not simply reflect these trends, they are integral to other much broader developments.

Our sink-or-swim conscriptions into such postindustrial economies are often thought to impart much less secure conditions upon workers, more so now that there is less safeguarding in the form of expensive and uncompetitive state-sponsored protectionism (the kind still favored in many a Western European country). Given all of the developments I have just outlined, it is not surprising that Keith Grint in *The Sociology of Work* should observe an awkward overlap in our processes of transition, one which also scars the mismatch:

> [S]witching from one form of production to another is not simply a question of replacing the technology and altering the organizational fabric. Technologies of production incorporate histories. . . . the longer an organizational system survives, the more sclerotic it becomes as privileged agents and groups surround themselves with material and symbolic forms of protection.[24]

These behaviors, as I illustrate in my case-study chapters, have indeed been rife in the last half century, and it is imperative that we sympathetically examine their motivations, the pain they cause, and their reshaping of our environment and the roles we play within it. Speaking more directly about workers' subjectivities and rights, another sociologist of labor, Huw Beynon, reflects:

> There is a lot of ambiguity and tension in these developments. In the context of a competitive economy which has displaced the producer from its centre, companies have to deal with the need to sell and to please their consumers. The market has taken an ascendancy which relegates the workings of offices and factory floors to subordinate status.[25]

One strategy that many countries, including Britain and the United States, have adopted in order to maintain their workers' status in the face of an inability to compete with cheaper manufacturing elsewhere has been to concentrate on specialist commodities that revolve around knowledge, service, technological invention, and information, with the media as one central component.

These approaches, this British and American dovetailing of national economic vision with a concern for cultural production, differ considerably from, for instance, many European countries' greater preservation of the Keynesian ideal. Economic restructuring of this order is by no means universal, and it is only in very specific geographical spaces, such as the United States, that someone like Presley could have made the journey from blue-collar worker to international mega-stardom so quickly. The necessary adjustments that opened up the business of entertainment were only a few of the many options available for keeping afloat amid, profiting from, and even promoting the turn to smaller-scale production, global competition, and worker insecurity. In his influential writings, Richard Florida has identified how technologies, infrastructures, ethics, and lifestyles afforded by both public and private investment have promoted the subsequent growth of a "creative class." Basing his statements on extensive statistical analysis, he notes:

> The *Creative Class* now includes some 38.3 million Americans, roughly 30 percent of the entire U.S. workforce. It has grown from roughly 3 million workers in 1900, an increase of more than tenfold. At the turn of the twentieth century, the Creative Class made up just 10 percent of the workforce, where it hovered until 1950 when it began a slow rise; it held steady around 20 percent in the 1970s and 1980s. Since that time, this new class has virtually exploded, increasing from less than 20 million to its current total, reaching 25 percent of the working population in 1991 before climbing to 30 percent by 1999.[26]

We should understand America and Britain not so much as "more imaginative" at present, but as shaped by the commodification and privatization of intellectual property, its rendition into goods. That "creativity" is now so central to economic agendas is just one extra reason that I am so keen to underscore the relevance of work as it runs through our understanding of the mismatch and the media at large. What is more, the entertainment industries, as my case studies will elaborate, have consistently favored some of the unpredictable, insecure, fragmented, decentralized, and small-scale models of production that are also common to post-Fordism, offering up a vital pattern book for understanding the far greater shifts promulgated of late. As I argue with greater intensity and detail in the chapters to come, such close-at-hand creative output offers its consumers a meaningful and engaging discourse on what it means to labor at a distinct remove from heavy industry and mass production in its most typical Fordist formats. If the shift into postindustrialization is confusing, even threatening to certain highly privileged consumers who are now set at a distance from more manual forms of wage earning and whose social roles and perceptions must adapt accordingly, then perhaps entertainment-as-labor offers some useful advice for making sense of their worlds. Presley's premature death could even function as a tragic cautionary tale. His overindulgences in food made him a casualty of this transition in labor history; his physical and psychological being proved incapable of weathering the shift from early life in a sharecropping family to a less impoverished or calorie-dependent form of earning.

Entertainment thus becomes not simply a crucial aspect of the economy, but also the means by which many of us can begin to take stock of the world and, among other things, how we are to earn our livings within it. I do not feel it is sufficient, however, simply to witness and learn from these commodities so that we might get used to the destructive impact of modern industrial and postindustrial life.[27] For better or worse, a whole range of broader strategies is being developed through, for, and according to them. Entertainment culture, for instance, often seems to bridge the divide between creative services and more concrete forms of manufacturing; in effect, it provides frozen, salable, and mass-produced variants of these services. As such, film-music commodities can act not just as helpful metaphors for understanding a confusing journey of transformation, but also as reliable exemplars of working conditions that are becoming more and more ubiquitous. Performers, as Stan Godlovitch argues, function as "brokers fulfilling a contract" between writers (of various types) and the audience.[28] In this sense, they are skilled tertiary workers par excellence, their labor accountable in ways unfamiliar to large-scale manufacture and so public that it becomes available for widespread discussion.

Paolo Virno, a theorist of post-Fordism, takes stock of the repositioned status of sectors like the media:

> [I]n the culture industry (as is the case, after all, today in the post-Ford era for industry in general) the finished products which can be sold at the end of the productive process are surely not scarce. The crucial point is, though, that while the material production of objects is delegated to an automated system of machines, the services rendered by living labor, instead, resemble linguistic-virtuosic services more and more. We should ask ourselves what role the culture industry assumed with relation to overcoming the Ford/Taylor model. I believe that it fine-tuned the paradigm of post-Fordist production on the whole. I believe therefore, that the mode of action of the culture industry became, from a certain point on, exemplary and pervasive.[29]

Consequently, the *work* of leisure reveals one of the significant ways in which employment continues to unfold in the current climate (the Las Vegas model, after all, is the one in which *Harum Scarum* chooses to leave us). With the expansion of the cultural industries comes a muddying of the distinction between labor and relaxation as they have traditionally been categorized. In its most fulfilling forms, media work can be a mode of earning money that stands in contradiction to other, more alienating forms of making ends meet. Creativity is often perceived to sit closer to the fulfillment of our imaginative urges and to complicate the ostracism of grueling toil from enjoyment. However, the mismatch of Presley's experiences in making *Harum Scarum* tell another story, one that speaks of a deeply fractured and devastating constellation of labor systems. Furthermore, the ethos of individualism that practices of creativity frequently encourage might also ignite a mismatch by way of a too-many-cooks appearance.

In terms of their organization of labor, then, the media industries have run ahead of the postindustrial game. For some time now, their modes of production and their commodities have allowed us to contemplate, as I shall reveal in the following chapters, the snowballing processes of decentralization, outsourcing, flexible working, and niche marketing.

Toward a Postindustrial Film-Music Scholarship

Given these historical developments and film-music production's role within them, what sort of methodologies are best equipped to adequately address the scope of the mismatch? Luckily for me, these newer divisions of labor and production have prompted, although they may not use the terminologies of postindustrialism, the appearance of a smattering of texts like John Mundy's *Popular Music on Screen: From Hollywood Musical to Music Video* and the anthologies *Celluloid Jukebox: Popular Music and the Movies since the 50s* (edited by Jonathan Romney and Adrian Wootton) and *Soundtrack Available: Essays on Film and Popular Music* (compiled by Pamela Robertson Wojcik and Arthur Knight). All of these books unpack the intertwined yet dispersed interactions of the film and music industries. To these, we might add the body of writings on musicals by the likes of Richard Dyer, Rick Altman, and Jane Feuer, which unmasks the hegemonic machinations of film-music harmony,[30] as well as the research of Krin Gabbard and Arthur Knight, which is preoccupied with the politics of the antagonistic arrangements of the two art forms.[31] All of these books admirably critique labor injustices while noticing ways in which film-music commodities also *undo* themselves as they simultaneously strain to wrap us into their specific projections of the world.

What I would like to contribute to this discourse is an approach that is more fully adapted to the decentralization and fragmentation of the postindustrial condition and which feeds these very characteristics back into a critique of how work is completed within this historical moment. It somehow seems in bad faith to evaluate what is hidden by the urge for consistency, discuss pervasive social fracturing, and then formulate arguments that lead adamantly and hypocritically into a similar cul-de-sac of conclusive description. Just as much as I find the unthinking vilification of the mismatch objectionable, I am loath to present a simple, oppositional reevaluation of it in response. Furthermore, surely there are ways of harnessing the energies held in (off-)balance within the mismatch for change as well as censure? Without even realizing it, the market as it stands exposes its own vulnerability and thus unwittingly sabotages itself a little every time it lets loose a mismatch into the world. How might we suspend the processes of castigation so that what "doesn't work" can give us a better chance of reorganizing our understandings and practices of wage earning and its inequalities?

In following through on some of these ideas, my project homes in on clashes between more immediate financial desires for capitalistic convergence and past or enduring histories of representation and production (ones that, by and large, encompass certain systems of domination). Therein often lies the mismatch. For example, film, as we know, carries many products within it, while paradoxically aspiring toward the type of streamlined identity that such multiplicity might scotch. The musical unit, which is often created in another decentralized zone, may stand out successfully as both an integral part of the film and an extractable component to be purchased—as so many commercially successful soundtracks do. Yet it can also scream its independence and market availability too loudly, meaning that we reject it, and its enveloping film framework, along with the threat of accelerated production fragmentation. This, for me, is a rich analytical seam to mine because, as politically objectionable as either force might potentially be, historical and contemporary demands may, in these instances, push each other toward a mutual subsidence. In essence, several of my examples incorporate products that destroy other neighboring products, working despite themselves against the maximization of profit, perhaps because of the extreme fragmentation that postindustrialization engenders. However, their innovative possibilities are regularly thwarted as a result of the desperate scramble to discredit any such confusions and to cast them off as failures. While such ordering allows us to function and discount the chaotic randomness of the world, it is also yoked to practices, I argue throughout this book, that may be interpreted or lived out as exploitative, debilitating, or harmful.

In thinking this through, I have been enticed outside the specific considerations of film scholarship and its treatment of music. While there are most definitely histories of sound on film that yearn for thoughtfully disjunctive audio-visual alignments (and these were particularly dominant during the dawn of synchronized-sound production),[32] my research has taken me to spaces where formal dissections and popular critical appraisals can meet the sociologies and philosophies of labor relations. Rather than trying to ignore or disable chaos, the thinkers with whom I connect aim simultaneously to discern the political root causes for the destruction of the mismatch and to stimulate methods for harnessing this commotion in order to rework our current, preferred, and rather stolid ways of perceiving and acting. Honoring the shuffle function that has juxtaposed some of the most inspiring and unusual musical choices that my computer files could muster throughout the writing of this book, my conjoining of subject matter and theoretical stances will be just as dismissive of the idea of right and proper counterparts. The approaches that have enthused me concentrate upon and are fueled by odd encounters; mismatches, some might call them. Thus, in the subsequent chapters, Karl Marx and Theodor Adorno will meet up with 1950s rock 'n' roll movies; Sergei Eisenstein with the composer biopics of Ken Russell; Jacques Derrida, Gilles Deleuze, and Félix Guattari with some horror movies banned from domestic consumption in Britain (referred to colloquially as "video nasties"); and Zygmunt Bauman with several unsuccessful cross-over performers. I will offer synopses of how this will work shortly, but, as a brief taste of my methodology, I want first to engage Georg Hegel with our old friend *Harum Scarum*.

What is particularly exciting about the writing that has been dedicated to such concepts as dialecticism, "undecidables," and ambivalence is that their initiators find fragmentation *everywhere,* but do not dismiss it outright. Through such thinking, the mismatch can well and truly be drawn out of the analytical hinterlands. Although Eisenstein is the only one of these thinkers to deal directly with film and music, all of them correspond well with the industrial and textual inconsistencies of "cinema" and "music," their jittery, amalgamating initiatives. These might include movies' editing processes, the alternation of verse and chorus in a song, or the juxtaposition of moods in the symphonic structure of movements—all formal conceits that refuse the possibility of stagnancy and total coherence. The ensuing theoretical trajectories of these writers, just like my case studies, are driven by the influence of Westernized modes of industrial (and postindustrial) capitalism, but have also been created with usefully farsighted vision that refuses to accept that anything can ever truly be held still. By working alongside these notions of what we might broadly call "dialecticism," I hope to perpetuate the idea that clashes, debates, and negotiations might underlie civilization as a whole and thus to expand my assessments out from and into specific film-music mismatches and their manifestations of labor. A more ubiquitous dialecticism should also hopefully instill confidence that my examples are not in any way isolated instances of dynamism. In pursuing their logic, I am not simply scooping away a small amount of territory from more oppositional or avant-garde rhetoric so as to endow my own case studies with a unique exceptionality. Instead, such moments can be seen as but small tremors within a much greater series of movements.

At the same time, for philosophers like Hegel or Marx, dialecticism is not something that can be "applied"—it is the very structure of history and should be treated as an insistent presence.[33] Transformation may well be activated from within, rather than forcibly introduced by a distant authoritative body. Dialecticism is not a tool, but a fundamental characteristic of life of which we must become conscious. Hegel, bemoaning the misapprehension of the activity, states:

> Dialectic is generally regarded as an external and negative procedure, that does not pertain to the subject-matter, that is based on a mere idle subjective craving to disturb and unsettle what is fixed and true, or that at best leads to nothing except the futility of the dialectically treated matter.[34]

The beauty of Hegel's inscription of the dialectic as omnipresent is that evolution and change are necessarily a part of how the world functions: affirmation–negation–negation of negation (retitled as thesis–antithesis–synthesis by Marx) affirms the ebb and flow of life, and this is of paramount value to my attack on the autocracy of the harmonizing principles of cinema and music's place among it.[35] Within this set of constant turns and motions, supposed incompatibilities come into alignment and reflect upon their relationship—or those who are conscious do so. Then a third, negotiated category comes into being, yet only by allowing the distressing and the injurious to make themselves known can real change ensue. A sense of (temporary) stability should be reached not by demonizing "the opposition" ("Hollywood" within the Elvis equation), but by acknowledging the productive and the positive in practices even more heinous than those Presley endured. In testing this proposition, Marx's dialecticism, for instance, dares to explore the benefits of slavery, and it is not too hard to think through Presley's inflexible Hollywood contracts in similar, although less dramatic terms. For me, the working through of all such "incongruities" of film and music—involving, of course, their industrial priorities and semantic inconsistencies—ideally pushes forward toward a new way of perceiving both the practices of combination and the state of the world more generally. This action, however, by no means always guarantees a more "advanced" state of being; the negotiation may lead, as it does in the social take-up of most of my case studies, toward a particularly oppressive, although transient, political end point. This sense of a project that is impossible to complete offers some hope to the politics of mismatch liberation.

What is also enormously valuable about Hegel's thought to the analysis of both the mismatch and the united yet distinct character(s) of the film-music industries is that he interrogates the very nature of oppositions or incompatibilities. In *Phenomenology of Spirit,* Hegel proposes that "the essence is neither an other than itself, nor the pure abstraction of the 'I,' but an 'I' which has the otherness within itself, though in the form of *thought,* so that in its otherness it has directly returned into itself."[36] He emphasizes the equivocating and paradoxical dimensions of any entity or process, the existence of contradictions within supposedly unified, "single" concepts, such as "individuality," which is, for Hegel, composed of universality and particularity.

Here is an easy example: the rendition of "Mirage" in *Harum Scarum*. After being drugged by Aishah (Fran Jeffries), Johnny awakens to find himself in a harem surrounded by beautiful women, whom he wastes no time in serenading. The lyrics include "Like a man in the desert, I am lost," "In the distance you call me like an oasis," and "I thirst for your lips," yet the music makes few concessions to the "Oriental" context. Instead, we hear typical Western tonalities and harmonies delivered by electric guitars, a piano, a drum kit, a lulling vocal chorus, and Presley himself. The encircling ladies are bedecked in outrageously gaudy, glitzy outfits, all gossamer, cleavage, and mid-1960s flip hair-dos. Through its insistent wedging of trite Arabesque themes into a no more cut and dried Western popular musical tradition, "Mirage" does the work of a dual deconstruction under its own steam. Its overwrought recourse to easily graspable symbols betrays the fabrication, rather than the consistency, of this "Arabian" mise-en-scène, while their association with the musical style of Presley, not to mention an entirely non-Arab supporting cast, throws open all number of questions about (the limitations of) our systems of difference and opposition. Indeed, the sequence itself also quietly bears the markers of such impossible stabilities. The number is set to a watered-down, more pop, and repetitive bossa nova–like beat, evoking Latin America and its past and present diasporas rather than the Middle East, a region whose only imprint might just be the faint sounds of rhythmic finger bells and the slightly *nai*-like reediness of the oboe that opens the song. Such indeterminacy is underscored by Johnny's deliriousness and, indeed, the title of the track; in not realizing whether or not he is fantasizing the harem, he inhabits another space that cannot be so rigidly defined as "one" or the "other."

Hegel's argument is also particularly enlightening when transported to the idea of film as a "whole": it becomes a text that reaches into perpetuity and is a part of it. Hegel's understanding of consciousness not only connects with the other (including such objects as film), but also mutates in relation to and is ultimately a compound of such entities; there is always a process of reflection and reconstitution at work:

> [C]onsciousness itself is the *absolute dialectical unrest,* this medley of sensuous and intellectual representations whose differences coincide, and whose identity is equally again dissolved, for it is itself determinateness as contrasted with the non-identical. But it is just in this

process that this consciousness, instead of being self-identical, is in fact nothing but a purely casual, confused medley, the dizziness of a perpetually self-engendered disorder.[37]

Central to Hegel's philosophy is the conviction that flux and interrelationship are the absolute basis not only of being,[38] but also for new modes of consciousness. For him, especially in *Phenomenology of Spirit,* the resolution of a struggle between supposed opposites is achieved most successfully through a growing awareness of the dependence of the one on the other, the fabrication of equivalences in this relationship, and the place of each in the manufacture of the ensuing reality.[39] This is, I would argue, a more assuredly complex way of understanding the energy that is created by a film-music association.

If we return to *Harum Scarum,* we can begin to interrogate the sense of agency that is central to the Elvis myth and to think through the utter codependency and changeability of the individual-versus-the-system face-off. When we enter into Hegel's mode of perception, we are readier to deal with the fact of Presley's little-discussed attachment to the movie, including his initial delight in the Johnny Tyronne role and his insistence upon wearing his "Arabian" costumes at home.[40] We are openly encouraged by Hegel's thought to acknowledge the more general performativity that drives rock 'n' roll celebrity with particular regard to how it might also draw from cinema-themed dressing up, thus confusing the dichotomies of work that have divided the construction of "Elvis." More broadly, through Hegel, we can start to unearth the affiliations and mutual lineage of not only "music" (and, here, "individualism") and "film" (or "alienating commercial structures") as they exist within entertainment culture, but also of "West" and "East," a binary that is splayed out across the entire movie and well beyond and finds so much of its inspiration from the labor injustices instigated by colonial exploitation. For Hegelians, such grand scope and its potentially positive outcomes are not to be lightly dismissed.

Hegel is compelled by two primary philosophical goals, which are distinctly more ambitious than and divergent from my own: to understand the Absolute (everything, the infinite, the god[-like] presence) through the particulars and to guide the dialectical movement toward telos/progress, a sensibility that rests on a firm belief that human development is evolving for the better.[41] In direct contradiction to these aims, my chosen examples bear the scars of attempts to obstruct their "forward" motion and to efface the anomalies of their working methods. Sometimes, as I argue, the potential for a negotiated third meaning, one that simultaneously acknowledges the flux of reality, is aggressively cut off, its teleological journey frustrated. At moments like these, the utopian projections of betterment that steer Hegel's work are met with vigorous and purposeful attempts at blockage. In a Hegelian schema of history, these may be minor stultifications, but they are nonetheless extremely damaging. Sorting through how these tangles happen, perhaps as a means of spotting repeated patterns and evading them in the future, encourages us to look deeper into time- and context-based particularities.

The Specific Aims of *Off Key*

Now that I have compiled a tool kit for picking away at the social conscription of mismatches, *Off Key* is ready to plunge purposefully into a set of synergies where music is often raucously independent of cinema culture (or vice versa), where its makers have stood aloof from film's presence and have, on many occasions, conceived their work without giving cinema a passing thought, perhaps even completed it before cinema was invented. All but my last chapter will deal with cinematic examples that integrate music that has been noticeably outsourced (be this in the form of borrowed stars, secondhand songs, or biographical treatments of dead composers) for the specific reason of pointing out just how distanced music and cinema can often be, especially in a more decentralized, post-Fordist climate. This quality is often discounted when the post-production soundtrack is cited as the key instance of music and film interaction, a practice that often seeks to erase the fragmented and decentralized characteristics of (entertainment) labor. Instead, my deliberately loose term, "film-music," comprises much broader understandings of aligned-yet-distinct "film" and "music" and, accordingly, within *Off Key,* there are explorations of rock 'n' roll film story lines, composer biopics, and cross-over stars. These cases lead us into an interdisciplinary domain, where mismatched music in cinema is not simply (often, not even) an inconsiderately put-together soundtrack that requires formalist deconstruction. To this end, the following investigation willfully deviates from the analysis of the contributions of song structure to diegetic flow in order to tease out other dimensions of film-music interaction, ones that allow for (largely by mistake) different modes of labor interaction and different orders of prominence and meaningfulness.

My initial case study in chapter 2, "'The Motion Picture You're About to See Is a Story of Music': The Migration of Cinema into Rock 'n' Roll," places under the microscope the stylistic incongruity brought about by Hollywood's desire to incorporate the increasingly popular music of rock 'n' roll into its narrative themes in the late 1950s. Here, a largely African American music-making process faced an even more stubborn tradition of exclusion in the film industry than it had perhaps encountered in the music industry, which is also a decidedly racist forum. Although it had been standard practice to divorce African American musical performers from films' narrative trajectories and to perpetuate a more disjointed review-style structure (with its African American musicians dangling on thin diegetic excuses which held them at a distance from the main plot), the new mania for rock 'n' roll exerted pressure for the music to be more fully incorporated into the films' themes. Significantly, although African Americans feature in the diegesis as performers, they are definitely not the characters who drive the story line, and this tells us much about how contemporary tensions encircling labor were played out through the depictions of entertainment work. I will argue that the consternation that these film-music alliances caused was provoked by a radical shift in modes of salary earning in America at this time. This included the greater acceptance of African Americans into the wage economy and various forms of internal migration for work that took place at the same time as sudden lurches toward novel forms of horizontal integration within the film and music industries. Although this decade lies outside the historical period many scholars associate with post-industrialization, it is easy to spot premonitory warnings of things to come in its niche market audience groupings: "teenagers," "African Americans." This tactic embodied a movement away from classic Fordism's saturated mass markets, as did the early rehearsal of the diffusion of manufacturing sites, which was to become typical of this shift.

The subsequent chapter, "'It's Not Only Trivial, It's Bad, Vulgar': Ken Russell's Composer Biopics and the Uneasy Realignment of Work and Culture," moves into the early 1970s, a more distinctly postindustrial time, and is intrigued by movies that use the rendition of a classical or Romantic composer's life as a means of exploring the formulas and clichés wielded to present artistic creativity. Such narratives unravel notions about the composer as heroic, rebellious, bohemian, libertarian, and, above all, vulgar. There is an almost irksome extravagance, a lack of subtlety, and a nonchalant selfishness to the protagonists of the Ken Russell–directed films I examine (*The Music Lovers,* 1971; *Mahler,* 1974; and *Lisztomania,* 1975)—features which contradict the way their music has been historically circumscribed within certain canons of taste and refinement. The lurid quality of these portraits and the translation of qualities which are entirely musically acceptable into a less tolerant visual and narrative register create a form of excess with which middle-brow critics quickly found fault. In addition, all of these films present a series of ideas on popular culture's relationship with high art, not least because they are drawing the latter into the mass-produced and mass-consumed world of cinema. This was an era marked by several states of emergency in the Western economies, most notably the

OPEC (Organization of Petroleum Exporting Countries) oil crisis, the opening up of free-industrial zones across the so-called developing world, and the ensuing rash of strikes in countries like Britain. This series of biopics and the responses to them inquired into the very nature of work and what it might be if it were to reform as something cultural rather than manual, which is one obvious survival strategy. The discomfort that these films induced speaks of a wider unease about class, productivity, culture, and individual liberties in crisis. In addition, in each of the texts, there are references, either in story lines or in extradiegetic signals, to spheres such as working-class entertainment culture and advertising which, again, were dubbed mismatches by various commentators. The resulting debate brought to the fore disagreements about culture's position regarding promotion, sales, and the commerce surrounding the supposedly rarefied creativity of art music. It placed practices of bourgeois consumption center stage—something perhaps anathema to many aficionados of such music— but did so alongside the prizing open of doors to a more overtly marketable economy of culture in an age of global competition.

My penultimate chapter is entitled "Troubling Synthesis: The Horrific Sights and Incompatible Sounds of 'Video Nasties.'" In the United Kingdom in the early 1980s, a high-profile newspaper campaign railed against a group of films that were soon christened "video nasties," movies whose home viewing was soon to be officially banned under the Video Recordings Act of 1984. What many of these films shared was a matching of graphically violent imagery with seemingly aloof and specially written synthesizer scores. This case study explores how one particular clash of music and moving image was politically circumscribed in terms of a proposed notion of morality based around the new status of movies as increasingly domestic objects. For those wishing the films to be banned, the nonchalance toward brutality they suggested (and the soundtracks were major components here) was at odds with a supposedly "correct" response to horror imagery. For supporters of these movies, this very ambiguity put forward a fascinatingly complex mode of contemplating and deconstructing the horror genre, one which transcended notions of identification and humanist pity. The fact that these films caused moral panic, parliamentary debate, and eventual illegality shows exactly how important a study of mismatching, in all manner of forms, is when trying to understand the mass media. At the heart of these debates were thinly veiled criticisms about the rise of the working woman and what the home might become in her absence. The negative reactions to these movies were similarly laced with concerns about technology, which were played out through the dismissal of synthesized music during a period when automation was a major cause for concern in the remaining manual sectors of the economy and the cause of no small portion of industrial action.

Last, chapter 5, "Pop Stars Who Can't Act and the Limits of Celebrity 'Flexibility,'" explores the consistent inability of many pop stars to pull off a successful acting performance amid present-day debates about short-term, unstable labor and the emphasis on multitasking. Cross-over stars' strangely recurrent inadequacy in translating charisma and dexterity from one medium to another (and the same can be said of many actors who try to launch musical careers) creates the final discordance that this book examines. This rather literal approach to synergy provides a particularly fascinating launch pad for unpacking each art form's ideological underpinnings and, in particular, their relative codes of professionalism. One key aim of this chapter is to acknowledge the connections between these modes of labor and those more widely experienced in the contemporary job market with its increasing emphasis on fame, chance, and media work. When the different conventions of celebrity and labor in film and music bump against each other, critics and audiences are often left so dissatisfied that they revel in aggression or ridicule. Why are responses to these performances so caustic? What might this unearth about our relationship not only to stardom and performance, but also to the dominant means of evaluating the quality of work itself within what are increasingly media- or knowledge-focused societies?

These four investigations help, through their diversity, to demonstrate the pervasive nature of the ambivalence that music's interface with film can provoke and to illuminate culture's deep rooting in apprehensions about what it is to work in some of the richer regions of the global economy. It would be entirely possible to select instances from narrower (or even longer) frames of reference, but this broad sweep across generic boundaries illustrates better, I would argue, the variety of faces that the mismatch assumes. Furthermore, there is something of the character of the mismatch in this rather incongruous arrangement of examples and, as I will contend, the productive potential of the odd juxtaposition is a capacity that we, as scholars, need to contemplate and benefit from in a more committed fashion.

Throughout these explorations, *Off Key* will abide by a historical materialism, one that is sensitive to the machinations of history, struggle, and production specificities and which will, although only scantly engaged in my introductory encounter with the Presley iconography, become central to activating the mismatch's inherent energy throughout the remaining case studies of this book. These are not the traditional histories of film-music creation; they are tales told about laboring in the past. Through a repositioning of events and influences, my analyses loop notions of work more centrally into how we might interpret these media productions.

Another reason for my turn to specific histories is to emphasize that some of the actions and ethics I analyze have resonated for longer than others. Upon closer examination, it becomes glaringly apparent that a mismatch is often the result of short-term avarice blundering its way into lengthier and more complicated narratives of dominance and oppression through representation. This may well account for the many jarring moments within the subject of my next chapter: the rock 'n' roll movies of the 1950s. Here, very simply put, cinema seemed eager to capitalize upon a widespread new youth craze for a type of music that was strongly coded as African American. At the same time, this move was at odds with certain older rules about representing "race" on screen, ones that evidently led back to a history of subordination rooted in labor-as-slavery. At moments like this, it is crucial that we look into the stratifications of employment that have shaped such inconsistencies of representation and enfranchisement. Interacting with a chronology of labor relations exposes the anatomy of these injustices (often obscured or disarmed by the action of labeling a "mismatch") and allows us to understand and perhaps adjust many of the political problems we confront not just in producing and consuming entertainment, but also in our broader everyday lives.

In general terms, the peculiar eruptions of film-music mismatches, as well as much twentieth-century cinema, are structured, in significant part, by the evolution and requirements of postindustrial capitalism, particularly the developments of decentralization, differentiation, specialization, and categorization, in terms of both manufacture and social status. The markers of these processes seem burned into the examples I will explore and the wider contexts which they inhabit. Recourse to a postindustrial periodization allows the second half of the twentieth century to be understood as a time period when movie production sought, or was forced, to draw from forms of creative labor which lay outside its more secure, long-standing grasp—although it must be stressed that the music and film industries have been commercially linked almost from cinema's inception. Evidently, there are times when these parallel compulsions (instances of diversification *and* specialization, for instance) can work against each other, create a mismatch, and, ultimately, confound our prior aesthetic training. This sense of contradiction is particularly central to any critique of film-music scholarship as it currently stands, a subdiscipline that all too often privileges classical linear production. When we fail to fully recognize all of these contradicting tensions, many revealing dimensions of entertainment culture are overlooked, and, as the rest of this book elaborates, ignoring the global shifts in manufacturing that have reshaped the entertainment industries along these lines is perilous.

One of the prime objectives of the subsequent chapters, then, is to sift through the kinds of ostracized sensory practices that have been formulated within my case studies, to journey back closer to their points of production (in terms of the labor of both aesthetics and physical assembly), and to understand how music and cinema's exchanges and commingling might actually be able to confuse the standard schema of construction and reception. What is usually happening in a mismatch is an unsuccessful effacement of labor. The failed expurgation of modes of production and their concomitant social and historical meanings significantly undermines the prospect of simple filmic absorption. Following these still-visible tracks through the practices of entertainment is the impetus for many of this book's journeys.

While doing this, the most pressing goal of this project, and its most transferable one beyond the ambit of film-music theory, is to scrutinize how entities and energies become more than the sum of their parts precisely because they are fragmented and in constant motion, just like contemporary workers. To understand how this might be possible, we need to penetrate deeper into specific historical changes themselves, past the formal conceits of film-music combination and their aesthetic rulings against the mismatch. From this perspective, heavily socially weighted meanings collide and conflict not only internally (breaking the rules of "harmony") but also externally (in that their historical legacies take us far beyond the mere product in hand). What follows will penetrate these interplays, in the firm belief that what is often thought to not work is both enormously politically revealing about labor, and crucial to the reformulation of that labor.

♦ 2 ♦

"The Motion Picture You're About to See
Is a Story of Music": The Migration
of Cinema into Rock 'n' Roll

How to deal with history? Loyalty to dialecticism demands that a spotlight be trained upon the *work* of history making, particularly the often-concealed labor expended on smartening up flows and consistencies, on wiping away the mismatches of the past's documentation. By distilling my argument through the apparatus of periodization, might I not be in danger of neatening the edges of "the postindustrial era" to create, at all costs, a smooth line of reasoning? As Hegel would have rejoined, this is an impossible venture: the shards of history do not easily fit together into uniform wholes, nor will they obediently remain in any given position. In response, the dialectical imperative provides enormous scope not only for acknowledging and questioning particular societal instabilities, but also for writing history in a manner that energizes the proposed periodization via ceaseless unexpected encounters. To start with, then, "the postindustrial era" needs to be understood as a messy and constantly renegotiated political entity, a constitution to which the diversity of my studies and their interdisciplinary methodologies adhere. There is much to be learned about social order from how a postindustrial or "post-Fordist" categorization can only hope to hold together countless localized adaptations and about-faces in policy.

However, as well as interrogating why exactly any such inconsistencies can be bonded together, I also want to expose and insist upon my own reasons for weaving a repeated set of concerns through this book. If I am not careful, this could be interpreted as a yearning for coherence that might outwardly seem to clash with dialectical reasoning. What I shall openly maintain is that the teleologies I construct search out certain unities of sentiment, ones that derive from ongoing (although constantly mutating) forms of exploitation propagated by the current regimes of labor. Hegel's dialecticism, after all, is no stranger to the concept of harmony. Indeed, as we have seen, he concludes with a belief in the unfeasibility of separating out "the one" from "the other."

Distinctions and divisions, then, are of human construction; so too are starting points. Mine for *Off Key,* in the simplest sense of where this opening case-study chapter situates itself most persistently, is the 1950s, a time before the classification "postindustrial" was in common currency. As such, the term will lurk in this chapter's background, waiting to spring into a principal position in the later sections dedicated to the 1970s and onward. But there is strategy as well as generic pragmatism to my selection of this decade: the 1950s weathered various (dialectical) collisions in working practices and did so perhaps more centrally in film and music production than in other sectors. This historical detail, situated, paradoxically, within a midcentury focus upon mass production and centralized governance, can consequently invigorate my propositions about the new economic and cultural status of the media. Drawing postindustrialism out of a Fordist heartland remains true to certain dialectical impulses, as does the ensuing chapter's concentration on various other ostensibly opposed ideas and entities, ones whose enforced ostracism opens up a debate on how film and music "don't work" together, and why. This energy then catapults us into more crucial disputes about labor injustices and the extent to which they invade, as this chapter recounts, numerous aspects of everyday life. So, now I shall "begin" and at a point that fleshes out the *Harum Scarum* references with which *Off Key* actually commenced.

The mid-1950s witnessed the appearance of a flurry of rock 'n' roll pictures, often starring and largely made for teenagers, huddled mainly around the various school holidays of 1956 and 1957. Considering that these were movies targeted at peak periods when work interfered less with leisure, they stand out because of their low production values, quick shooting schedules, and lack of trained top-name actors. Their sparse story lines revolved around the music industry with a heavy weighting of musical performances in clubs and television studios, particularly toward the films' denouements. Theirs were certainly not the working methods of prestige pictures. Although commercially successful, the cycle was far from championed by anyone beyond its newly amassing niche market; it was a source of real apprehension for many cultural commentators.

A contemporary *Look* magazine article, for example, blurts out its "racial" and generational concerns about the musical genre all too clearly: "Going to a rock 'n' roll show is like attending the rites of some obscure tribe whose means of communication are incomprehensible. An adult can actually be frightened."[1] Frightened of what, exactly? Unmistakably, such vague yet panicked responses to rock 'n' roll events functioned as a protective shell whose cracking exposes a microcosm of writhing political anxieties ready to be probed. For the most part, academics have identified the key fears as juvenile delinquency; the policing of fraught American "race relations"; and the then morally condemned "crudeness" of rock 'n' roll.[2] Considering the resulting media furor and the ruckus caused by the audiences of *Rock Around the Clock* (Fred F. Sears, 1956) in the mid-1950s, these are understandable scholastic triggers.[3] Blazing the trail for the many rectifying tactics and pontifications that followed in the wake of the explosion of rock 'n' roll, a good number of the movies themselves—including *Don't Knock the Rock* (Fred F. Sears, 1956), *Shake, Rattle and Rock!* (Edward L. Cahn, 1956), *Loving You* (Hal Kanter, 1957), *Mister Rock and Roll* (Charles S. Dubin, 1957), and *Rock Baby: Rock It* (Murray Douglas Sporup, 1957)—did their utmost to impress upon their viewers (and detractors) that the genre provided nothing but good clean fun. The rock 'n' roll mismatches to be smoothed over by these gestures seem to be those bringing the aspirations of short-term wealth accumulation into closer company with the injuries it can cause, most centrally the corruption of youth.

In order to expand the scholarly and popular formation of "rock 'n' roll movies" so as to get a grip on the longer strands of economic policy and to knit all of this into a logic of accumulating post-Fordism, I feel it would be wise to position the film cycle amid contemporary practices of labor and exploitation. Consumer citizenship and decentralization, as provoked by certain forms of internal migration and antitrust action, should feature more prominently if we are to rise above an us-versus-them dichotomy and harness the

43

power of a host of dialectical interchanges.[4] These are the topics of the current chapter. Responding to these broader politics and social geographies, how did the industry constitute itself as a set of philosophies and practices in relation to rock 'n' roll? The leading trade journal of the time, *Variety*, which I shall be using extensively, offered not so much voguish moral judgments about the movies, but no-nonsense financial advice to industry insiders about the financial state of play among cinema, music, and the buying public. If a publication like this acknowledges a mismatch of sound and image culture, then it is often based on projected earnings that relay a great deal of crucial information about politico-economic doctrine, often at the national level and beyond. The dialectical tensions that emerge when our perspective is widened in these ways include the "racial" absences and presences that unsettle the steady flow of classical film narrative tradition; the standoff between more Fordist modes of entertainment assembly and a greater move toward decentralization; the uneasy borders that enacted the spatial and "racial" zonings of the time; and the confusion over how youth should or should not enter the practices of consumerism.

The Politics of Narrative Placement

It was at the level of the story line that these movies provoked the most spite from the mismatch labelers. With a few exceptions, like *Untamed Youth* (Howard W. Koch, 1957), their diegeses take little care to gently introduce their musical numbers; the songs stand out conspicuously. Outraged critics commented: "the plot is thrown out the window,"[5] "[t]he tunes are tied together by a flimsy story of high school romance,"[6] "the plot is really beside the point,"[7] and, most alarmingly, "[t]he string of rock 'n' roll turns is pieced together by a script that's as primitive as the music."[8] *Variety*'s assessment of *Jamboree* (Roy Lockwood, 1957) appositely likened it to a revue movie of the early sound era recast in the more contemporary form of a jukebox cueing up a line of hits.[9] With songs played and filmed in full and occupying much larger segments of screen time than was typical of feature films, rock 'n' roll appeared to its opponents as "monotonous and more than slightly cacophonous."[10] These reviews disclose a strong, unwavering faith in the directional story line and all it stands for in terms of cinematic dominance, a principle threatened by the implantation of a more concert-like atmosphere. Rock 'n' roll probably *was* the main attraction above and beyond the previously so-hallowed plot or actors; maybe music culture was now so strong that it could break free from the compliant position within cinema to which, as the previous chapter noted, it was so often relegated. Yet what these accusations about mismatches reveal is a critical resistance to not only the insertion of profitable new cultural influences into film texts but also, perhaps, their derivation from shifts within the (entertainment) labor market that severely jeopardized the standards and values set in place by the classical Hollywood system. A form of decentralization, so much the bulwark of postindustrialization, was becoming apparent, and its impact will be investigated on various fronts throughout this chapter.

What did it mean for a musical form often historically dominated by African American labor to be positioned so pivotally, to become one of the high points of the cinematic experience, to be respectfully left to play out in its entirety in all of the featured songs, to even give its name to a cycle of films? How could one have seen a "story of music,"[11] of rock 'n' roll to be precise, when that "story," its characters, its plot particularities, its historically determined structures, had long been ignored or, at best, offset by the apparatuses of American cinema? One could claim that the market demand for rock 'n' roll inspired another chapter in the manual of how African Americans might appear on screen: as headlining stars of movies aimed squarely at a "racially" mixed audience, as *workers* of a different order from those in Hollywood's past. Might the fact of the rock 'n' roll *narrative* have reshuffled certain hierarchies, even functioned as a symbolic and literal enactment of radically new reorganizations of labor in the United States? Fundamental to an understanding of this period is the fact that the United States in the 1950s, as Krishan Kumar notes in *Prophecy and Progress: The Sociology of Industrial and Post-Industrial Society,* had just become the first country in the world to have a majority of its population working in the service industry.[12] How might these rock 'n' roll movies, with their plethora of African American stars (and thus more privileged service workers than in days gone by), have complicated a steady transition into this labor configuration by disturbing certain "racial" hierarchies of old?

Taking into consideration this new twist both in the economy and in the politics of representation, how strange it is that rock 'n' roll movies have received scarce attention from scholars of the African American presence in film culture. Survey books like Donald Bogle's *Toms, Coons, Mulattoes, Mammies and Bucks: An Interpretive History of Blacks in American Films,* Ed Guerrero's *Framing Blackness: The African American Image in Film,* and Jesse Algernon Rhines's *Black Film / White Money* omit these pictures from their chronologies of African Americans in cinema. The *American Film Institute Catalog: Within Our Gates: Ethnicity in American Feature Films, 1911–1960,* which claims, "[i]n this volume we have selected nearly 2,500 feature films in which a significant focus has been on the depiction of members of American ethnic groups,"[13] only mentions *Rockin' the Blues* (Arthur Rosenblum, 1956), an all–African American musical review, and *The Blackboard Jungle* (Richard Brooks, 1955), which stars Sidney Poitier.

There is evidently something disquieting, something of a mismatch for these writers of more recent times, perhaps, in the insistent musicality of African American figures in movies, a topic with which Arthur Knight's *Disintegrating the Musical: Black Performance and American Musical Film* deals expertly. From the troubling blackface of cinema's earliest musical, *The Jazz Singer* (Alan Crosland, 1927), to the wholly musical allowances of all–African American features like *Hallelujah!* (King Vidor, 1929), *Cabin in the Sky* (Vincente Minnelli, 1943), and *Carmen Jones* (Otto Preminger, 1954), music has operated in a ghetto-like fashion for African Americans in Hollywood, which is not to deny the extraordinary creativity emanating from the ghetto space. In musicals like *The Pirate* (Vincente Minnelli, 1948), for example, African American performers (in this case, the Nicholas Brothers) were set at a distance from the story's flow in "specialty numbers" so that their appearances could be edited out for screenings in the American South. African American song-and-dance folk are frequently huddled along the sidelines, functioning as a chorus, as they often do in the rock 'n' roll cycle. The Platters' delivery of "You'll Never, Never Know" in *The Girl Can't Help It* (Frank Tashlin, 1956), to take an instance from the period under discussion, merely underscores, as the classical Fordist soundtrack would have done, Tom's (Tom Ewell) obliviousness to Jerri's (Jayne Mansfield) affections. Just as a particular chapter of the civil rights story was getting under way, complete with heroes and heroines like Martin Luther King, Jr., and Rosa Parks, narrative "progress" was folded back into a more enclosed, often cyclical structure. The repetitive organization of the African American performers in the rock 'n' roll movies instead matched the particular stylistic constraints of that genre of songwriting, with its alternating rather than strictly processional A–B–C patterns. Film aesthetics, then, mirrored the more restrictive models that were available within African American representation.

The relationship of these rock 'n' roll performers to the story line activates very particular working associations. In film after film, named and distinguished musical figures were never allowed to roam far from their musical pretexts. They were always to play "themselves" rather than characters in the more fantastical dimensions of these often digressively un-narrative narratives, ones that prefer the musical revue scaffold to plots with more spatial and incidental variety. The curtailment of possibilities for African American dramatis personae was not a new phenomenon. In the 1930s, Duke Ellington and Cab Calloway had appeared on film as "themselves"[14] and continued to do so for most of their lives. Should the 1950s audiences feel that they were drifting away from this tradition, dialogue references and advertising posters in the mise-en-scènes of these newer films asserted the real names of most of the members of the cast. In all sorts of calculated (but obviously not total) ways, this world was allied as closely to "reality" as possible, replicating its commodities and ensuring that we remember how to distinguish them without condoning the entrance of any such performers into our matrices of empathy or identification. In essence, these performers are continually "on the job," inscribed indelibly as workers and nothing much besides, rather than being granted an expanded imaginary life. While the ubiquitous white impresario Alan Freed plays himself too (most blatantly in his autobiographical film, *Mister Rock and Roll*), his performance aggrandizes his existence to much higher levels of cinematic importance: his life is worthy of immortalization, unlike the jobbing African American musicians who make up the cast lists.

The ways in which each of the musical performers is captured on film repeatedly enact some of the most noticeable and pressing tensions of the time. Although rock 'n' roll assumes a thematic and structural centrality in these movies, unless a live concert is taking place, there is very little in the way of, for instance, reaction shots or eye-line matches that secure the musicians into either the filmic space or the suturing processes of mainstream cinematic audience engagement. It is not atypical for performers to shift their eyes restlessly away from the camera, settling upon no particular focal point so as to avoid staring directly into its lens or at any given character. Often, the camera is set at an angle to avoid the possibility of visual engagement and, in the rarer medium shots of single singers (such as during the Moonglows' rendition of "I Knew from the Start" in *Rock, Rock, Rock* [Will Price, 1956]), such intimacy is avoided at all costs. Throughout his turns in *Don't Knock the Rock* and *The Girl Can't Help It,* Little Richard sidesteps the issue by adopting a characteristic thousand-yard stare off to one side, something that plausibly extends the mad-cap persona he wields throughout these movies and elsewhere.

That said, the same techniques are clearly tendered to and by white musicians like Bill Haley and his [*sic*] Comets in *Don't Knock the Rock* and Jerry Lee Lewis in *Jamboree*. The implication is not that African Americans alone must never presume a more intimate connection with viewers. Instead, this is a prohibition on the rural working-class lock, stock, and barrel, the kinds of people who were, as we shall see, moving into the metropolis, but who would not exactly have been welcome in the newly developing suburbs, where many of the films' protagonists seem to dwell. In this respect, perhaps a framework of migration rather than segregation is more useful for our understanding of these movies; it certainly helps to explain various overlaps of experience that shaped the production and reception of the rock 'n' roll cycle. Furthermore, a migration model clarifies the uneven treatment of these stars as workers, rather than as potential friends or neighbors in a shared space. The chronicling of migration's history, including how it contributed to the diminution of the rural economies that made way for postindustrial production, is worthwhile at this point then.

In the lead-up to this era and in a repeat of the 1914–1918 period, labor shortages caused by war had provoked another stream of migration out of the rural South and into the cities of the North and West, as well as the more built-up areas of the South itself. Unlike in the preceding set of relocations, however, where most of those moving were African American, this era saw whites transferring to the cities too. Further workers continued to arrive there throughout the 1950s as educational opportunities continued to weed more and more people out of the still-booming blue-collar sector. Eric Avila's investigation of cinema at that time yields some highly pertinent statistics:

On the eve of World War II, 70 percent of American blacks lived in the South, whereas only 53 percent lived there thirty years later. The number of black urbanites, moreover, increased dramatically in the United States between 1945 and 1960. During that period, New York's black population increased two and one-half times, and the number of blacks tripled in Detroit. The West, however, experienced the greatest growth in its African American population. Los Angeles, a city with a relatively small black population until 1940, saw an 800 percent increase in its black population, from 75,000 to 600,000.[15]

There were serious reasons behind this exodus. Postwar developments in tractor, mechanical picker, and pesticide technology had rendered cotton production less labor intensive. So too did federal programs encouraging a 40 percent reduction in cotton acreage and a minimum wage for farm hands.[16]

The subsequent relocation of many rural/southern white and African Americans out of a sharecropping economy and into a wage-earning one in urban centers must have transformed the notions of work and leisure. How was the inevitable exploitation of these migrants' labor to be weighed in correspondence with their inculcation into the rights and practices of consumption and citizenship? Certainly, organized labor was entirely ambivalent about the balancing of this equation in many of the struggles it undertook. White workers' rights in terms of pensions and health care were privileged, and many trade unions, such as that of the bus drivers, proved unwilling to offer their support in the fight for freedom.[17] The anxieties about working-class migrants penetrated so fully into the national psyche that they bob to the surface incessantly throughout this body of films.

Untamed Youth is the rock 'n' roll movie that engages most explicitly with these issues, despite and because of its all-white cast. The year's bumper cotton harvest is in peril because of, a radio broadcast informs us, an "acute shortage of labor in the south-west." In response to this scantly explored repercussion of migration, the film's villain, Tropp (John Russell), hatches a dastardly scheme to seduce the local female judge (Lurene Tuttle) into providing him with unfairly sentenced youths to work on his prison farm. The ruptures of worker relocation are explicitly projected onto vulnerable teenagers (more about them later), the very audiences for these films. The protagonists are fed dog food and kept from their freedom by a system of indentured labor that leaves them in perpetual debt to their employer. "I thought Lincoln got rid of slavery," Janey (Lori Nelson) exclaims, while in the fields they defiantly sing (along with Eddie Cochran, no less):

> You ain't gonna make a cotton-picker out of me,
> You can make me sweat, make me steam,
> You can make me rock, rock, rock 'til I scream,
> But you ain't gonna make a cotton-picker out of me.
> You can make me poor, you can make me rich,
> You can make me want the seven year itch,
> But you ain't gonna make a cotton-picker out of me.
> You can make me sing, make me dance,
> Make me rock right out of my pants,
> But you ain't gonna make a cotton-picker out of me.

Replicating the hierarchies of slavery, working in "the house" is regarded by the captive teenagers more favorably than toiling in the fields, but positions them closer to the roving hands of the boss. In a bizarre alternative and largely uncontextualized citation of African diaspora culture and its geographical loci, the tale ends when Penny (Mamie Van Doren) performs "Go Calypso" in a mock Caribbean accent, on a television show.

Similarly, *Jailhouse Rock* (Richard Thorpe, 1957) is haunted by references to an unfinished (African American) journey from enforced to manual to service work, the close-to-hand specters of slavery seemingly breathing down the necks of the white characters too. "You know I'll be your slave if you ask me to," proclaims Vince (Elvis Presley) in his song "Treat Me Nice"; Vince retorts to Hunk (Mickey Shaughnessy) at one point, "I ain't asking you to shine my shoes"; and the number that is performed in their shared prison cell runs:

> I'm up in the morning with the rising sun,
> Work like a slave 'til the day is done,
> Just workin' and sleepin' and nothin' more
> And every day is just like the day before.

In *Shake, Rattle and Rock!* at the point at which Nelson (Mike Connors) fears that his television show may be canceled, he turns to June (Lisa Gaye) and asks, in a parody of a southern accent, "Can you just picture yourself the wife of a poor but honest laborer, a poor cotton picker, for instance." Her reply: "I love cotton-picking cotton-pickers." A fear of a return to agricultural poverty, although tinged with anxious comedy and nostalgia, seems to leach messily and uncontainably from all of these allusions, revealing distinct uncertainties about working relations. In *Don't Knock the Rock,* disquiet about the shifts in labor practices and, perhaps, the instabilities of media employment are expressed by the older generation when a father good-naturedly remarks to a group of rock 'n' roll revelers, "In the old days, the kids used their energy for picking corn."

Evidently, the deeper patterns set in motion by job reallocation and internal migration to more media-oriented urban centers within the United States are central to both the development, recording, and filming of rock 'n' roll and, of course, the building momentum of social desegregation. What is all the more striking about these movies is that they arose from a set of industries that still largely functioned according to Fordist techniques and that were themselves breaking away from established traditions of laboring in order to enter a parallel phase of relocation.

"Be Sure and Watch Alan Freed's Television Program Tomorrow Night": The Decentralization and Diversification of the Media Industries

The disjunctive flow of people into service professions took place in a highly perceptible dialectical climate. The United States' relatively self-contained national economy still largely functioned according to Fordist mass production. This ethic's very heartbeat can be heard throughout the formulaic replication of these genre movies[18] and the tight, industrially rhythmic structures of many rock 'n' roll songs (think, for example, of the regularity and forthright predictability of "Jailhouse Rock"), not to mention the restrictive stratifications of labor that had historically justified racial segregation. From numerous perspectives, mid-1950s America was engrossed, as it was through much of the twentieth century, in a Keynesian economic conviction: bureaucratic regulation, even state intervention, strived to cultivate stability—all to the advantage of the healthy longevity of capitalism.

But this drive met its dialectical adversary, particularly within the entertainment industries, in the form of an urge for deregulation which challenged existing monopolies. The story runs thus: the Paramount Decree of 1948 had thrown the once-secure Big Eight film studios into a more unpredictable world infested with unwanted competition. These antitrust laws dictated the disassembly of the industry's vertically integrated structure, but the impact of this legislation was only truly beginning to be felt in the mid-1950s. Ironically, Hollywood now hankered after protectionism in an otherwise proudly expansionist arena. By opening up exhibition to outside investment, the Paramount decision paved the way for a flurry of new film-viewing enterprises, notably the long-maligned drive-in theater. The Hollywood majors refused to fully cooperate with these businesses and charged them exorbitant rental fees, unwittingly strengthening the trade between the drive-ins and the exploitation companies, many of which made rock 'n' roll movies and held no prior resentment toward the outdoor "ozoner" venues. To the evident dismay of the big budget film producers, Hollywood expertise hardly seemed to be missed by visitors to the drive-ins,[19] who were more drawn to the diversified experience of the environment itself, with its babysitter-free convenience, playgrounds, restaurants, and other leisure activities, including, on occasion, rock 'n' roll shows.[20] The demise of the studio system, the collapse of vertical integration, and the simultaneous loss of the large-scale family audience sparked a rescue mission. This saw Hollywood wading into more uncharted waters, ones of outsourcing, decentralization, short-term contract work, and appeal to smaller, more-specialized markets, the very hallmarks of the fast-approaching post-industrialism.[21] As will become clear later, rock 'n' roll films, fragmented from their very points of assembly and no more coherent when they reached viewers, provoked concern and mismatch accusation, largely because they threatened older labor traditions.

This narrative of deregulation wended its way through other spheres of entertainment too. By the end of the decade, all manner of analogous antitrust actions had been flung around the music business. Perhaps one of the most long-standing and spiteful was the campaign instigated by the licensing giant ASCAP (American Society of Composers, Authors and Publishers) against BMI (Broadcast Music, Inc.). Once small-fry, BMI had come to imperil ASCAP's market share through the unpredicted rise in popularity of the types of artist it represented. Significantly, these musicians were predominantly from the genres of rock 'n' roll, rhythm and blues, and country and frequently heralded from the traditional rural blue-collar non–service sector classes. What is more, their output also appealed to the escalating teenager market. These two factors, I shall illustrate, were locked together in the moral panics of the time and also help to explain ASCAP's erratically concealed plea for the protection of youth from BMI's largely African American influence, which eventually led to congressional hearings in 1958 and 1960.[22]

Interestingly, the muddled dialectic of monopoly control battling against divestment interacted, in various and quite surprising ways, with the United States' contemporary concerns about the politics of desegregation. In a long *Variety* editorial, Arthur L. Mayer, with no small measure of confusion coloring his analogy, argued that the Paramount Decree should be reversed:

> [W]e must regain our faith . . . in the Supreme Court's capacity to even reverse the Supreme Court, as in the segregation issue where segregation approved 60 years ago was in the light of humanitarian progress and world opinion held unconstitutional. . . . Thank God we live in a free economy where nothing is static; in a democracy where nothing—not even a Consent Decree—is irretrievable.[23]

Untrammeled "advancement," "racial" and capitalistic, should rule the day.

Despite these pleas, though, no such intervention took place, and the way was paved for less stable, more horizontal coalitions that matched, in many senses, a broader social shift in working practices in mid-twentieth-century America. Following through on this particular economic and institutional history, we witness a mighty blow dealt to traditions of laboring. Crippled by their lack of control over exhibition, the former Big Eight rapidly sold off many of their assets and let a good proportion of their permanent staff go; in 1956, there were only twenty-four contracted writers working in the industry.[24] It was noted by *Variety* in December of that year that the major studios "more and more are engaging in partnership deals with independent producers."[25] The emphasis had turned to the brokering of deals with free agents, which set in motion a chain of events that Thomas Doherty outlines in his classic book on youth movies, *Teenagers and Teenpics: The Juvenilization of American Movies in the 1950s*:

> Once Hollywood lawyers and agents realized that capital gains were taxed at a lower rate than salaries, they urged their high-priced clients to back private production companies and reap the benefits of corporate profit sharing rather than take a studio salary. Attracted by freedom as well as finance, big-name producers, directors and stars rushed to form independent production companies . . . [whose] share had risen to at least 50 percent [of Hollywood output by 1958].[26]

The tide was certainly turning toward what we might now call post-Fordism.

It soon became apparent that the major studios were a lot worse off financially without their exhibition wings and that production was slowing down. Left high and dry without as diverse a range of movies, small picture houses, like the drive-ins (which, logically, had proliferated after the antitrust legislation), would often turn to the quick-buck fare at which the exploitation companies excelled. The working traditions of the Hollywood majors were leaving them behind and, consequently, *Variety* noted "the sudden willingness on the part of the major companies to turn out more films . . . [which should be] seen in the light of their realization that the survival of the small house depends on the delivery of volume product that can be turned out at very low cost."[27] Thus, simply in order to provide the necessary stock, MGM teamed up with the small independent Avon Pictures for *Jailhouse Rock* and Warner Brothers with Vanguard for another rock 'n' roll picture, *Jamboree*, which, notably, was filmed in New York and suggests the simultaneous *geographical* decentralization of the movie business.

These films embody the expedient deal struck to counter the built-in sluggishness of conventional film manufacture: as *Variety* also observed, they were the outcome of labor-saving horizontal affiliations with independent equivalents from the world of music.[28] The manufacturing flexibility, single-mindedness, and greater, more organic knowledge of the niche markets of the independent music companies were paying off, ensuring a much weightier margin of success in the charts than had been evident a decade earlier—much to the annoyance of ASCAP.[29] The standing of Hollywood's major studios within media culture appeared to be diminishing, while the popular music markets were on the rise, but in both spheres, the majors found themselves taken somewhat unawares by the more elastic approach of their junior competitors. While elsewhere in the country, intense Fordist manufacture, the type that is charted so astutely and articulately in many a rock 'n' roll song, prospered, the imperative to revamp these modes of production at pain of perishing gnawed away at and into these media institutions, creating, so the critics bemoaned, a string of often highly uneven movies.

It is now time to throw a broader, politically reflective element into all of these divergent flows, to add the voice of one of my core theorists of dialecticism to this inquiry into working and what "doesn't work." In his sociopolitically charged exploration, *The Poverty of Philosophy*, Karl Marx reflects precisely upon financial dealings like these, thinking beyond the aesthetic rough edges that are often their outcomes in order to unlock their impact upon workers, both as producers and consumers:

> This juridical relation, whose form is the contract, whether as part of
> a developed legal system or not, is a relation between two wills which
> mirrors the economic relation. The content of this juridical relation (or
> relation of two wills) is itself determined by the economic relation.

Here the persons exist for one another merely as representatives and hence owners, of commodities. . . . Men are henceforth related to each other in their social process of production in a purely atomistic way. Their own relations of production therefore assume a material shape which is independent of their control and their conscious individual action.[30]

A sense of human alienation looms large, pointing us toward interpreting film–music connections as something more than attempts of varying success at structural harmony and compelling us to unpack these allegories of subsumed, unfair labor. Contracts of these kinds helped to overcome and to benefit from the divorce of the spaces of production and consumption and were, as will become apparent, a core anxiety that was threaded through the rock 'n' roll cycle.

The explosions of these profitable alliances, which were detonated across the breadth of the entertainment industries, rumbled through these movies, damaging, for one, their structural consistency according to standard patterns for the delivery of narrative. Traditionalists were quick off the mark with their pejorative statements about mismatches which we would now call product placement, a rupture in the text that might lead potential customers off toward other merchandise. *Variety,* for instance, complained upon *Mister Rock and Roll*'s release that it "runs off like an unadorned filmization of one of Freed's typical stage shows."[31]

Radio shows profited from similar plugs, or, rather, the movies regularly drew upon the allure of radio DJs, with *Jamboree* casting a lengthy list of twenty-one different regional radio hosts, all of whom also contributed specific, locally targeted trailers.[32] Another advantage of the DJs appearing on screen was the naturalness with which their patter clearly announced which performer was which, enabling viewers to easily distinguish any artist whose records they might later wish to buy.

Even cinema itself became a beneficiary of these emphatic, plot-diverting statements. Film footage is used as evidence in support of rock 'n' roll in the "trial" in *Shake, Rattle and Rock!* and there is mention of "MGM Records," the movie's parent company, in the story line of *Jailhouse Rock*. Soundtrack albums had persistently been the bestselling genre in long-playing records so it seemed a logical progression to lead cinema in a musical direction and to promote music through coordination with the hype of a movie's release (as was the case with Chess's marketing of the *Rock, Rock, Rock* soundtrack).[33] Any supposedly tidy diegetic world became merely a nodal point in a network of real purchasable commodities, especially ones linked to up-and-coming markets.

While television may have been one of the most aggressive rivals to film culture in the 1950s, it is merrily welcomed in this set of movies. Musical performances on television are crucial plot developments in *The Girl Can't Help It; Loving You; Rock, Pretty Baby* (Richard Bartlett, 1956); *Jamboree; Jailhouse Rock; Shake, Rattle and Rock!* and *Untamed Youth;* ideas are delivered by it and names are made on it. *Rock, Rock, Rock*'s finale becomes an out-and-out promotion for Alan Freed's television show, which is being shot at Dori's (Tuesday Weld) school that week, foreshadowing its actual national syndication in July 1957. Interestingly, critiques about a lack of regard for format specificity followed the Freed franchise into television when it was claimed by *Variety:*

> Freed makes no concessions to the tv medium. If it's rock 'n' roll that ABC-TV wants, then it's what he's giving them all the way. . . . Freed came up with a strong roster that should appeal to the kids who go for this type of music. But if any unsuspecting adults tuned in by error, they weren't likely to be won over to the stomping, screaming and just plain caterwauling styles common to the performers.[34]

Unfazed by these criticisms, Freed blatantly disregarded the traditions of expertise in any given area, trampling over their regulation of labor and output in order to become a master of the cost-cutting and profit multiplication inherent to cross-promotion. Alongside his vastly popular radio show and numerous film appearances, he put together box office record-breaking live performance packages where films like *Don't Knock the Rock* were screened as warm-up "acts" before the stars of the movie performed and where soundtrack LPs could be purchased from concession stands. Freed negotiated a 10 percent cut of *Rock, Rock, Rock* as well as securing appearances by artists signed to Coral Records, in which he had a hand, and the rights to fifteen of the movie's twenty-one songs.[35] Throughout his career, Freed walked the thin lines between cross-marketing and attempts at a monopoly economy, exploitation (in all of its semantic incarnations) and corruption—distinctions that were clarified by the payola scandals of the latter part of the decade, which implicated Freed irrevocably.

All of this mirrors Marx's understanding of financial manipulation and his observations about the division of sensory perception, which is, for him, "a labor of the entire history of the world down to the present."[36] The splitting off of commodities for the ears and for the eyes works both in the service and as a result of capitalist modes of production. We wrench them from their contexts, objectify and catalog them, and make a naturalized leap from believing that we own our perceptions to asserting our rights to lay claims on their object stimuli as potential commodities. Thus, sensory perception becomes not only divided, but also ideologically circumscribed. As a consequence of this placement and diversification of the senses, more products for our delectation are made available, and we become increasingly dependent on the idea that the commercial satisfaction of these senses is something with which to indulge ourselves. Most important for Marx, however, "This *material* immediately *sensuous* private property is the material sensuous expression of *estranged human life*."[37] The labor expended upon the object or the subsequent suffering or misuse that its manufacturer may have experienced are obliterated by the ethics of ownership and most aesthetic appreciation: the concentration on the sensuous qualities of the object leads to the belief that it has been "earned." Although there is nothing new to all of this, there is something particular to the way that frozen labor is then patched back together in these rock 'n' roll mismatches. They edge dangerously close to revealing how alienated from each other all of these practices of working actually were, and this is something that comes dramatically to the fore when the films' narratives are damned for their lack of unity.

What one can also discern in the reactions to these movies is a similar desire to criticize the very work for which the new geopolitical arrangements made way, namely, the further integration of all sorts of prior underclasses ("black" and "white") into the growing and profit-generating service industries. By asserting the importance of professional mastery, newcomers were belittled for their ignorance and its implications for "product inferiority." The critics' gleeful pointing out of a lack of technical finesse[38] (in effect, that certain work should deftly remain unnoticed) emerged as a desperate smoke screen to obscure a genuine alarm that modes of manufacturing were changing and threatening previously stable institutions.

Proper Work, Proper Leisure, and the Teenager

In 1956, one edition of *Variety* concluded:

> [T]he market is wide open and hungry for the former, regular flow of product which is now being filled by the quickies. My argument isn't that they can't make money—because they certainly can show a good profit on a low investment—but rather, being of indifferent quality, such pictures are apt to hasten the demise of an already wobbly section of exhibition.[39]

There was certainly a palpable fear in the air that Hollywood was being priced out of the market by "novices." This included not only producers, but also performers.

Another recurrent observation being bandied about was that the cinema's rock 'n' roll output was devoid of stars.[40] This was not at all the case: the confusion arose because those with top billing were musicians not actors, and many of them were African Americans with proven track records in music sales. There was a cruel double irony awaiting these performers who, once they had finally arrived center stage in the insistently racist medium of cinema, looked around to find it evacuated of "stars." However, the title sequences of these movies readily acknowledged all of their names, usually before many of the actors; if these were "no-star" vehicles, then at least the musicians were first in billing and mentioned in detail in most of the contemporary reviews. All the same, scores of critics failed to acknowledge their standing, reinstating familiar restrictions, ones duplicated by the circumscribed diegetic spaces of performance within the rock 'n' roll movies, an aesthetic conformity which was often at odds with some of the more expansive, unreservedly exploratory registers of the packages' song structures.

Many of the contemporary industrial concerns about these products were projected onto their consumers, as if the teens themselves were to blame for a restructuring of the employment market. Mitch Miller, then director of Columbia Records, spleenfully and dismissively announced that "the kids don't want recognized stars doing their music. They don't want real professionals. They want faceless people doing it in order to retain the feeling that it's their own."[41] Although he was just as likely to be referring to the more "manufactured" artists of the time than to the progenitors of rock 'n' roll, the attempt to de-skill contemporary popular stars is telling. Similarly, the untrained delivery of creaky segue lines like Bill Haley's "Hey, how about hearing my new tune?" in *Don't Knock the Rock* received trouncings according to unsympathetically traditional means of appraisal.[42] In a sector whose most commonsensical strategy was to turn back to a tried and tested template of successful production when that was one of its few remaining assets (conservatism, some would call it), it is hardly astounding that notions of "quality" became "the mainstream's" strongest weapon. The expended energy and creative agency were thence drained out of the rock 'n' roll merchandise by more established and respected industry folk. To make matters worse, especially for African Americans, the fact that their singing was rarely "spontaneous" in these narratives and took place within service sectors, such as clubs or rehearsal rooms, where they were consistently positioned as employees, brought the issue of (failed) labor even more fully into the frame. These criticisms thus yet again fail to contextualize and politically scrutinize the economies of African American work, one of the country's most monetarily lucrative and troubling legacies.

Attempting to expose this history, Brian Ward in *Just My Soul Responding: Rhythm and Blues, Black Consciousness and Race Relations* points out:

> [M]any black artists were locked into extraordinarily exploitative contracts which substantially reduced their capacity to profit from even the records they did sell. When lawyer Howell Begle investigated claims by a number of r&b veterans that they had routinely been deprived of proper payment by their record companies, he discovered that in the 1940s and 1950s most had contracts which paid royalties at a meagre rate of between 1 and 4 per cent of the retail price of recordings sold, or else provided one-off payments of around $200 in return for performances which sometimes made millions of dollars. Such practices retarded black capital accumulation within the music industry and ultimately had a chilling effect on the extension of black ownership and economic power.[43]

Johnny Cash and Carl Perkins, in addition to Elvis Presley, were similarly hoodwinked, although not to the same degree (they rarely received one-time payments). And, furthermore, Alan Freed, a star of many of these films and one of rock 'n' roll's most ardent promoters, unjustly attributed to himself songwriting credits for money-generating hits like "Maybelline" and "Sincerely."[44]

Rock 'n' roll artists fared little better in independent movie production. American International Pictures' (AIP) "no-stars" policy conveniently sidestepped these performers' musical fame in order to pay them minimal wages that would not have satisfied white singers like Pat Boone.[45] Shooting schedules, such as *Rock, Rock, Rock*'s lean two weeks,[46] were partially made possible because the musicians were already polished; their rehearsal time did not encroach upon the films' budgets.

This ability to garner increased profit from already-established money earners lies at the heart of what "exploitation" meant in the industry parlance of the day. The term came to denote, on the one hand, the creation of maximum revenues from a minimum of expenditures, and, on the other, successful cross-marketing. Both depended upon, if we return to Marxian priorities, the injustice of our isolating and uneven interrelationships of labor, governed as they were by unequal evaluation, worker exploitation, and the obfuscation of human pain and toil into such abstractions as money or commodity fetishes.

The indies parted company from Hollywood, however, when they chose to deliberately unmask these very practices of entertainment capital by refuel-

ing on negative commentary and all that it proclaimed about media manufacturing. "Exploitation with a Flair from Bel-Air. A profit making line-up for
the 1956–57 season . . . crammed with action, drama, adventure!" claimed an
advertisement for the production company responsible for *Untamed Youth*.[47]
In the unabashed responses to attacks from more established producers, the
makers of the cycle foregrounded just how much shoddiness and exploitation
capitalist revenue generation can get away with. AIP, which put together *Shake,
Rattle and Rock!* routinely churned out its wares for a slender $50,000 to
$200,000[48] in a matter of weeks in order to capitalize on particular, perhaps
short-lived trends.[49] Producer Sam Katzman, who later went on to make
Harum Scarum, never lost money on a movie, and similarly flagrant attitudes
toward disposability laid bare the capitalist principles that are often more carefully hidden in entertainment fare. By acknowledging this rule of the game
during a tender moment of transition in the consumer statuses of adolescent
viewers, African Americans, and even white rural migrants, these companies
evidently provoked much annoyance in various sectors of society, not least
among the increasingly threatened entertainment stalwarts.

Furthermore, such business interactions are key to the movies' plots, laid
out boldly for the audiences themselves to examine. By far the most prevalent
scenario in this group of films is the performer (successful or on the rise) and
his or her dealings with the music business. *Carnival Rock* (Roger Corman, 1957)
depicts the unrequited love of a comedian for a singer, while *Rock Around the
Clock; Rock, Pretty Baby; Loving You; Jamboree;* and *Jailhouse Rock* spin tales of white
youngsters trying to make it in show business, buffeted from all directions by
an endless whirl of contracts, salary negotiations, and exploitation exerted from
all sides, including their own. Arnie (Alan Dale), the hero of *Don't Knock the
Rock,* is exhausted from a heavy performing schedule and pleads with his manager for a holiday; his reluctance is matched by *The Girl Can't Help It*'s Jerri,
who is pressured into a life on stage by her gangster fiancé. In all of these stories, business and pleasure mix (usually via heterosexual, white love matches)
in challenging and fulfilling ways that are captured by *Jamboree*'s culminating
song, "24 Hours a Day." The relentlessness of entertainment industry struggle
is neatly equated with the enduring love that can be found within it. Other
songs also insistently discuss the interplay of work and its rewards: "It's Satur-
day night and I just got paid," divulges Bill Haley in "Rip It Up," which is
showcased in *Don't Knock the Rock.* Even the jokes center their fun around
wage economies: "I always thought freedom of the press was someone who
ironed your shirts for nothing," says Haley in the same film. While music is
more of (although not entirely) a backdrop in *Rock, Rock, Rock* and *Untamed
Youth,* it has to be noted that the former is almost entirely a parable about teen

money management and the latter has a protagonist who just happens to be called Penny.

What was the point of narratives that damned exploitation from an overtly exploitative position? I do not wish to pass judgments of praise or damnation on this seeming contradiction, but to prize it apart and see what can be learned from it. Does the repeated eagerness to contemplate corruption, workplace inequality, and the subjugation of performers' personas to market forces in any way, for instance, allow for a veiled audience identification with (African American) artists, again through the heavily loaded formal structures of musical and filmic commodities? Certainly there is an awkward mismatch written into any empathy that equates what W. T. Lhamon dubs the "wanton squandering of energy—in decibels, pace, and unstable motion"[50] (not to mention the "rebelling without a cause") of the stereotypical, largely white and middle-class, 1950s teenager with the unerring abuse of the (sometimes African American) performers who feature in these movies. In many ways, a line that carved out categories of labor, a line drawn out by even some of the presentational customs of the rock 'n' roll movie cycle itself, was being crossed by viewing practices. Although more of a shared investment than the activation of equal rights or opportunities, might these interactions have shaken up dialecticism's momentum as a means of transformation? Partially so: the affluence of the decade definitely redrew any such demarcations, allowing a greater inclusiveness and enfranchisement, while simultaneously maintaining a particular type of separation.

Here we confront a hub of dialectical epistemology where the social construction of oppositions, the possibility of their very existence, and their dependence upon our habit of fencing off meanings, entities, and presences are confused by these denigrated film cultures. To be sure, as is ever the case within advanced capitalism, there were successful attempts to inculcate spending practices unequivocally into the political ideals of continued production,[51] but, at the same time, these actions severely compromised some of the more robustly maintained distinctions of the work-leisure dichotomy.

"Told the Way They Want It Told": The Question of Teen Leisure Expenditure

In *Consuming Youth: Vampires, Cyborgs, and the Culture of Consumption,* Robert Latham stresses the fraught nature of this balance and the way it was cast onto the figure of the adolescent:

Fordist capitalism from its origins saw in "consuming youth" a potential for cementing the increasingly fractured activities of labor and of
leisure, yet this "resolution" did not eliminate the ethical contradiction
between these realms that would in the postwar period become a
source of profound cultural crisis.[52]

Such oppositions of work and leisure, production and consumption are similarly embodied within the narratives of the rock 'n' roll movies, making their
plots anything but meaningless.[53] This somewhat uneasy tension between spending and earning is tellingly central to parenting self-help manuals of the time,
like Paul H. Landis's *Understanding Teen-Agers,* which incorporated long sections on youth money management. Perhaps as a consequence, the figure of
the young musician on screen simultaneously earning a living and having fun
functioned as an effective means of understanding this inconsistency.

It is hardly surprising that youth-oriented films of this time sought ways of
coming to terms with the balance of labor and leisure, given the somewhat
novel suspension of this portion of the population from the workforce proper.
In his wide-ranging study, *The Rise and Fall of the American Teenager,* Thomas
Hine points out that it had only been a couple of decades previously that the
majority of adolescents had begun enrolling in high school; it was at this time
that the underemployment and intense competition for work which arose
from the Depression rendered legislation against child labor much more plau-
sible.[54] In the not-too-distant past, teens had provided essential extra income
for their families and, in fact, this practice had not entirely died out, particularly in poorer families. By the mid-1950s, though, adolescents largely appeared
to be more "profitable" as consumers, but ones requiring the vital infusion of
a future spirit of work.

The more vibrant economy which granted the inhabitants of this phase of
life heftier disposable incomes was also, as has become apparent, characterized
by various forms of decentralization and fragmentation that had begun to assemble subgroups like the "teen market" and the "African American market."
This revamping of consumption set adolescents at a greater remove from other
sections of society, something that attracted all kinds of differently received and
projected connotations. Landis's handbook for parents easily rationalizes this
reconfiguration of the populace in terms of evolution: "One has to go to a very
backward country indeed to find any gathering at which all age groups are together. The teen group has its own meeting place in town. . . . In a real sense,
the teen-age group is self-sufficient now as in no previous generation."[55] Adolescent notions of autonomy stemmed not so much from numbers (the baby

boomer generation had not quite reached this age yet) but, more likely, from the shared experience of a universal high school education and a fair spread of affluence that advertisers estimated was worth $9 billion to the market per annum, and set to rise.[56] The emotional absorption in spending on clothes, candy, and jukebox tracks that is all but the only concern of Dori, much to the chagrin of her father (Jack Collins), in *Rock, Rock, Rock* was not only rising but becoming commercially significant.

It did not take the music industry long to realize that its recent high grosses were thanks to this social group; Elvis Presley alone, apparently, was responsible for 50 percent of RCA's profits,[57] and Decca had seen a 20 percent increase in sales by March of 1957.[58] However, it was noted within the film industry not only that the teen audience, with its own particular tastes, was one of its most reliable consumer groups, but that cinema was "behind" in spotting the favored trends and, as *Variety* saw it, "borrowed occasionally from other entertainment media, picking up for film exposure a teen hero or heroine who had already obtained a degree of acclaim via disk outings."[59] Hence the contracting of the independents.

Given the widespread cluelessness about the youth market, the trade press took increasing care in its movie reviews to point out to the entertainment business at large exactly how this newly developing group might react to the rock 'n' roll cycle. "It has the ingredients that cater to the whims and fads of America's most publicized age group";[60] "[b]ouncy musical drama with plenty [of] appeal to teenagers. Special handling can lure extra b.o. coin";[61] "this pic is aimed straight at the teenage disk fans";[62] "[t]he entire setup is slanted at the young filmgoers"[63]—all of these statements suggest an increasing realization that this sector was worth exploiting. *Variety*'s review of *Rock, Rock, Rock* barely contains its cynicism nonetheless: "Unimpressive rock and roller quickie concocted for some fast b.o. cash—With the trend to 'pictures for teenagers' it follows that one emphasis would be on rock and roll subjects. That doesn't mean all will be good ones, or that teenage draw will give them a sustained market."[64]

The independents went to great lengths to comprehend the needs and concerns of the teen body, indicating a sensitivity to audience tastes that was perhaps not as familiar to the previously vertically integrated studios. Samuel Z. Arkoff of AIP, for example, invited teens to his house to discuss their preferences and to screen his latest films for them, while the print advertisement for *Rock, Pretty Baby* proclaimed the movie to be "told the way they want it told."[65] As has already been noted, particular attention was paid to where and when films were screened: *Rock, Pretty Baby* and *Love Me Tender* (Robert D. Webb, 1956) coincided with Thanksgiving, and the releases of *The Girl Can't*

Help It; Don't Knock the Rock; Rock, Rock, Rock; and *Shake, Rattle and Rock!* fell in line with the winter break from school.

What, then, did it mean for the indies to exploit the newfound wealth of these social groups in their films' depictions of the working practices that drive entertainment? Teen audiences were considered to be at risk in all manner of ways, their recent buying power rendering them both vulnerable and powerful[66] and their entry into various marketplaces subsequently involving them in a set of new dialectical subjectivities.

The content of these movies did little to assuage any worries about the vulnerability of youths, but what it did achieve, conveniently, was a projection of their exploitation into the world of work, rather than leisure. The uncertainty about the spending power of the niche grouping was being displaced elsewhere, onto the perhaps more teen-oriented music industry, a realm, of course, that incorporated an appreciably greater proportion of intercultural contact, at least at the level of the commodities that were exchanged. Almost all of the white characters fall prey to unscrupulous employers or self-proclaimed "exploitation men," from Penny's naïve vulnerability in the hands of a sexual predator who might further her career in *Untamed Youth* and Sherry's (Jennifer Holden) "cooperation contract" that insists she date her leading man in *Jailhouse Rock,* to Arnie's weary speech about his disposability in *Don't Knock the Rock:* "It's just a name, if it wasn't me it'd be someone else. Kids just pick someone like me and wave it like a flag, they wanna hold me in front of their parents' noses like a pair of red britches in front of a bull." How startlingly close this comment is to both the observations of estranged major record label bosses and the philosophy of Karl Marx. The difference, of course, is that Marx is adamant that the dislocation of worker from product should not be repeated through the mechanisms of consumption. In contradistinction, these films also urge a greater *protectiveness* toward white youth, but do so by encouraging their spending practices. The hegemonic category of "youth" was perceived to be at great risk, and its entertainment cultures (including rock 'n' roll and cinema) became a crucial site for tussles undertaken in the name of adolescents. Throughout all this, it is worth considering Robert Latham's claim that "Fordism had begun to conceive of youth not merely as an empirical category but as an ideological abstraction."[67] Stuffed into the term "youth" was a whole host of other political ideals with which teenagers had to contend.

Driving onward in the opposite direction, perhaps unwilling to confront such a loaded term, were certain factions from within Hollywood. Certainly, "mainstream" Fordist-derived movie production was slow to realize that the broad-based family audience (whom it had consistently thought of as the customers for the majority of its products) was no longer so reliable, but maybe there were greater social issues at stake too. The marked difference between *The Girl Can't Help It* (a Twentieth Century Fox release) and the more independent rock 'n' roll pictures is that the former, by poking fun at the world of music manufacture, was both hedging its bets more than the others and trying to offset the distancing of adolescents, providing, as one contemporary review concluded, "entertainment for both adults and teenagers"[68] during which "Charleston-age oldsters can delight in the ribbing and enjoy the show, too."[69] There are family-friendly dimensions to the narratives of some of the other films and even some less baldly rock 'n' roll musical numbers.[70] Their aim was perhaps to win over a diverse audience to the harmlessness of the teen sensibility and to downplay the utter alienation provoked by a newly segmenting market.

Why, then, the ambivalence about teen separatism, the desires to defend a body largely understood as young and white, to encase it within particular symbolic formations, or to corral it back into more supposedly secure enclosures like "the family"? One answer to this may be that the teen market did not necessarily obey the segregated stratifications of yore and that racism may well have motivated some of this concern. While the battle for the white teenager was being waged, the moves toward niche market economies also seemed to be repositioning African Americans more fully within this same citizen-consumer model. Ironically, the upshot of mass market productivity, to which African Americans contributed greatly as both workers and buyers, and which had maintained their unequal access to rights through a sort of social Taylorism, demanded an increased consumer base that now cautiously embraced them in order to meet its manufacturing costs.

In many senses, the targeting of smaller buying groups allowed for the maintenance of "racial" distance. When white Americans became the assumed audience for television, radio often directed its attentions more readily toward African American listeners. As a largely domestic technology, radio logically appealed to groups who had more limited access to public sphere leisure opportunities. According to Kathy M. Newman's careful research into 1950s black radio audiences, "By 1957 . . . there were over six hundred radio stations targeting 30 to 100 percent of their programming to African Americans in cities all over the country."[71] Commercial in the main, their owners found the market lucrative enough to provide for it thoughtfully and specifically, something which, as Newman continues,

> forces us to reconsider an accepted wisdom about the 1950s: the notion that advertisers were only interested in a homogeneous, white, middle-class market. Secondly, the story of the forgotten fifteen

million [listeners/consumers] challenges the accepted wisdom that African Americans were completely excluded from national advertising markets until the 1960s and 1970s.[72]

There was also an increase in African Americans' expenditures on cinema at the same time. African American theaters regularly brought in profits during the mid-1950s crisis years,[73] and, furthermore, the teen element was prominent within it, particularly if the film involved rock 'n' roll.[74] It was surely not entirely without thought for these audiences that such an expensive picture as *The Girl Can't Help It* was shot or that African American teenagers themselves, like Frankie Lymon, featured in this cycle of movies. Congregating around the peripheries of these musical spaces could also be found African American dancers, such as Jimmy and Javada in *Don't Knock the Rock,* and DJs like Jocko Henderson, who wittily appears dressed as a Martian in *Jamboree.* The swankier joints that house rock 'n' roll in these movies, particularly in *The Girl Can't Help It,* are testament to the hefty fee earners on their bills; at the time, Fats Domino was said to be earning up to $12,500 a week,[75] although he would have been an exception to the rest of the cast members. Remarkably, as Brian Ward's research shows:

> By the late 1950s median black teen income in New York State was actually 131 per cent that of the equivalent white cohort. Of course, much of this income was dedicated to buying the bare necessities of life, but estimates suggest that blacks spent much the same proportion of their earnings (3.5 per cent) on recreation as more affluent whites (4.1 per cent).[76]

While these figures register that the suspension of middle-class youth outside the gates of responsible adult spending was not a state to be taken for granted, such statistics simultaneously open a window onto the opportunities afforded by the multidirectional forces of migration. Largely through these movements, African Americans were entering the wage-earning consumer economy with more regularity than ever before. In conjunction, they were gaining greater, although entirely fraught, involvement in the processes of political enfranchisement. As LeRoi Jones (later Amiri Baraka) attested, "The Negro as slave is one thing. The Negro as American is quite another. But the *path* the slave took to 'citizenship' . . . the one peculiar referent to the drastic change in the Negro from slavery to 'citizenship' is his music."[77] Perhaps, then, this is why the music industry received the brunt of the criticism in these films and in contemporary popular discourse. As W. T. Lhamon argues in his astute interpretation of Chuck Berry's material (which is heard in movies like *Rock, Rock, Rock*), the divergent forces of "fifties consumer fetishism vying with blues determinism"[78] are boldly explored, placing the shift out of total disenfranchisement, the proximity of African American lifestyles to white teen concerns, right within unavoidable earshot of any casual listener.

However, if these reorganizations of consumer rights were muddling certain hierarchies, then plans were afoot in the geographical fabric of postwar America to reinstate the boundaries.

Creating and Negotiating the Suburb

During the 1950s, more solidly middle-class, white Americans were also on the move—to the suburbs—and, of all those making the journey, people in their late teens and early twenties were a dominant group.[79] At the same time, a number of financial and urban planning measures were underhandedly put in place in order to discourage African Americans from moving into these spaces and to persuade them to settle in the very heart of the metropolis, leaving this particular migration a sitting duck for the nickname "white flight."[80] In the suburbs, then, we see the "geographized" refusal of social, economic, and "racial" dialectical mixing. The aim was toward homogeneity rather than generative oppositions; suburbanization embodied the thorough casting out of "the other" so that interaction in the form of physical shared experience was as minimal as possible. The frameworks for promoting this type of settlement, just like the denial of the film-music mismatch, point out how utterly manmade (and, here, legislative) oppositions and aggressions can be. These developments, like mismatches, are then camouflaged in more intricate ways. A return to Marx illuminates this tendency:

> From the moment that the development of the dialectical movement is reduced to the simple process of opposing the good to the bad, of posing problems tending to eliminate the bad, and of giving one category as antidote to the other, the categories have no more spontaneity. . . . There is no longer any dialectic; at the most there is only pure ethics.[81]

A range of excuses were given for this zoning, including ones reliant on that old chestnut of reasons: safety. In his detailed book on the subject, *Crabgrass Frontier: The Suburbanization of the United States,* Kenneth T. Jackson notes how the Cold War provided a suitable pardon for such developments: "In 1951 the

Bulletin of the Atomic Scientists devoted an entire issue to 'Defense through Decentralization.' Their argument was simple. To avoid national destruction in a nuclear attack, the United States should disperse existing large cities into smaller settlements."[82] And with ethics like these also came whole value systems and ways of being that were eagerly fed back into the machines of cultural production.

The leisure habits of the suburban population, dictated as they were by particular circuits of mobility and white family structures, greatly impacted upon how media commerce was conducted. According to a contemporary survey carried out in Milwaukee, the downturn in conventional cinema attendance could largely be attributed not only to television, but also to drive-ins (themselves an out-of-town experience) and the effects of suburban planning on the behavior of the nation more generally.[83]

While film spectatorship was suffering an overall downturn, drive-ins were flourishing, bringing in almost a quarter of Hollywood's revenues.[84] Construction costs were low because of the lack of building required and the cheapness of land on the cities' outskirts. The animosity toward the drive-ins from the Hollywood majors was, one would imagine, in part initiated by film producers' grudging acknowledgment of just how much convenience was at a premium and how well placed the "ozoners" and the neighborhood theaters were in these practical stakes.[85] No wonder, then, that an unprecedented move was made to launch *Jailhouse Rock* at neighborhood rather than downtown theaters in New York.[86] Now that manufacturing and other types of business had been dispersed to outlying areas,[87] automobile sales and highway construction plans were rising thanks to a mighty pro-road-building lobby,[88] and a housing boom in the suburbs had been supported by financing from the Federal Housing Administration (which included the substantial underwriting of a good many mortgages), the entertainment industries needed to readjust both their foci and loci. Just as cinema, radio, and music recording were launching unlikely expeditions toward each other, so residents of the suburbs were traversing their locales in ways that had less to do with the periphery-to-core journeys of before.

This was symptomatic of a more sustained turn away from the established geographical centers, one that also included, for film production, an opening out to cheaper shooting options (both within the United States and overseas) and that, it was argued, also accelerated Hollywood unemployment.[89] What is surprising in all this is that Hollywood, itself once the epitome of geographically decentralized production, had taken so long to adapt to the new practices and mindsets. Likewise, developments in recording technology had made music production equipment cheaper and more compact, enhancing the capabilities of smaller, more provincial enterprises and bringing a body of more regionally accented work into the fray. All of this comes together in the rock 'n' roll movies, many of which were shot in multiple locations. Frequently, a musical sequence shot in New York was pasted into a Los Angeles–created story line, a fact that also helps to explain the jolts within these narratives and the decrease in techniques like eye-line matching—as well as the literal segregation of cast members.

In effect, all of these developments marked a reshaping of the geographies of cultural creativity and reproduction. At the same time and in response to the national persuasion of television, the larger radio networks were giving way to smaller companies, local in their advertising, focus, and material. As a summary of some contemporary industry research, *Variety* argued at the time:

> Every other form of entertainment is becoming nationalized, while radio has become regional and local. . . . radio sets outsell television sets and there are more stations than ever and everybody listens. . . . Television . . . does not have a cluster of groups and cannot afford to develop its programming to suit one group. Television must have a "cross-cultural" appeal because no one cultural group can deliver an audience large enough to pay for the production.[90]

While television expanded its borders, radio hoped to capitalize on those who had not yet purchased a set, including, for the first time on so wide a scale, African American listeners.

What was at work here was a concurrent and paradoxical interplay between localization and nationalization of the media, and rock 'n' roll movies, which often sat within both circumscriptions, interrogated the possibility for their assimilation. Despite the turn toward decentralization in the film and music industries, there was still an ambience of state collectivity in the air, even if the leadership was hell-bent on funding the processes of geographical dispersal through federally financed road building and suburbanization. Following a Keynesian logic, the Eisenhower administration had turned around a recession by lowering interest rates and taxes, spending 18 percent of the Gross National Product (GNP) on government projects in the 1954–1964 period.[91] However, it has to be noted that such developments also greatly accelerated a particular privatized and atomized national sensibility: 75 percent of the outlay on transportation during this period went to highway construction, with only a measly 1 percent dedicated to public transportation,[92] and a great deal of resources went toward developing the seclusionist infrastructures of the suburbs.[93]

In trying to square up these ideals of capitalism and country, Brian Ward argues that "consumption became virtually a civic and patriotic duty, as well as a means to satisfy more personal desires"[94]—the balance between the national and the individualistic remaining paramount here. It is in this framework that we can begin to understand not simply the inconsistent attitudes toward teen earning and spending, but also how the new geographies were inscribing their politics of "the public" and "the private" as they were experienced by young people. The surge in (suburban) home ownership, along with the affluence of the mid-1950s, provoked a worried *Variety* to inquire, "Is prosperity bad for the box office? . . . This is the age of the all-electric kitchen—and mortgage payoff. . . . In short, the film industry has to plan its selling for the future in terms of new living habits."[95] There are a range of hugely extratextual jokes about this in the heart of the rock 'n' roll movies, particularly in Jerri's nesting urges in *The Girl Can't Help It;* her yearning to settle down as a housewife, to cook, and to clean is the platform for many of the film's gags.

Although shared by many new suburban residents, these fantasies were not only responsible for the precarious condition of 1950s cinema but were also precisely a motivation for teenagers (at the very least) to attend movies in the first place. Just as these "new living habits" coaxed closer alliances with the more domestic media, they also propelled many people who might not have found themselves particularly "at home" in their new environments into new patterns of consumption. In the increasingly postindustrial suburban landscape, there were plenty of folk who were dissatisfied with its palpably unyielding inscriptions of the private sphere, many of them from the younger sectors of society.

Likewise, within the urban heartlands dwelled a sizable population whose sense of alienation aided in the creation and purchasing of the sorts of decentered and destabilized narratives and products of which the rock 'n' roll pictures were a part. The rewards of migration, it must be stressed, were starkly "racially" irregular. Contemporary sources confirm that the inner-city "ghetto" that developed in response to exclusion from the suburbs was characterized by overcrowding as centrally located housing was demolished in the name of renewal and more and more rural families moved in, establishing fairly homogeneous clusters as "racially" defined "communities" sought security in numbers.[96] In the meantime, their landlords took advantage of the diminished housing options for their clientele, leaving their buildings in increasing ill repair.[97]

The metaphorical echoes of this situation reverberate through the cramped framing, tight budgeting on camera set-ups, and squeezed back-to-back performances of the revue sections in rock 'n' roll movies. Chuck Berry's rendition of "You Can't Catch Me" in *Rock, Rock, Rock,* for instance, articulates these paradoxes of contemporary urban life. The tale conveyed by the lyrics is one of abandoned speeding in an automobile along, presumably, the very roads developed to enable suburban segregation. Yet the vocal riffs and guitar and piano stabs are brief, stuttering, and constrained in their vigor. Berry seems restless within the featureless set in which he performs, the camera framing him at a distance through a full body shot, imprisoning him within a highly restricted and bleakly minimal space which he is never encouraged to transgress. These stylistic allusions are perhaps the only traces within the cycle that acknowledge African American living conditions. *Untamed Youth* is an exception here in that its last reel contains a hasty plot line about the importation of illegal Mexican laborers who, along with the prisoners, are there to bolster the failing rural economy.

Film and music consumption, then, did not simply provide a mode of escape, spatially and textually, it also charted any number of contemporary migrations and their resulting understanding of both work and what works. Within this were caught particular patterns of commerce too, ones taking place in specifically policed public areas like cinemas, cafés, and music venues. A good deal of adolescent social activity required the space (physical and psychological) that was often not available at home. It is not hard to surmise how the separation required for autonomous development and the related impulse to purchase niche consumer goods might have been fulfilled by the drive-in, the car (although "parking" was still illegal), the jukebox-equipped teen "niteries" that were springing up,[98] and the neighborhood theater whose sound system was more thrillingly loud in its rendition of rock 'n' roll than any home record player. In each, there were safeguards to comfort parents (if not other patrons) that order and expected conduct would be maintained, including, of course, in so many regions, the insistence upon the racial segregation that also created a reason for African American cinemas. "Privacy" away from African Americans, and from this we must read an urge for the spatial as well as emotional separation that is redolent in the detached single-family suburban home and car, was rarely breached in these public spaces, although it was beginning to be in terms of the commodities on sale there. Likewise, the niche marketing of radio that had seen a rise in African American stations meant that such programming could also casually drift over into suburbia, complicating the more concrete spatial zoning of the U.S. conurbations. This is not to say that all forms of cultural communication were becoming increasingly more imaginable, nor that inner-city working-class African Americans and middle-class white teenagers were willing to merge in blissful color-blind unity. Devices like the radio and the jukebox might actually have diminished departures from the suburbs because of what they conveniently channeled into them. Rather, both groups were perhaps on different cutting edges of the same historical moment,[99] one that, at the same time, brought their cultural predilections into readier proximity with one another, as is evident from the mainstreaming of previously more margin-alized musics like rhythm and blues.

The locations which featured elements of rock 'n' roll, whether as actual events or as ethereal radio waves, were thus also symbolic battlegrounds where struggles over mobility and ownership were staged that also spoke of the greater commercial, civil, and political enfranchisement of African Americans. As such, the products peddled in these spaces were nowhere near as meaning-less as the press and general public often assumed. Rock 'n' roll movies repeat-edly insist upon the legitimacy of their music and its venues, of which one of the most common is the television studio which broadcasts such material straight back into the suburban living room. In this way, the neuroses over the weighty connotations of "home" and "outside" (and, more important, their detachment or dialectical interplay) are addressed head on. To what extent the internation-ally staged "riots" and journalistic moral panic provoked by screenings of *Rock Around the Clock* was a deliberate response to these validating discourses or vice versa is impossible to discern. If teenage car ownership privileged hot rod ex-perimentation and cruising over the pragmatic practicalities of traveling from A to B, and if street corners transformed into the breeding ground for so many successful vocal groups, the reclassification of these other spaces also marks a historical shift in social interaction. It is in the mismatches thrown in here by rock 'n' roll culture that the inscription of these supposedly zoned spaces be-comes anomalous, even "dangerous." The particular geographies of physical, audio, and visual intercommunication set in motion the dialectics that refuse a tidy "racial" specificity, as does rock 'n' roll, although this does not preclude "racial" politics from forcefully determining its complexion. These social changes also made space for new forms of mobility for different people in different ways. The jukebox and the drive-in, for example, utterly resituated rock 'n' roll and demanded altered modes of engagement from those, say, that had been ex-pected by the classical Hollywood plot. However, one major worry, it seemed, was that the adolescents would not return "home" from the other side of the fabricated theirs-versus-ours equation.

In terms of audience statistics for rock 'n' roll movies, there was now more common ground between the more affluent white teens of the suburbs and the African American high school students on the front lines of southern school desegregation, which began with the *Brown v. Board of Education* deci-sion of 1954, but which had to battle hard against the de facto prejudices im-planted by zoning and the concomitant distribution of resources.[100] That some of the musicians featured in these rock 'n' roll movies were also adolescents is not without great significance, and that a good number of them were African

American is even more pertinent, given the conventions of U.S. film representation and consumption up until that moment. It was also in the very expansion of African American (teen) work, though, and the broader implications of African American wage earning, as has become clear, that these unions were becoming even more concrete. Might these factors have acted as fuel (and continue to do so) for the journey toward a more egalitarian rendition of not only culture, but also social interaction itself? If it is indeed fuel, then it works partially through a process of combustion, of volatile elements reacting in precise ways with each other. Could not this also be a metaphor for dialecticism itself? Certainly, there is more that such a way of thinking about history and human action can contribute to my study, so I want to pour more of these elements into this chapter's engine now.

"Rock 'n' Roll Is a River of Music Which Has Absorbed Many Streams": The Dialectical Possibilities for Desegregation

Marx always adamantly emphasized that, while dialecticism should lead to diversity and a realization and reconciliation of difference, contradiction is frequently and wrongly suppressed in order to project a misleading sense of foreclosed unity. The same is true of Theodor Adorno, who also immersed himself in debates about dialecticism throughout his career, particularly in *Negative Dialectics*. The critical rejection of these films according to an adherence to the typical principles of narrative continuity stands out as just one example of this stalling tactic. Adorno, however, demolished such attitudes by questioning the very notion of singularity, and his comments can function to undo both the sense of cinematic consistency and the segregation acted out through the discourses encircling the rock 'n' roll cycle and their wider social frameworks. It is worth quoting Adorno at length on this issue:

> The name of dialectics says no more, to begin with, than that objects do not go into their concepts without leaving a remainder, that they come to contradict the traditional norm of adequacy. . . . It indicates the untruth of identity, the fact that the concept does not exhaust the thing conceived. Yet the appearance of identity is inherent in thought itself, in its pure form. To think is to identify. . . . Dialectics is the consistent sense of nonidentity. . . . We are blaming the method for the fault of the matter when we object to dialectics on the ground (repeated from Hegel's Aristotelian critics on) that whatever happens to come into the dialectical mill will be reduced to the merely logical form of

contradiction, and that (an argument still advanced by Croce) the full diversity of the noncontradictory, of that which is simply differentiated, will be ignored. What we differentiate will appear divergent, dissonant, negative for just as long as the structure of our consciousness obliges it to strive for unity: as long as its demand for totality will be its measure for whatever is not identical with it. This is what dialectics holds up to our consciousness as a contradiction. Because of the immanent nature of consciousness, contradictoriness itself has an inescapably and fatefully legal character. Identity and contradiction of thought are wielded together. Total contradiction is nothing but the manifested untruth of total identification.[101]

Dialecticism consequently announces the fabrication of opposition and fragmentation, provoking us into understanding these insistences as a means, among other things, of exploitation.

Marx likewise urges us to fathom the historical movements that bring about strife and to dismiss the rationales that present these factors as commonsensical or innate, rather than, for him, the results of bourgeois self-perpetuation. Crucial to my own investigations is the fact that, to Marx's mind, the asymmetries of labor practices, of political and commodity structures that are padlocked into these constrained stabilities are all precariously balanced in favor of those in control of the means of production, figures who hold as tightly to these reins as possible, but cannot sustain their stasis.[102] While the contradictions that inhabit these movies about rock 'n' roll have been presented by their critics as inconsistent, quixotic, the upshot of human discrepancy, each, as I have argued, is composed of condensed aesthetic, political, and moral debates. The Marxian insistence that we treat all such structures as determined by relations of power has seemed entirely suitable, especially given their status as commodities. As with any Marxian analytical procedure, the collusion of discourses such as "common sense" or "aesthetic suitability" with the histories, values, and representational regimes of the ruling elite becomes increasingly apparent the more one interrogates their assumed neutrality. What a sense of dialectical impact adds to all of this is an observation of how certain reliable capitalist strengths are frequently and unexpectedly dissipated (through interpretation or even practice) when placed, as they so often are in rock 'n' roll movies, within new relationships. Might these apparently quite random communions somehow lead us to a more equitable reformation of labor? This is a question worth asking of this material, although I will leave more sustained responses to it until this book's conclusion. For the meantime, following Marx involves a dedication to revealing inconsistencies within capitalism so that working practices might eventually be revolutionized. As has emerged, in their producers' greed to incorporate as many youth and rock 'n' roll commodities as possible into one supposedly coherent unit *and failing* (the various mismatches I highlight throughout), an inability to control meaning and response becomes baldly obvious.

Within Marxian praxis, then, dialecticism's propensity for process, communication, change, and transformation can alert us to ways of altering our material conditions—but turning dialecticism against itself is, ultimately, a defensive tactic. In the end, dialecticism's emphasis on division insists that observers become vigilant of the fact that the drama that is played out between any given cinematic and musical presences can simply lead fans into investing more in the singled-out commodities that seem to them the most worthy, the ones that lure them, say, to niche market or segregated social group identification. The greater structure that pits these two essences or modes of exploitation against each other is often overlooked. As Adorno points out, "dialectics is the ontology of the wrong state of things. The right state of things would be free of it: neither a system nor a contradiction."[103]

And yet, caught up as we are in the tides of these capitalisms, an awareness of the dialectical dramas embodied within a host of media products is no bad thing, especially when there is little space for something more revolutionary to materialize. The situation was hardly ideal in the 1950s, and compromised modes of struggle had to be instituted. Such a move is evident in the group of numbers delivered by Fats Domino in *The Girl Can't Help It, Shake, Rattle and Rock!* and *Jamboree.* In all of these examples, and unlike most other African American performers in these films, Domino veritably flirts with the audience, coyly smirking as he gazes directly into the lens, "working" the camera and breaking the fourth wall. In *The Girl Can't Help It,* he delivers "Blue Monday," a number whose verses roll repetitively as he details the drudge of his working week, but which breaks out into thumping, rising chords as he revels in the joys that his salary provides on weekends. The dialecticism between labor and leisure that is rewarded by the basic structure of a rock 'n' roll song becomes patent at moments like this. More broadly, in the appeal for identification in his gaze, the "for us" quality—whether oblique or as direct as Fats Domino's fixing stare outward—the status of the entertainer-as-worker (and nothing more) is somewhat confounded. Perhaps it is his portly demeanor and older look that allowed him to get away with these responses, but Fats Domino was similarly no stranger to trouble in the heady days of early civil rights protests. In August 1956, a "riot" had broken out at one of his concerts in Houston, fueled by indecision over whether the white or African American sections of the audience would be allowed dancing rights. The African Americans being the majority,

Fats Domino refused to play if they were marginalized, causing a certain amount of tension that was largely directed toward the concert's promoters and the assembled police.[104] What is at issue in all of these episodes is Fats Domino's ability and desire to break down the false barriers of the mismatch, to interact with and encourage identification from a mixed audience while simultaneously insisting upon certain egalitarian rights. It is this dynamic that provides for the reconceptualization of the niche market according not to "racial" boundaries, but to ones that ask audiences whether or not they will engage more fully with African American culture. The literal mismatching of the concert attendees with those in charge of patrolling it (perhaps a generational more than a "racial" divide) offers an insight into how these consumer groups might begin to amass according to different politics.

While it would be hard to ascertain whether these actions achieved any recordable political effects, Fats Domino did deliver a direct condemnation of the spatial segregation of work and leisure under the excuse of protection and privacy. This move opposes broader forms of governance that James Baldwin, in *The Devil Finds Work,* observes as being reflected through cinema:

> The private life of a black woman, to say nothing of the private life of a black man, cannot really be considered at all. To consider this forbidden privacy is to violate white privacy—by destroying the white dream of the blacks; to make black privacy a black and private matter makes white privacy real, for the first time: which is, indeed, and with a vengeance, to endanger the stewardship of Rhodesia. The situation of the white heroine must never violate the white self-image. Her situation must always transcend the inexorability of the social setting, so that her innocence may be preserved. . . . But the situation of the black heroine, to say nothing of that of the black hero, must always be left at society's mercy: in order to justify white history and in order to indicate the essential validity of the black condition.[105]

This is exactly the kind of condition that Marx suggests leads to human estrangement (Baldwin's "privacy"), an objectification of the world and an "externalization of consciousness."[106] With a startlingly effective perversion of its working traditions, Fats Domino reconjures the for-us-ness that usually (and profitably) detracts from these feelings of isolation, while also frustrating the conventional patterns of cinema's formal and "racially" political "coherence." His actions show us that, when alienated objects are later rebranded as "ours," the results are by no means predictable. Furthermore, among such discrepancies, there may be clues about how to forge new arrangements, ones that may not be as harmful as some of the capitalist exchanges that are currently in operation.

Such partial yet nonetheless brave reworkings were utterly vital to the state of play in mid-1950s America. On the one hand, migration and greater media prominence sanctioned a larger social, economic, and political enfranchisement among various sections of the nation's people, although access was definitely an uneven issue here. On the other, various legislative preconditions, especially in the South, were tugging these progressive gestures in another direction and aiming to stymie their potential. As late as the summer of 1956, a new law in the state of Louisiana paid special attention to leisure practices, banning "all interracial dancing, social functions, entertainments, athletic training, games, sport or contests."[107] This act must be set alongside the Montgomery bus boycotts of 1955–1956 and the attempted desegregation of southern schools following the *Brown v. the Board of Education* decision of two years previous. A wide range of consumer opposition from white Americans to cultural integration in the South was reported by *Variety* throughout the 1956–1957 period. This ranged from boycotts of pictures like *Island in the Sun* (Robert Rossen, 1957), which tested the reception of one of the first on-screen inter"racial" romances since the axing of the Production Code's "miscegenation" clause, to the forced cancellation of Nat King Cole's television show.[108] In one particularly virulent display of prejudice from within the slipstream of the accelerating violence in the region, the three Louisiana senators who had proposed the bill outlawing desegregated entertainment railed against "the Communist technique of brain-washing for racial integration by bringing into private homes in this state harmful [television] programs designed to affect the minds and attitudes of juveniles and thereby contribute to juvenile delinquency."[109] Once again, teenagers were being used to justify certain norms of moral (or rather economic) decency, their leisure practices prevailed upon to reinforce age-old retrogressive and labor-related hierarchies.

All the while, African American spatial isolation, as I have pointed out, was rapidly increasing,[110] a situation that was unkindly paralleled by the way rock 'n' roll sequences were filmed far away from the Los Angeles industry centers. Despite their vanguard position in throwing traditional viewing practices off-kilter, drive-ins were as segregated as their regions demanded at the time with, if expected, separate entrances and facilities for each group.[111] Not until the early 1960s were standard movie theaters completely desegregated and, even then, it is up for speculation whether the stratification and unofficial bounding of town space made for a more de facto form of separation that set in place a whole range of self-sufficient services that, in their own way, carved the path for the African American niche market.

In response, the National Association for the Advancement of Colored People (NAACP) and famous figures such as Sidney Poitier and Harry Belafonte made various high-profile statements about the media to the industry press.[112] An equivalent pressure was exerted through antiracist commercial boycotts of films and television stations that sought to mimic in form and reverse in politics the embargos against African Americans that were happening across the South.[113] The African American consumer lobby was now, it seemed, a force to be reckoned with, as was international disinterest in segregated movie narratives, rendering the South less of a viable influence to pall the entertainment industries in the global marketplace.

Certain writers have claimed that these tensions provoked nervousness about how movie narratives themselves should react to the political situation, something which apparently led to an arm's-length approach,[114] but there were also those odd precious flashes, like Fats Domino's performances on screen, that continued the struggle. Might we consider fragile mobilities like these to issue from the dialectical possibilities activated by the very survival tactics of the entertainment business, its decentralization and niche markets coincidently liberating movie semantics from prior traditions and making them answerable to new audiences? In *Rock, Rock, Rock,* against a backdrop of bands that are kept at a distance from each other by sequencing, shooting schedules, and editing, Alan Freed delivers a speech celebrating the rich interracial roots of rock 'n' roll.[115] It is not to be forgotten, however, that Freed's real television show was canceled when its producers failed to edit out a shot of Frankie Lymon dancing alongside a white girl and that Freed was quickly brought to ruination by the payola trials at the end of the decade. Elsewhere, in *Shake, Rattle and Rock!* it is the white Tommy Charles, rather than any of the more renowned African American singers on the fictional bill, who is performing when the police target the staged riot at the rock 'n' roll concert, implicating him rather than the other musicians. One of the film's most sympathetic characters is the white Axe, who functions as a cipher for the absence of African American figures in the diegesis through his consistent use of "jive talk." Though these were hardly revolutionary acts, they do speak of a quiet resolution of the ambivalence to cultural and labor segregation, something that can also be interpreted from the inclusiveness of the Jimmy Bowen number "Cross Over" in *Jamboree.*

The same aspirations toward the occasional scratching away at often rather conservative veneers can be observed in *The Girl Can't Help It.* Comedy is used as a façade, allowing the movie to get away with statements against the debilitating strictures of its contemporary environment. The film draws on its director, Frank Tashlin's, reputation and experience within the world of Warner Brothers cartoons to make a number of rather pointed allusions that leave the

African American musical cast's dignity more thoroughly intact. The lurid colors, the repeated sight gags, the names of the protagonists (Tom and Jerri), and, above all, the balloon-sculpture figure of its star, Jayne Mansfield, combine to create a live-action approximation of an animated landscape. The abstractions expected from the average commodity are blown out of proportion, highlighting their constructedness. "Pretty is just how good you apply your base," Jerri tells Tom in just one of the many moments where 1950s femininity is exposed as a charade. At the same time, middle-class whiteness, with its ludicrous estranging rituals (like the habits of the suburban homemaker whom Jerri so idolizes), also becomes a distinct and often laughable "ethnicity." Just as Jerri's world is a social fabrication, so too is her singing career reluctantly built. It is at the level of vocation that she runs headlong into conflicting expectations.

The photography, even with its Cinemascope possibilities, barely seems capable of squeezing her anatomy into the frame, suggesting a dual sense of containment that is shared by the musicians she encounters along her way through the story line. Her almost preposterous white otherness, her suburban dreams of homemaking and child rearing despite her sexpot appearance, codify another difference. What a shame it is that the psychological difficulties provoked by her alienation from gangster and entertainment employment remain purely within her own experience, although comedy and identification do, at least, allow her dilemmas to leach outward so that audiences can contemplate with her what it means to understand whiteness and femininity through models of work. Certainly, *The Girl Can't Help It*'s world is deliberately removed and cartoonish so as to discourage the appeal of the productivity and commodity carousels upon which many of the other films place us. Yet the movie's effectiveness is entirely dependent on its regular interjection into these spaces of the very real topographies of teenage and African American existences, including their music.

Analogous to *The Girl Can't Help It*'s deployment of style, the musical numbers of all these movies—their textural dimensions (vocal flourishes or the odd wink and nod), rather than their structural ballasting—drive some particularly explosive eruptions out of these restrictively contained narrative frameworks. Consequently, the new prominence of the song provides, or at least corroborates, certain ideas about representational and social struggle. The skyscraping melismatic lurches in, for example, Little Richard's rendition of the title song to Tashlin's picture, particularly in its more "meaningless" enclaves like nonlinguistic screams and "nonsensical" lyrics, speak of the dialectical potential of thinking concurrently about work and leisure, migration and containment, fragmentation and collectivity. The regular and driving rhythms of factory life that this song shares with the average rock 'n' roll track and its endless rehearsal on screen are met halfway by incongruous lyrics about hedonism or ecstatic yelps that contradict typical conscriptions of the work ethic. Coming from the other direction, the realms of trouble-free pure pleasure are, at the same time, encroached upon by the concerns of labor (note the constant references to slavery and exploitation in the lyrics). Within this range of mass-producing media industries, then, these subjects devised ways to at least express dissatisfaction with work and entertainment while still necessarily immersing themselves in their multiple economies. One has only to listen to the songs that the press and much of 1950s society were so eager to downplay as meaningless to hear *entertaining* dialectical negotiations very definitely *at work*.

If these film-music examples both issue from and discuss a jerky and often mismatched transition into what was to become postindustrialization, then the next chapters situate us very much in the thick of these labor-related priorities. Service employment, decentralization, and niche groupings all played their part in how the rock 'n' roll cycle was made and received. In the twenty-year gap that separates this chapter from the next one (with *Harum Scarum* standing as a midway point), such labor strategies became increasingly more crucial and problematic to how work was carried out. What was more a particularity of media history (deregulation laws, for the most part) in this chapter came to overrun the economy at large in chapters 3 and 4's time frames. By chapter 5's era (the mid-1990s to the present day), as will become clear, it is not so much that production models hailing from the entertainment industries can seem concordant with postindustrial work, but that the media themselves are crucial to financial stability. This subtle renegotiation of a specific balance in labor connects the developments charted in this chapter to the more solidly postindustrially situated ones that we have now reached.

◆ 3 ◆

"It's Not Only Trivial, It's Bad, Vulgar":
Ken Russell's Composer Biopics and
the Uneasy Realignment of Work and Culture

When Conservative leader Edward Heath won the UK general election of 1970, he brought to Ten Downing Street, along with all of the paraphernalia of domesticity, a small rosewood Steinway grand piano. A year later, he was in front of the London Symphony Orchestra conducting Edward Elgar's *Cockaigne Overture*. Although these actions were, in many ways, merely the whims of an individual, they were also deeply resonant on a politically symbolic level.

The previously stalwart colonial and manufacturing economies of the country, this chapter will emphasize, were being increasingly coaxed, if not bullied, into obscurity. As a replacement for these losses (both financial and emotional), the United Kingdom tried to renew and renovate its dependency on cultural achievements, to position them much more centrally within its economic policies and ethos. The choice of Elgar is not without significance here. Elgar presents us with an image of Britain that is self-affirming: subtle, yet spiritually invested in the landscape; patriotic, even parochial at times, but also appealing across borders and equivocal about nationalism.

The year 1970 was also when Tom Lupton and Robert Hamilton of the Manchester Business School felt confident enough to claim: "The status of the industrial worker has changed little since World War II and is, in the nature of things, likely to change little in the future."[1] With hindsight, how wrong they were and how caught up in a particularly British, perhaps complacent, comprehension of the island's stability. The years to follow were marked by a radical restructuring of how (and if) people worked, how they thought about work, and how they churned all of this back through their relationships with culture. There was also a specific reconfiguration of culture as a somewhat fraught and experimental replacement for other declining national industries. If the regroupings of the entertainment industries in the 1950s had gone some way to foreshadowing broader reorganizations of labor and society according to "post-Fordism" and decentralization, then these trends had galloped on single-mindedly in the intervening years into a landscape of global competition that was utterly bewildering, if not traumatizing to the average Briton.

Almost a decade earlier, Ken Russell, then a director for BBC television, had made his name with his fêted dramatized documentary, "Elgar," the runaway hit of the 1960s.[2] Elgar was enveloped into the bosom of bourgeois taste as a result, his regained popularity perhaps spurring on Heath's selection of the *Cockaigne Overture*. Although Elgar had perhaps seemed a dusty anachronism to many in the midcentury, Russell's film breathed new life into his oeuvre, presenting a composer deeply invested in a reinvigorated sense of Britishness and how, most crucially, it could be processed and conveyed through the arts. Sections of "Elgar" (Ken Russell, 1962) insist that we revisit the composer's work with a different eye and ear: as the famous "Pomp and Circumstance" marches play, we are exposed to contrapuntal images of blinded World War One mustard gas victims followed by accumulating shots of graves that undermine the jingoistic connotations that have been heaped onto the "Land of Hope and Glory tune."[3]

These techniques recall the work of Sergei Eisenstein, a thinker and film practitioner whose ideas have much to offer in the analysis of Russell's films and the critical tirades that plague them. Eisenstein, especially in his early career,[4] drew an awareness of dialecticism into the very heart of cinema, fashioning his films and critical writings in an overtly disjunctive, yet semantically and politically productive manner.[5] Through his direct treatment of the medium, and particularly his treatises on montage, Eisenstein's work is invaluable as a set of strategies for dealing with forced or fabricated aesthetic and labor-related divisions in the production, dissemination, and consumption of mass entertainment. Russell's own work carries on in this vein of inquiry.

By the less affluent and less confident 1970s, Russell had ventured from TV into feature films, persisting with his preoccupation with biographies of prominent classical composers that had generated for the BBC such programs as "Béla Bartók" (1964), "The Debussy Film" (1965), "Delius—The Song of Summer" (1968) and "The Dance of Seven Veils" (1970). Yet, although his television documentary audiences had repeatedly applauded his sensitive and poignant matching of picture to soundtrack, of musical aim to visual rendition, the three theatrical releases that followed elicited a sourer attitude. *The Music Lovers* (1971) treated Tchaikovsky (Richard Chamberlain) as if he were the misunderstood protagonist of a turbulent melodrama; *Mahler* (1974) wound Nazi iconography around a flashback biography of the composer (Robert Powell); and *Lisztomania* (1975) saw its hero (Roger Daltrey) as analogous to a contemporary rock idol. An Eisensteinian imperative prevails once more, but not one that could be tolerated unquestioningly. Out streamed a cacophonous polyphony of historical ideas gorged on a range of influences from more popular entertainment forms like slapstick comedy and recent popular music. Similarly, in Eisenstein's modus operandi, art is defined by such collisions and struggle, by pitting elements against each other, and by sweeping those contemplating this melee right into its core so compellingly that they realize their role within, for him, a revolutionary collective. He argues:

> The basis of this philosophy is the *dynamic* conception of objects: being as a constant evolution from the interaction between two contradictory opposites.
>
> Synthesis that *evolves* from the opposition between thesis and antithesis.
>
> It is equally of basic importance for the correct conception of art and all art forms.
>
> In the realm of art this dialectical principle of the dynamic is embodied in
>
> CONFLICT
>
> As the essential basic principle of the existence of every work of art and every form.

FOR ART IS ALWAYS CONFLICT:
  1. because of its social mission,
  2. because of its nature,
  3. because of its methodology.[6]

For Eisenstein, "The sphere of the new film language will, as it happens, not be the sphere of the presentation of phenomena, nor even that of social interpretation, but the opportunity for *abstract social evaluation*,"[7] and herein lies the political power of cinematic montage. However, in contravention of this objective, Russell's films were rarely received in the spirit of dialecticism. His boisterous and jarring cinematic ruminations on, as will become apparent, the stature of high art and the more widespread dilemma of how "labor" might be remodeled, were instead roundly admonished as a direct affront to good taste, a conservative stance that clearly upheld so much within the British context.

John Coleman of the *New Statesman* compared Russell's relationship with composer biographies to that of "a rapist with a victim,"[8] while David Robinson of the *Times* felt *Lisztomania* was "execrably silly."[9] Even across the water, *Esquire* claimed that *Lisztomania* was "sheer loathsomeness";[10] the *grande dame* of film criticism, Pauline Kael, registered her disgust, and Peter G. Davis of the *New York Times* spewed, "Rage. . . . That was my immediate reaction to 'Lisztomania,' Ken Russell's latest and most perversely self-indulgent 'music appreciation' fantasy."[11] Although *The Music Lovers* had turned a surprising profit in a flagging climate, respected British film critic Alexander Walker (himself no fan of Russell) attested to the commercial failure of the following two films: "*Mahler*. . . cost a mere £193,000, and by 1984's figures had lost only £14,000. *Lisztomania,* on the other hand, escalated to £1,200,000 and has been largely written off."[12] What such responses reveal, I argue, is a pointed aggression toward Russell for opening the doors of culture and shepherding in all sorts of influences that these gatekeepers would rather remained outside, but which may well have become the saviors of the economy during Britain's bumpy ride into the "postindustrial" age.

The attacks are personal, but so too were many of the perceived production processes. This chapter does not have an auteurist focus as some kind of salute to an unacknowledged maestro, but because, as will be uncovered, there is something pertinent about this means of understanding work in the 1970s. Likewise, it illuminates the vigor with which class-based ethics and aesthetics are espoused by journalistic workers whose incomes are fairly low and unpredictable and for whom cultural capital, itself a transforming category, is paramount.

Yet even within the reviews of Russell's films, there is equivocation and conflict—both within individual responses and among the members of the press as a collective body. Michael Dempsey wonders why "*Mahler* is especially bewildering; rarely has one movie been so extraordinary and so godawful at the same time."[13] The bulk of critics postulated that these films would divide audiences,[14] echoing Marjorie Bilbow's analysis of the lively divisions that Russell's work stimulated:

> Whoops, here we go again. Cannon to the right of Russell, cannon to the left, with the Fors and Againsts hurling insults at each other across an abyss of non-communication. The trouble is, it's becoming increasingly difficult to review any of Ken Russell's kaleidoscopic portraits without implying ruderies directed against those who hold the opposing point of view.[15]

Furthermore, the movies themselves are only one possible starting position for tracking a dialectical logic: one might just as easily begin this journey with the music they feature. Mahler, for instance, was a composer so absolutely absorbed by opposites like life and death, their synthesis and their transcendence, that it is unsurprising that he should figure in Russell's cinematic examination of what the director thought to be "the union of the spirit and flesh, body and soul," rather than "bio-pics or social tracts."[16] Such pretensions would doubtless have seemed ludicrous to many a critic of the day, but interchange through struggle, ambivalence, and opposition plays itself out in other ways in their journalistic diatribes.

The push and pull initiated by the three films and their hasty resolution in the form of particularly damning and belittling reviews from many fronts execute the kind of closure of which we should be intensely skeptical. The specific damnations of Russell's films lock us away from *The Music Lovers, Mahler,* and *Lisztomania*'s urgent explorations of some of the most pressing political concerns of the time. The narratives, I shall demonstrate, involve themselves dialectically with the treatment of employee isolation as against collectivity; manual work versus its increasing opposite, service and cultural labor; the annexation of "past" and "present"; elite and popular art's wary distance from each other; and the fluctuating conversion of "public" to "private," especially as they relate to policies of arts funding during this decade. All of these forces impacted upon the way that work, particularly creative work, was done at this time. The discourses encircling Russell's oeuvre demand a weighing of both the central role that media play in the construction of (their own) history and the increasing importance of media representation in the recording and re-drafting *of* history. Just as the highly noticeable zooms that Russell uses hurtle us from the wider environment into a closer framing of the individual artist, a similar movement from macro to micro, from history to creativity, pivots around the artistic protagonists. Liszt, in particular, is caught up in the broader political currents of Hungarian and German state formation, which allows the film to establish a connection between artistic accountability and other, more social developments. Through these moves, unconsciously or not, Russell's films impress upon us how vital cultural production is to political activity.

But we should be careful not to construe these propositions as merely a *reflection* of more expansive historical trends. Eisenstein impresses upon us an understanding of dialecticism that sees art (and everything else) as capable of and responsible for the fabrication of history. The hermetic sealing of "the film" and the obsessive tidiness of the continuity system, for instance, are dispelled by Eisenstein, who argues that any of the film's elements can forcibly spill out of and into multitudinous political and social arrangements. As with Hegel and Marx, these Eisensteinian dialecticisms sprawl outward; they are forces to be revealed, harnessed, or exposed, rather than solely exerted as a methodology for formal film-music analysis, despite Eisenstein's clear focus on the cinematic. Thus, movies like Russell's were active participants in what was happening at the time, and we can intuit their sensibility in even the most general accounts of the era.

The Fragment and the Whole: Russell amid 1970s British Politics

Writing in 1970, Zbigniew Brzezinski postulated that "the paradox of our time is that humanity is becoming simultaneously more unified and more fragmented"[17]—a summation that could refer equally to the formal and thematic patterns of Russell's films and a history of the nation's varying labor practices as they settled around specific geopolitical dealings. In the United Kingdom, the 1971 Immigration Act had made it distinctly more difficult for overseas citizens to settle in the country. Yet, at around the same time, Britain became a member of the Common Market, the European Economic Commission (EEC, now the EU),[18] just as Russell was exploring three distinctly non-British composers. All of these films delight in international culture's situation as inherent components of British taste (and beyond). More bleakly, *Mahler* forthrightly and anachronistically parallels the composer's conversion to Catholicism and career-furthering submission to the Viennese elites with a concession to National Socialism. *Lisztomania* again invokes Nazism to investigate Richard Wagner's (Paul Nicholas) anti-Semitic designs and, as such, the film has little positive to say about nineteenth- or twentieth-century nationalist exclusivity.

Drawing upon the prerogatives of economic history, we benefit from understanding the 1970s according to the aspirations of the General Agreement on Tariffs and Trade (GATT). Its aim was to legally and institutionally amplify global free trade, which gained more and more momentum throughout the decade, allowing for the expansion of multinational corporations that, although often located in specific countries, carried out production and sales across borders with greater ease. The GATT had insisted upon the abolition of local film quota systems in Britain and had allowed for American penetration of the market alongside, in the 1950s and '60s, U.S. investment in UK production. This situation allowed for what was, in effect, the Hollywood outsourcing of *The Music Lovers* (backed by United Artists and distributed by Warner Brothers), a furtherance of the decentralization explored in chapter 2, which was followed by a lack of financial input for the two biopics that followed. By this point, the Vietnam War–impoverished U.S. government took to providing subsidies for those shooting within its own borders in an attempt to revitalize its own media economy.[19] As a whole, then, American money was being drained away from Britain as Russell continued his career. Alexander Walker described the activity in 1970 as follows:

> MGM announces its British studios will make between 10 and 12 films a year, but this does not allay rumours of imminent studio closure.... Closure of MGM's British studio announced in April.... Although 70 films are in production in 1970, their budgets are smaller, their shooting schedules shorter, more are made on location. Columbia is only American major in Britain to maintain former level of production with six films; United Artists, only two; MGM, three; Paramount, two; Universal and Twentieth Century–Fox, none at all.[20]

By 1972, investment was down from £39.22 million the previous year to only £8.44 million, and January 1975 saw no film shoots on the horizon.[21]

In a similar but more pervasive fashion, initiatives like the GATT were clearing the ground for a massive reorganization of production, one that was to seriously endanger the competitiveness of British labor and take its toll on the sorts of assumptions and practices that the Russell mismatches, as I will illustrate, obliquely highlight and embody. Jeffrey Harrod explains:

> Free Industrial Zones (FIZ)... were created in many third-world countries during the 1970s. By the early 1980s there were more than 300 FIZs in about 66 countries. The country setting up a FIZ usually provides an economic infrastructure, company tax incentives, and

other advantages and invites foreign companies to develop an "export processing capacity" in which goods are exported from mainly imported materials and technology. The majority of FIZs are subject to special national legislation that either prohibits or severely restricts the activities of trade unions. In effect, the state guarantees that unions and bargaining forms of social relations will not be permitted within the FIZ. Foreign companies may, therefore, take advantage of the lower wage rates without fear of union intervention. . . . This type of legislation, as well as the use of socially disadvantaged labor and small enterprises, means that employers begin to regain absolute power in these zones reminiscent of the power they had in Europe of the nineteenth century.[22]

Hand in hand with this came a turn toward multinational companies' (MNCs) exploitation of less large-scale manufacturing within regions where economic poverty and less protective working conditions drove down costs. Buoyed by massive borrowing enabled by banks reliant on the revenues of new oil-exporting countries and the subsequent low interest rates, industrial development continued at speed in distinctly new centers of production. Michael Piore and Charles Sabel provide statistics for this swing: "The upshot of this shift in the epicentre of economic growth was that from 1971 to 1974, manufactured exports from the developing countries increased at an average annual rate of 25.6 percent; in the developed countries, the rate was 11.2 percent."[23] Even movie industry personnel started drifting to more lucrative or competitive locations overseas, with the 1970s seeing a steady emigration of stars and the shooting of films like *Walkabout* (Nicholas Roeg, 1970) and *Don't Look Now* (Nicholas Roeg, 1973) increasingly taking place in other countries. What impact would an even more distanced form of commodity assembly than ever before have upon the world? In the most symbolic of fashions, this question is answered by the structure of *The Music Lovers,* a narrative that follows the patronage of Tchaikovsky by a woman, Madame von Meck (Izabella Telezynska), who refused to meet him. While their relationship is easily idealized by the fantasies that absence (and their removed communication through the medium of letter writing) permit, it is ultimately destructive in that control is relinquished, harsh working conditions are unacknowledged, and, in the end, Tchaikovsky is abruptly stripped of his income when von Meck discovers that his moral codes (his homosexuality) contradict her own. Distance allows a blind eye to be turned for only so long; whims easily dictate where the money is next redirected, and insecurity rules the day.

If we penetrate the history writing on multinational capitalism, it becomes apparent that, while British MNCs (which were second only in number to America's) sought to advance their interests overseas, their ambitions were mismatched with the needs of workers at home. In essence, manual labor was being relocated, leaving various vacuums in countries such as the United Kingdom. As James Hinton points out:

> Between 1960 and 1976 Britain's share of world manufacturing exports was nearly halved. The British economy appeared to be caught in a vicious cycle which led from recurrent financial crises, to deflation, to slow growth, to undercapitalisation, to export weakness, and back to crisis again.[24]

Simultaneously, James E. Cronin notes:

> For industrial workers, particularly men, this meant a heightened sense of insecurity. Between 1966 and 1979, the size of the Labour force remained constant but the percentage of men at work declined by more than 5%. From 1966 to 1979, 2.9 million jobs were lost in production industries, and about 3/4 of these had been held by men.[25]

The desperation that this state created for workers is threaded through the Romantic era preoccupations of Russell's three composers, themselves also the victims of job insecurity. None are working for guaranteed salaries, and each makes enormous sacrifices in order to stay afloat: Tchaikovsky denies his homosexuality in order to curry favor with patrons; Mahler converts from Judaism to Catholicism to secure a post at the Vienna Opera; and Liszt's career is based more on populist cash-generating concerts than intellectually taxing composition. Under harsh conditions, work is inevitably compromised.

"One response to increasing uncertainty," Piore and Sabel continue (in relation to the resituation of production), "was conglomeration: the large corporations tried to hedge risks in their primary (or original) market through diversification into others. This was done either by founding new subsidiaries or by merging with going concerns."[26] Was this not much of the impetus behind the horizontal integration that marked the rock 'n' roll movies? By the late 1960s, one of the larger film companies in Britain, ABPC (Associated British Picture Corporation), had been folded into EMI (Electric and Music Industries Ltd.), which was, among other things, a music firm. Subsumptions like this led to diversification enclosed within a monopoly structure. As Sarah

Street reveals, for 1972, "the circuits controlled 32 per cent of cinemas, which generated 52 per cent of total takings."[27]

The ensuing economic slump also brought about a downturn in the purchasing of mass-market goods and in large-scale manufacturing. In response, besides the conglomerations and mergers, small-scale production arose as a survival strategy. In many ways, the Russell films were tailor-made for or, rather, were a response to this environment. Without U.S. (or local) studio backing, *Mahler* was produced by the director's Goodtimes Enterprises, shot in the United Kingdom on entirely British money for a paltry £160,000. It formed part of an increasingly post-Fordist cinema economy, where films were financed on a singular basis, the money raised in a more entrepreneurial fashion than had previously been typical. As was the case for the Romantic composers Russell depicts, steady backing was simply not available. At best, filmmakers could only hope for what really amounted to an outsourcing deal that mirrored the globalizing model: *Lisztomania,* for example, was made fairly independently and then bought by Warner Brothers for distribution, with much of the investment risk falling on the shoulders of Goodtimes itself.

Films like this, spotting the more general trends away from mass commodification, often aimed themselves fairly squarely at niche audiences, the kinds that had been developing solidly from the period of the preceding chapter. All three of these films—due to their subjects, but also perhaps due to their cheapness of production—were less inclined toward the average consumer (whatever Russell may have desired), fitting more comfortably into the art-house bracket that the British industry as a whole felt to be a national specialty and strength. Cinemas noticed the shift too, as Stuart Laing relates:

> Between 1970 and 1980 the seating capacity of British cinemas fell from 1.46 million to 0.69 million; at the same time the number of commercial cinema screens marginally increased. This apparent paradox is explained by the fact that between 1970 and 1980 the proportion of cinema buildings with two or more screens rose from under 5 per cent to over 60 per cent, with a very considerable saving in fixed overheads and running costs per screen. This arrangement effectively recognized cinema's new role as a provider of specialist or occasional entertainment for small and diverse sets of audiences.[28]

Many reviews of the time commented on how Russell's films would fare well at selected theaters or screens, either as art films or in their appeal to the "adult" audience through their liberal use of sexual themes and nudity,[29] although this, as I shall soon relay, was also their downfall. Racier content was evidently a bandwagon upon which an increasing number of producers were leaping with a later policy document observing that X-rated certificates increased from 98 in 1960 to 212 in 1970.[30] In such hard times, there was little faith in a broad international viewership for British output; mass and expensive high-end manufacture no longer seemed possible, and other enticements were proffered.

As large-scale planning and production dwindled (not just in cinema, but throughout the United Kingdom), it is hardly surprising that themes of solitude and alienation enter these films, particularly *The Music Lovers* and *Mahler.* This economic state of affairs is shared by the historical period that Russell portrays, and both tap neatly into what music scholar Charles Rosen calls "the Romantic Fragment."[31] In formal terms, one key example of this is the musical leitmotif: a short phrase that is perfectly self-contained and repeatable, yet somehow aborted in its brevity and lack of confident development. Wagner, who features prominently in *Lisztomania,* was, of course, a major proponent of this style. Russell, although often keen to indulge in lengthier sequences, translates the leitmotif into his work too. The silent-comedy theme that kick-starts *Lisztomania* (concluding with Liszt and his lover trapped inside a piano on the railroad tracks) is drawn once more into the filmic corpus when a pastiche of *The Gold Rush* (Charlie Chaplin, 1925) is later employed to convey the early years of Liszt and Marie's (Fiona Lewis) relationship. The sequence is accompanied by the piano piece *Liebestraum,* which itself echoes throughout the film in a similar manner. Rosen evocatively compares the "fragment" to a hedgehog:

> [It is] an amiable creature which rolls itself into a ball when alarmed. Its form is well defined and yet blurred at the edges. This spherical shape, organic and ideally geometrical, suited Romantic thought: above all, the image projects beyond itself in a provocative way. The Romantic Fragment draws blood only from those critics who handle it unthinkingly. Like its definition, the Romantic Fragment is complete (this oxymoron was intended to disturb, as the hedgehog's quills make its enemies uncomfortable): separate from the rest of the universe, the Fragment nevertheless suggests distant perspectives. Its separation, indeed, is aggressive: it projects into the universe precisely by the way it cuts itself off.[32]

Just as this stylistic form may well have suited artists experiencing the disorder of a confusing world, so it must have fitted the 1970s workplace (cultural or otherwise) in its protectiveness against the onslaught of global and local displacements and reorganization.

There is a sense, too, that Russell mocks this short-term stylistic defense mechanism. When Tchaikovsky's wife, Nina (Glenda Jackson), takes male lovers to distract her from Tchaikovsky's absence, she fantasizes that they are great Russian composers, such as Borodin and Rimsky-Korsakov, and the encounters are soundtracked by the most easily recognized morsels of these artists' greatest hits. Just before Wagner reveals himself to be a vampire in *Lisztomania,* one of his leitmotifs hyperbolically announces the dramatic about-face. It is as if Russell were taking a swipe at Hollywood's own jarringly obvious and crudely terse musical promptings, but it is moments like these when critics most felt that the debasement of canonical work was Russell's aim. Jay Cocks of *Time* called *Mahler* "discombobulated, flatulent"[33] as a rebuke rather than a compliment of Russell's deconstruction of the ultimate futility of what the leitmotif might offer. To make fun of a gilded means of fighting off the horrors of alienation and distance, to open up its more facile forms of comforting was, to many, an ultimate mismatch.

Continuing along this line, Russell also interrogates the bolstering of "the self" inherent in the artistic movement. Romanticism, as the self-absorbed characters in these films often testify, prized direct individualism as a response to an uncaring although increasingly interconnected world. These figures are more concerned with themselves, their biographies, and their (what we would now call) identity politics—particularly in the case of Tchaikovsky's homosexuality—than with larger, more macro-political concerns (the exception being the nationalism of both Liszt and, more dangerously so, Wagner). The lone maverick stance is to be spotted both in Russell's attitudes and in the working practices of David Puttnam, his producer for the latter two pictures, who was a commercial entrepreneur rather than a stable studio head at this point. Yet the volatility of such positions manifests itself in a cynicism toward greatness, one that is evident through the less-than-likable traits of these composers and, indeed, in the eyes of the critics, in Russell himself. Russell is here either the victim of, or the sacrificial lamb to, an unsettling reconfiguration of the self enforced by the radical changes in working conditions.

Notably, Russell's responses to the many often-personal torrents of critical abuse have always been dismissive and suitably eccentric, signaling again appropriate new adaptations to the vacillating conditions of contemporary labor. His stance, like his oeuvre and its critical reception, is infused with an auteurism that speaks of a more fragmented, less rationalized Fordist mode of production, one that reflects the project-by-project output of a more entrepreneurial take on movie making that is apposite to an industry in near-crisis. Likewise, in focusing upon a single director, I aim to understand how the trope of individualism functioned alongside practices of (self-)employment during this specific period, particularly in Russell's congruent selection of biographical material that steeps stories of personal artistic development in grander historical currents.

The sensibility of self-reliant free-floating is also a variation on the themes of other economic developments of the time, if we listen to their recurrent motifs with a particular ear. In 1971, the year of *The Music Lovers'* release, the Bretton Woods Agreement, which pegged the monetary exchange rate to gold, was abandoned, leaving currencies adrift and the ability to forecast their worth, and thus an enduring mass production economy, much hazier. In 1976, as the period of these films ended, Britain was reduced to appealing to the International Monetary Fund (IMF), and Labour Prime Minister James Callaghan had to admit that the once unquestioned state-managed economy of Keynesianism was no longer effective in the uncertain global marketplace.[34] Historian Trevor May records the following developments:

> In 1974, prices rose by 19 per cent, and wage rates by 29 per cent, as groups of workers, who had got used to annually rising real incomes, fought to maintain their position. In the third quarter of 1975 inflation peaked at 26.5 per cent. More troubling even than this was that a situation had developed which orthodox Keynesian economic theory had seemed to hold impossible—high levels of inflation were accompanied by high levels of unemployment. "Stagflation," as it came to be called, presented the government with problems that Keynesianism seemed unable to solve, for any moves to curb inflation were likely to exacerbate the unemployment situation, while attempts to reduce unemployment stoked the fires of inflation. The economy thus floundered along at a low rate of growth while the high rate of inflation continued to make British exports uncompetitive.[35]

The most basic of economic variables were no longer reliable and a dialectic of unfathomable future effects was playing out. Global competition created problems for British protectionism, its fair wages, unemployment benefits, and other state support. It seemed increasingly likely that MNCs, rather than nation-states, would act as market stabilizers in the future, mobilizing whatever ethical or unethical means they saw fit to advance their expansion. The ensuing chaos appears to have dealt a major blow to British workers, particularly in the manufacturing industries, and, in a climate when trade union power was influential, the tactic of collective action seemed an appropriate way to confront fragmentation and dissolution. The fault lines dividing communal struggle, big business, and small-scale, even individual endeavor generated tremors across Russell's narratives, rumbling through them like (and by way of) complex symphonic structures. They also took their toll on how Russell's films were received, and it is therefore crucial to survey the foundations of Russell's critical castigation from within the groundswell of industrial action.

Using a variety of statistics from the *Employment Gazette,* Keith Grint summarizes that 1970–1974 saw 2,380 workplace stoppages, with 1,567,000 workers involved and 14,039,000 working days lost. There were, at this point, 11,390,000 trade union members amounting to a 49 percent trade union density.[36] By 1979, this had increased to 58 percent.[37] Throughout the period, then, organized labor exercised considerable disruption, with dockworkers, builders, and miners holding prolonged strikes. The year 1971 saw a forty-seven-day postal strike, somewhat ironic as a backdrop to the letter-writing exchange between Tchaikovsky and Madame von Meck that shapes *The Music Lovers'* narrative structure and that pits private (privatized) encounter against the composer's later impoverished resort to conducting and public performance. Neither the 1970–1974 Tory government nor its successors from the Labour Party fulfilled their aims of sweeping labor reforms, such was the central position of the unions in more general political decision making. Still, throughout the decade, measures were taken to enfeeble union muscle, to orchestrate splits between state and labor, the sort of fabricated dialectic that finds its way into how "the worker" is rendered in these three films. Although a collective language was being used to define the strike periods, these were times marked by a collapse in consensus politics, the kind that also features in the discussion of the Romantic fragment and the decline of the supported (cultural) worker.

There seems to have been a tangible concord between the contents of *The Music Lovers, Mahler,* and *Lisztomania* and the broader histories with which they interacted. Might this harmony with downright chaos have helped to prompt the films' labeling as mismatches? If Russell's movies weren't working, neither were so many other elements in Britain. Just as measures were taken to upbraid his directorial labor, on a much wider scale, forms of worker control were also being reconfigured. Starting with the 1969 white paper *In Place of Strife,* the UK government had tried to nudge toward more legal and corporatist modes of controlling industrial relations and, ultimately, the unions. These ideas provoked widespread outrage and were withdrawn even before Labour lost the general election of 1970 to Edward Heath, who had an even more stringent approach to trade unions. The year 1971 witnessed the Industrial Relations Act which, again, attempted to corner industrial actions within the frameworks of law. A National Industrial Relations Court (NIRC) was instituted to handle unfair practices, but it could also monitor and intervene in collective bargaining and individual union regulations. The act ended the closed-shop framework for most unions (although not, significantly, for Equity, the actors' union) and put many barriers in the way of direct striking, especially if it were seen to damage the national economy or public order—foggy concepts at the best of times. The new approach to controlling collective action and worker relations was by then clearly imprinted as a possible solution in the political mindset and would be developed further, as will become apparent in the following chapter, by the Thatcher governments of the 1980s. Public opinion, however, could not be swayed into a capitalist and corporatist resolution to economic decline and thus ensued, as has been observed, the rash of strikes of the early 1970s. Opposition to legislation had stimulated a three-day week that brought down the Heath administration, but led to only a small Labour majority. The act was repealed in 1974 by the in-coming Labour government and replaced by the milder Trade Union and Labour Relations Act. This chain of events tugged production this way and that, scarring too the layout of creative practices.

Another nail in Heath's coffin, very much a reason for the reduced working week and an event that bore a greater connection to musical mismatches than we might first imagine, was the 1973 leap in oil prices. Domestic fuel now being in very much greater demand, the National Union of Mineworkers (NUM) used this leverage to refuse to work overtime. There was now not enough electricity to consistently power the country, although, incongruously, a stripped-down television schedule did momentarily prompt healthier cinema box office figures.[38] The fuel crisis can be interpreted to have arisen from the Arab-Israeli or Yom Kippur War of October 1973. Oil embargos were imposed on Western nations by Arab states in an attempt to curb their support of Israel, while, at the same time, the money from Arab fuel revenues was rarely spent within the Western economies. In the somewhat bizarre memoirs of Edward Heath, *Music: A Joy for Life,* where the focus of his premiership seems geared more toward encounters with performers than the nitty-gritty of policy, the prime minister of the time related the events around the crisis:

> Isaac Stern and Pinchas Zukerman were both coming to play a programme of violin duos on 27 October, the same programme that they were giving at the Royal Festival Hall two days later. Alas, earlier in October, the Yom Kippur War broke out and brought tensions between the Israeli and British governments. Pinchas Zukerman felt unable to play but Isaac Stern, for the sake of his friendship with me, and even though it might expose him to criticism, decided to take part.... This concert showed once again how music can triumph over the conflicts and indeed the agonies of mankind.[39]

Perhaps within this odd seed of idealism and even Heath's concern for micro-relationships lay the clue to the future of the British economy. Perhaps culture would lead the way, and the desperate need to set agendas for it—as expressed by Russell's work and the responses to it—were not quite as incongruous as they at first might appear.

With its costly manufacturing and the financial license of its colonial influence both in decline, Britain was forced to strategically reposition itself within the global economic infrastructure. As such, it comes as no surprise that films like Russell's should debate what exactly it might mean to work and to create saleable goods within another potentially profitable sphere: that of culture. Was culture a more stable commodity for Britain to turn out, given the country's recent inability to maintain competitive mass production? While all of the interconnections between the economy and the media that I have charted seem merely to place the latter in tune with the former, the true dialecticism of every one of these elements, their clashes and exchanges, comes to the fore through an examination of the financial status of culture (as a prop to certain modes of capitalism and as its merchandise). This, however, requires an understanding of how and why culture might have become more central to the commodification process in the 1970s.

Reshaping the British Economy:
From Manual Work to Service and Culture

The expansion of the global marketplace and its sites of production, the fragmentation of manufacturing of all kinds, the industrial actions, and the fuel crisis had all dealt an enormous blow to a once financially secure nation. By the 1970–1975 period, inflation was up by 96 percent, and government debt had zoomed from zero to £9 billion by 1976.[40] In this inhospitable climate for borrowing, innovative entrepreneurialism had stalled and large-scale manufacturing had flown elsewhere. Even British giant Rolls Royce was declared bankrupt in 1971. It is thus revealing to see just how many of the reviews of Russell's films use the language of "lost potential" and "wasted talent" to condemn the three biopics.[41] Thwarted productivity and economic failure infuse claims that, for instance, *Lisztomania* was "intellectually bankrupt."[42] The country was beginning to realize that it could not depend upon old ways of earning money, but it was still debating exactly how to drag itself out of this depression.

One response is evident in how these films, in a direct replication of Romanticism's similar yearnings, nostalgically turn back (albeit in a satirical manner) to a now long-diminished agrarian way of life. Mahler is trying to distill "the very essence of nature," siphoning cow bells, bird song, and folk songs into his symphonies. Yet there is an air of comic impossibility to these fusions, reiterated by an overly idealized pastoral fantasy sequence which accompanies the premiere of Tchaikovsky's *Piano Concerto in B-flat Minor*. In the 1970s, the agricultural and manual sectors were in decline, and James E. Cronin observes instead, along with the swelling ranks of trade union membership, an increase in white-collar employment, particularly in the public, educational, service, and cultural spheres.[43] Such workforce transmutations brought about a change in how culture was to be perceived and consumed, but they also required careful balancing as many British citizens made the switch between professions or suffered the repercussions.

Interestingly, given this transition period, Russell's depictions of composers (as well as his own practices) are laden with references to physical effort. When Tchaikovsky is at the piano, we see the sweat pouring off him. Not for Russell the cunning close-ups that disguise the actor's inability to perform; instead, the full force of a driven performance is captured in complete body shots, Tchaikovsky's energy rendered through exhilaratingly frenetic and jagged camera work. In choosing to study Liszt, Russell takes on a composer whose repertoire exploited the full gamut of manual dexterity and vigor. Liszt's revolutionary new techniques demanded draining physical interaction with the piano itself. Both Tchaikovsky and, in particular, Mahler were profligate with manpower, writing large-scale works that increased musical employment to new symphonic heights. Even Russell himself was itchy to muck in. David Puttnam relates:

> If Ken arrived in the morning uncertain of his next move, he'd set
> up a complicated tracking shot and by the time the rails were laid
> he'd have had it all worked out in his head. The important thing is
> *activity*—do *anything,* but keep active.[44]

Given these preferences for arduous labor practices, it is startling to note how often critics hurled at his biopics the word "vulgar,"[45] a term carrying connotations of both excessive corporeality and working-class "tastelessness" and one to which I will return presently.

At the same time, Russell's selection of more famously creative, rather than manual workers points out that a tide was turning. The 1971 census made it known that the majority of British citizens were now employed in services, with relatively few (compared to in the United States) remaining in industry.[46] This does not, of course, mean that mass production declined as a whole, but that in Britain a caesura had been reached, and such work was now largely carried out elsewhere. In 1973, Daniel Bell had characterized the postindustrial phase as one with an increased emphasis on service, technical expertise, and knowledge. Hopeful that the coming age would realign the problematic struggle between labor and capital through a decreased emphasis on material goods, Bell was less attentive to the ways in which practices would become increasingly privatized and exclusive, maintaining older class divisions.

Bell's vision does not account for how a flailing economy would manage to enlarge the scope for cultural capital to replace, in a sense, a lack of solid economic capital. It was also unclear to Britain how culture, as a subsection of service, might become a boon to the nation's finances, especially when areas like cinema were evidently in crisis. Given the slump that the United Kingdom was enduring, it was certainly worth a shot. By the period dealt with in chapter 5 (the 1990s onward), the country had governmental policies in place to support and promote the "creative economy." For the meantime, however, various groups had yet to thrash out whether culture could flourish in such a manner and, either way, how cultural output was to interact with the very real increases in service personnel. Could and should culture serve to hegemonically shore up a recently repositioned social class? As Pierre Bourdieu argues:

> The new bourgeoisie is the initiator of the ethical retooling required by the new economy from which it draws its power and profits, whose functioning depends as much on the production of needs and consumers as on the production of goods. . . . It finds ardent spokesmen in the new bourgeoisie of the vendors of symbolic goods and services, the directors and executives of firms in tourism and journalism, publishing and the cinema, fashion and advertising, decoration and property development.[47]

From this perspective, film becomes a battleground for the concomitant struggle to realize an ethics and habitus that could match the drastically realigned economies and methods of labor. It is in Russell's concessions to change that the critics found fault, but, in many ways, his biographies are often fairly reasonable, even middle-brow in their propositions.

Russell's movies are often far from absorbed by the clichéd conceit of the Romantic artist rebelling against the bourgeoisie, although this did not stop the bourgeoisie from disliking *him* on occasion. It is only on the most personal and finicky of whims (such as Mahler's obstreperousness) that these composers challenge the elite; in fact they do much to hide what it is about them that sets them at a distance, such as Tchaikovsky's homosexuality and Mahler's Jewish heritage. In essence, when in public, the protagonists are often fairly eager to please and to be accepted for what they do, perhaps an insinuation about the compliant behaviors of a newly transmogrifying and expanding labor sector.

The representation of the work of composition in relation, perhaps, to the changing social status and legitimization of nonmanual economies is much more prominent. All three movies start in medias res when the protagonists are adults, although childhood flashbacks feature in *The Music Lovers* and *Mahler*. The biographical subjects are largely constituted through their professions rather than more random events in their lives. For the most part, the narratives circle around how the composers make money from their art and what that then entails for their private, emotional, and moral existences. Liszt, in particular, lives by his wits in order to fund himself, exploiting his sexual charms as much as his musical talent to guarantee sponsorship.

The spaces and times of artistic creativity are also explored. Tchaikovsky is saved from the noise of Rubenstein's (Max Adrian) annex and then Nina's clumsy intrusions by Madame von Meck's patronage, complete with his own house on her grounds. Mahler escapes to his gazebo by the lake, although he is often plagued by family members, and he is forever bothered by interruptions during the train journey that structures the plot. Like many cultural workers, they are situated in decentralized spaces, as was the case with the musicians recording in separate cities who featured in the preceding chapter.

Inspiration is rarely treated as an effortless occurrence, and artistic frustration is very much to the fore. Although Mahler is seen to be aroused into activity by his natural surroundings, this is a somewhat tongue-in-cheek take on the standard Hollywood biopic rendition of the creative process (the kind that sees the "tick, tick, tock of the stately clock" in Cole Porter's lyrics of the title song of *Night and Day* [Michael Curtiz, 1946] motivated by a nearby timepiece and the "drip, drip, drip of the rain" by the storm outside). Instead, the emphasis is on slow investment in practice: "Genius calls for scales, scales, scales," Mahler's teacher Sladky (Otto Diamant) admonishes him. Like the more Marxian-inclined precursor biopic, *The Chronicle of Anna Magdalena Bach* (Jean-Marie Straub and Danièle Huillet, 1967), effort is taken to capture the laboriousness of cultural work and, on occasion, these three films continue along the lines of *Chronicle*'s lengthy unedited performances of full pieces, which refuse to give audiences relief from the musical work by simply throwing in particular musical climaxes (as the later *Amadeus* [Milos Foreman, 1984] so readily does). If similar employment were to become more essential to Britain's success, then details of its working processes and ideas about how to value and measure the efforts expended would need to be laid down.

Unlike *The Chronicle of Anna Magdalena Bach,* however, we *are* privy to psychological impact, the interior life of the protagonists that renditions of

Romanticism more wholeheartedly invite because of the period's concentration on the self in relation to creativity. The artist is someone who shapes his work and inflects it with individuality, but this does not mean that composers are above reproach. Russell argued:

> People call *me* self-indulgent but he [Tchaikovsky] was the most self-indulgent man who ever lived, insofar as all his problems and hang-ups are stated in his music. Some might say overstated but then they never experienced what he went through and wouldn't have the guts to put it down on paper even if they had.[48]

His engagement at this level resituates the crises of 1970s labor, collectivism, and declining protectionism and allows them to resound through the stylistic decisions made through the films. The camera is often "too close" in *The Music Lovers,* perhaps distastefully so, and it is eager to thrust Tchaikovsky's self-obsession into our faces. This also mirrors a gossipy inquisitiveness that plagued the composer's life while promoting a fascination for intrusions into the private sphere (for want, perhaps, of a reliable social structure) that marks both Romanticism and more contemporary fandom. How, then, were all these anxieties and behavioral priorities to be assumed into a wider social ethics of work?

The clues might lie in the movies' consistent reference to Romantic conditions of creative labor. Following an era of exquisite rule-bound dexterity (exemplified by classical composers like Mozart), Romanticism sought to increase the musical palette, to weave itself into the uncertainty, chaos, and change of nineteenth-century industrializing and social-scrambling life through recourse to, for example, more unexpected key changes and an expansion of what harmony could be. Might not the further opening up of global trade competition in the 1970s, the various financial crises of the decade, the industrial development of certain nations, and the ensuing lack of prominence of others have understood an affinity with nineteenth-century patterns of progress and the music that explored its swelling and disorienting interchanges? Both periods witnessed dramatic reinventions of what "productivity" could mean and how the commodification of art fitted within this matrix. Could not the legacy of Romanticism—deployed so often in an idealized form to reaffirm a particular set of values—now address a collapsing status quo in labor, announcing a repetition of similar crises and conflicts in a specifically dialectical mode?

Caryl Flinn in *Strains of Utopia* ponders the allure of Romanticism to classical film scorers and offers some enticing correspondences between wage earning in the cultural sphere and the philosophical preoccupations of Romanticism that have relevance to the mismatches that critics found in Russell's biopics.

For her, Romanticism was born of a more freelance economy brought into play by the loss of royal and religious patronage, a condition that haunts composers and filmmakers even more in the post-Fordist period. Romanticism's mechanisms for coping with this included an aggrandizement of the individual, the nonconformist genius ground down by, but acutely sensitive to, the ruthlessness of an increasingly industrializing and dehumanizing world. The various alienating conditions of 1970s work similarly provoked such a reaction, one would imagine. If Romanticism was familiar to cinema (if only as a default scoring style), might not its affection for the hero figure also seem ripe for readaptation in the standard delivery of the filmic narrative structure? It is surely not coincidental that Russell should act and respond to the 1970s environment, and particularly the personally directed criticisms of his work, with the confidence of a misunderstood revealer of contemporary hypocrisies.

However, unlike in later composer biopics such as *Amadeus,* genius is no excuse for bad behavior in these treatments; a class system does not protect the depicted composers' idiosyncrasies so readily, although social instability has inflamed them. In the 1970s, just like in the Romantic period, cultural workers had to prove themselves and survive within new conditions that offered less support than they had historically come to expect. Consequently, all three composers are reprehensibly selfish, especially in their treatment of women, who were, in the 1970s, less susceptible to the shift in labor patterns and often the victims of male frustration. In periods of augmented competition and with fewer safety nets, this is an understandable response. Thus, Mahler is unremittingly cranky and rude to almost everyone he encounters; Tchaikovsky inconsiderately dismisses his wife, her mother (Maureen Pryor), and the Moscow art scene; and Liszt moves from one financially indulgent sexual partner to another with little deep concern for the psychological consequences. Yet overwhelming self-indulgence is also wholly intrinsic to their work. Mahler puts his compositional career before everything—family and religion—turning his wife into an unwaged copyist. Later he complains that "duty destroys, duty always destroys": both his to his family and Alma's to him as he grows sick. The investment that so many workers had made in careers at this time, often in vain, echoes through these responses, asking whether a reconception of the employee-to-job relationship (or lack thereof) might not be worth searching out.

The fact that these protagonists are disagreeable at times is not simply a reflection of their working methods, but also a forewarning of the realities of a creative economy. Personality traits like these have been deliberately latched onto a film genre that has sought to be, by and large, quite complimentary about artists' psyches. With "genius" displaced somewhat, these characters became approachable and understandable (if not necessarily likable) for a contemporary, more creative industry–ready world, but their emotions seemingly debased them to many a disparaging critic. In all sorts of ways, Romanticism opens up a window for thinking about the projection of self within a cultural consumer economy, but we are also warned that this process is as vain as it is alchemical. *The Music Lovers* comically and emphatically intercuts between ballerinas performing *Swan Lake* and Nina, who, while watching the show, has tightly knotted her own biography and feelings to the events on stage. The film's audience is tipped off to the ludicrousness of overinvestment in cultural work and its commodification by artists and fans alike. Throughout the narrative, Nina cannot truly come to grips with the seriousness of art, yet here she falls for it in the most facile of ways and, as such, she acts as a cipher for the implications of an expanded cultural economy. With the future of service and culture work demanding ever-increasing investments of the self (as chapter 5 will testify), these sequences also caution against the sense of meaningfulness that is engendered by cultural work. How might commodification and alienation from the point of production complicate the exalted qualities of high art's status, themselves emblems of successful commercial validation?

In moments such as this one with Nina, the absolutism, the abstraction of music that is so precious to many is undercut. Its magical quality, which upholds unfathomable genius, is portrayed in terms of chance, necessity, and often misplaced individualism. Subsequently, the wardens of that tradition are divested of a certain amount of their power.

"You and Your Ideal Love Will Die": The Desecration of the Romantic Greats

After *The Music Lovers'* unflinching exploration of Tchaikovsky's tortured homosexuality and *Mahler's* implantation of sauced-up Nazism into early twentieth-century Vienna, the self-appointed bastions of elite tradition the Liszt Society wrote an anxious letter to the magazine *Film and Filming:*

> We are naturally concerned at the prospect of Franz Liszt being
> subjected to the Ken Russell treatment. Our apprehensions are
> heightened by the news that the music has been rearranged in
> rock style and that the story contains scenes of rape, blood sucking,
> exorcism and castration. . . . If you wish to check with us for our
> reactions to the film or for any specialised advice, we shall be pleased
> to help.[49]

The society's sense of assumed authority to relate Liszt's life is exposed in this correspondence and felt to be under direct fire from the often humorous, complex, and camp liberties that the movie was to take with the composer's (and Europe's) history. No doubt, certain bodies perceived their territory to be threatened, not just by *Lisztomania's* particular perspective, but also, arguably, by larger currents that were reforming how work and its attendant class and leisure structures were composed. At the same time, once fairly stable and confidently expert high- and somewhat middle-brow presses were distancing themselves with celerity from the tabloids.[50] This distinction allowed the broadsheets and "quality" magazines an even grander and markedly more defensive isolation throughout this decade, one that saw Russell's work as a worthy target for wrath especially because of its mismatching of canonical music with various elements of film style, referencing, and narrative composition.

These reviews embedded themselves within the customs and validations of a particularly British morality that Russell-as-individual, rather than the machinery of postindustrialization, was charged with troubling. In a spiteful exchange between film critic Alexander Walker and Russell, Walker accused the director of making "porno-biography,"[51] a statement that reiterates countless accusations about the "vulgarity" of this trio of films and which is ruefully picked up and bounced back in Rubenstein's comment that Tchaikovsky's *Piano Concerto in B-flat Minor* is "not only trivial, it's bad, vulgar." Russell's off-screen rejoinder was, "If Mel Brooks or Fellini had done what I do, they'd [the critics] like it, but one of their own is expected to respond to their very favourite word—*restraint*. If I were American, who would want restraint?"[52] Certainly there has been much critical marginalization of the tradition of British cinematic hyperbole, from Gainsborough melodramas to the luridness of movies like *Black Narcissus* (Michael Powell and Emeric Pressburger, 1946) and Hammer horror films. These are works that question the limitations of professed tastefulness as required by certain high-brow material. It is the provision of excess that disturbs, especially when the overindulgences are felt to be too concrete and forthright. Perhaps this dismissal betrays unease about productivity itself: the manufacturing of standard physical commodities versus the often more intangible forms created through and for intellectual engagement, a very different type of work altogether. Although this struggle appears to be playing out at a removed register here, its cultural location must have been crucial to the search for how film and music might slot into an augmented nonmanual economy.

What seems to have been most shocking for the critics were the "mismatched" *visual* manifestations of some particularly harried and unsettled musical compositions in these films. *The Music Lovers* provides one such moment when Tchaikovsky and Nina, emboldened by alcohol, attempt intercourse on a train. The sequence begins with abrupt whistles and train chugs, signaling that we are in a private compartment on board. The camera lurches into extreme close-ups of the couple, as seemingly inebriated and off-balance as are the protagonists and eager to particularize their disheveled, sweaty bodies and reactive facial gestures. When the swinging overhead light intermittently exposes their forms from pitch darkness, we confront a naked, lolling, and desperate Nina and an utterly terrified and revolted Tchaikovsky. All the while, the music engrosses itself in a state of hyperbole and turmoil, its positioning breaking away from Russell's more typical modes of musical tallying. The opening section draws upon the high point of the *Sixth Symphony's* (*Pathétique*) first movement, but then, when confronted with this piece's decrease in frenzy and shift from B Minor to Major, the soundtrack makes a dramatic leap, for the sake of heightened intensity, into another composition altogether: the twice-repeated and equally fraught coda from *Manfred*. As the two works are in the same key, they chime with each other on one level, but the mismatch is evident to anyone knowledgeable about Tchaikovsky's oeuvre. In one sense, the splice is both sensationalist in its desire for drama over structural variation and anachronistic (*Pathétique* was written many years after Tchaikovsky's marriage, his last major opus before his death). Yet the train sequence is extremely cunning in the way that it barges biographical implications into the heart of Tchaikovsky's overall output. *Pathétique* was dedicated to Bob Davidov, his nephew and probable lover, and seems to many an exposition on the travails of illegal homosexuality, while *Manfred* involves itself diegetically with forbidden love of another order: incest.[53] When tied to this scene and, in particular, to the shots of Nina's cavernously vaginal, upturned crinoline as she undresses and Tchaikovsky's expressions of disgust, explicit statements are made about the composer's sexual orientation. All of the "abstraction" of the music is undermined as the sequence suggests the torment of Tchaikovsky's ill-placed attempts to deny his homosexuality. Whatever other loose associations that the music might have held for the refined aficionado of the classical canon are temporarily usurped. A literalness of narrative/biographical information, one of unreserved tumult that bursts forth from the music, forbids other, looser (perhaps class-supporting) associations from running their course, including those that respect the temporal interplay of fuller symphonic structure. A mismatch comes to the fore for those who feel awkward about such a union of long-respected music with messy sexual imagery. In many senses, the guardianship of these artistic expressions against what Roy Armes calls the "glib oversimplifications and facile symbolism"[54] destabilizes a particular historical trajectory of engagement, one that favors, I contend, some socioeconomic classes over others. What, then, has been invested in this music and by whom?

The Music Lovers, Mahler, and *Lisztomania,* as I have made evident, take liberties with the past, just as most composer biopics do, particularly such distinctly non–high art Hollywood fare as *A Song to Remember* (Charles Vidor, 1944), which presumes to detail the life of Frédéric Chopin. What matters to my own arguments is how "historical truth" ballasts the debates about ownership that sparked the mismatch condemnation and how all of this interacted with the changing working conditions of 1970s Britain. Robert A. Rosenstone's investigation in *Visions of the Past: The Challenge of Film to Our Idea of History* provides, in more general terms, some clues to the exigency of the critical responses to Russell's movies:

> Question: Why do historians distrust the historical film? The overt answers: Films are inaccurate. They distort the past. They fictionalize, trivialize, and romanticize people, events, and movements. They falsify history. The covert answers: Film is out of control of historians. Film shows we do not own the past. Film creates a historical world with which books cannot compete, at least for popularity. Film is a disturbing symbol of an increasingly postliterate world (in which people can read but won't).[55]

That these films were also about artists of exalted status only added grist to the mill. The protection of their heritages by another, often affiliated elite group has much to say about the control, formation, physicality (or not), and moral hegemonic frameworks that these communities wished to maintain. As any composer biopic is truly an intersection of ways of retelling and benefiting from the past—a life rendered as narrative, a fictionalized set of facts, a new vision of something primarily musical—it cannot help but set a series of dialectical adventures and problems into staunchly enforced hierarchies of sociality and meaning.

The three Russell-directed films also examine how art might be symptomatic and how its resonances might ring throughout lengthier historical periods in different forms, forms that undercut the stability of "meaning" that often embalms classical music for the perpetual, staid contemplation of a more unified class tradition. It is as if Russell were saying, as Tchaikovsky's male lover Count Anton Chiluvsky (Christopher Gable) does while explaining the themes of *Swan Lake* to the newly married Nina, "You and your ideal love will die," pointing out just how compromised such sentiments ultimately are. Russell's insistence on certain alliances across history disturbed many of his detractors because certain emotions and states of flux cannot be buried in the past or archived so as to bolster a particular class privilege. In his essay on Russell's biopics, Robert Kolker argues that these films play

> the "facts" against the romanticized myth that has grown up around the artist. Thus, the typical Russell subject is composed of three personae: the historical figure, the myth the figure has created, and Russell's own vision of the subject, which exaggerates the historical figure in order to play it off against the myth. The result is, obviously, conflict. . . . Ultimately the biographical figure is turned into an actor in history and destroyed by his act and the historical moment that cannot contain him. After his death, he is further destroyed by his mythic persona, that *version* of himself created by the admirers of his art.[56]

Just as *The Music Lovers* has Tchaikovsky haunted by his mother's death and *Mahler* presents continual psychologically unresolved flashbacks of its protagonist's youth, so the ghostly forms of industrial and creative labor history revisit more contemporary cultural products.

Romanticism too, in its many incarnations, was also preoccupied with a form of double temporality, one that yearned for the archaic, the natural, and the remnants from the past (such as deserted ruins) while hurtling full tilt into the uncertain contemporary, which it did through stylistic innovation and new modes of understanding the self. These films work within a similar dialectical paradigm. Historical veracity is snarled, at times suggesting a complicity of art in future (sometimes destructive) developments. Russell argues that "historical films are often made as if the people living in the past thought of themselves as part of history already, living in a museum";[57] not for these pictures the closed carapace of "pastness" that protects the viewer from troubling continuities. Both *Mahler* and *Lisztomania* discuss the future, anachronistic rise of the Nazis in ways that critics found irritatingly crude, yet without too much of a sense of what such historical dialecticism could offer an understanding of culture's increasing claims to social centrality. On one level, *Lisztomania*'s intimation about Cosima Wagner's (Veronica Quilligan) proto-Nazism is a (perhaps too) obvious statement about responsibility and implication across the ages. On another plane, *Mahler*'s rendition of goose-stepping soldiers and swastika-clad dancers into a sexualized Busby Berkeley-esque organized spectacle reminds us of the proximity of media culture to all kinds of vastly important historical progressions. This was a point to be taken with great seriousness if countries like Britain were to place culture more prominently in their economies.

Much to critics' disgust, Liszt was recast as a rock star, pointing out the similarities between both modes of musicality in delightful disregard of the barriers that often freeze these two genres in an opposition.[58] This is an almost Eisensteinian plea for egalitarianism through a uniform investment in all of the movies' formal components. For Eisenstein, elements such as shots and sounds become "of equal rights, of equal influence and equal responsibility in the perfect film."[59] Mirroring the greater practices of labor, of which filmmaking is just one tiny fraction, movie manufacture is a dialectical process that is aware of the injustices of capitalist inequality and tries to debate the nature of status. While both Eisenstein and Russell evidently hoped for a resolution of such conflicts in the thinking and acting audience, the way in which many critics refused to engage with this clashing material tells us much about the ruling tastes of the world at that time. This depiction of Liszt questions the reasons for distancing the represented modes of artistic expression. It also asks, through deliberate anachronism and flagrant ripostes to blinkered notions of fidelity, how history writing might interact with more popular methods of storytelling or disengage from traditional forms of historical authority and elitist cultural-capital custodianships.

Furthermore, the overlapping of the structures of history writing and media narrative reshapes the semantics of each sphere of production. History is invited to absorb some of the preoccupations of the increasingly prominent (mass) cultural industries, perhaps an inevitable outcome of a certain hegemonic shift within deindustrializing Britain. The struggle of such critics, then, is one that challenges the power of the media to establish history, to omit, to elaborate, and to narrativize it in its own particular registers. There is a particularly stringent set of expectations to which one is held when depicting a once-living person of stature, and these maintain a range of sociopolitical agendas that are no longer so strong in a post-Fordist globalized climate.

"I'm Doing Franz Liszt Meets Richard Wagner. It's Going to Be Rather Like Frankenstein Meets Godzilla": The Increasing Prominence of the Media and the Devolution of History Telling

Throughout these films, then, the very fabric of historical recounting, along with understandings of cultural worth, are permeated by the values and traditions of art and popular culture itself.[60] Other types of history must come to the fore. When academic Russell Lack declares that "Russell weaves a kind of cinematic pulp . . . straining within the envelope of a conventional bio-pic,"[61]

Richard Mallett of *Punch* deems his work "third-rate melodrama,"[62] and Michael Dempsey calls it "hyperthyroid camp circuses,"[63] there is little sense that compliments are being offered about the types of *work* that are being fashioned. Such claims of a mismatch of historical narration and popular culture marginalize the creative outcomes that might be brought forth from this type of connection. What, exactly, does it mean to feed history through the machinery of more popular discourses? How and why would this have been seen as a harmful ambition? What imbalances to the traditions of labor are set in motion?

The blending of class-defining markers of taste as they map across various planes of cultural production are central to the Russell method. *Dr. Kildare* heartthrob Richard Chamberlain, for instance, is cast in the lead role in *The Music Lovers,* and the film as a whole often has an emotional ambience more fitting to primetime soap fare, although with a much more adult sensibility made possible through cinematic screenings. *Mahler* draws in imagery from the film *Siegfried* (Fritz Lang, 1924) for the composer's conversion scene, complete with appropriately pastiched intertitles. Earlier, the *Fifth Symphony,* used so famously in the movie *Death in Venice* (Luchino Visconti, 1971), starts up, and we see look-alikes of its two lead characters waiting at the station where Mahler's train pulls up. There are also, as has been observed, the silent-comedy references in *Lisztomania.* The film's most sustained welding of "the popular" to "the artistic," however, is the composer's first concert scene, where the audience is made up of nineteenth-century teenyboppers, screaming for "Chopsticks" and drowning out the complexity of the more intellectually challenging pieces in his program by mobbing him. Casting rock star Roger Daltrey in the lead role and Ringo Starr as the pope firms up all of these connections, as do little touches of mise-en-scène like Liszt's rock-like strutting with an Orphean lyre, the pictures of Daltrey's fellow band member Pete Townshend in Carolyn's (Sara Kestelman) room, and the pope's robes detailed with images of classical Hollywood stars. Rock musician Rick Wakeman, who also rephrased Liszt's work for the soundtrack on synthesizer, provides a humorous portrayal of Thor: part Frankenstein, part comic book superhero to match Wagner's kitschy understanding of the master race.[64] Daltrey lends his interpretation of the composer's famous *Liebestraum,* complete with somewhat syrupy American-accented lyrics of "oh love, sweet love" and rock-like vocal inflections. Like Liszt's own compositions, then, the film is full of reinterpretations, paraphrases, and reworkings of culture bearing seemingly insufficient gravitas akin to Liszt's beloved folk songs in his day. Just as Liszt had done, Russell also riffs on his own work. Mahler declares knowingly that his œuvre is "for music lovers everywhere," and there is also a scene featuring a boy (Mahler) on a white horse, an iconic snapshot from Russell's television hit "Elgar."

In this way, culture from across a much wider spectrum is used to underline itself. This is not, however, as George F. Custen argues of Hollywood biopics, one sphere of production colonizing another so as to exert its newfound control in the making of public history. It is more a process of affirmation that opens up the means of recording and discussing the past to a new alignment of working practices and its economies. Eisenstein himself may well have approved. He tested his theories to the limits, a breath-taking range of subject matter ricocheting in and out of his expansive and incorporative approach to topics, including those that lay well beyond the boundaries of consciously leftist cinema such as his own.

Like Eisenstein's material, these movies are far from hierarchical in their exchanges; they also repeatedly allow musical form to lead more populist-tinged interpretations. The whole of *Mahler*, Russell claims, follows a rondo structure (A-B-A-C), which is also, one could argue, the routine that many pop songs follow.[65] Music strikes up, just as it does in Hollywood movies, as a cue to every flashback, but, in allowing the music to lead at a more fundamental level, he appears to be poking fun at this lazy standard device. Music is not merely an accompaniment or a commentary; it is the aesthetic lifeblood of and rationale for the film. There are ten full minutes free from dialogue in *The Music Lovers* when Tchaikovsky is performing his *Piano Concerto in B-flat Minor*, and the fantasies that the music prompts lead the visual track. This gesture not only respects the gamut of artistic endeavor, it also tries intently to weave a tighter, more complex fabric from various, often ostracized cultural practices, not least ones that, like classical concert music, were at the time fighting for their financial survival. If the sphere of culture was opening up to greater numbers of workers, then it had to also expand its repertoire to all of the possibilities of production and profit, using each to propel the others into new realms. As an endeavor to grapple with some of these issues, this oeuvre is far from Michael Dempsey's comment about Russell's "growing emphasis on razzle-dazzle as an end in itself."[66] It clears space, just as his carnivalesque visual style does, for a renegotiation of the high-low art encounter.

By devaluing Russell's work in terms of deportment and vulgarity, a whole series of possibilities is closed down. Uneasily commercial they may seem (for example, in their casting of popular entertainment stars), but surely this aesthetic speaks of a new economy for culture that has everything to do with Britain, or the West's, turn to the production of less physical commodities. What the films seem to aim for is not simply a prototypical "postmodern play," but a concrete manifestation of the practical necessities of postmodern (or rather post-Fordist) *work*. Mass culture, through such movements as pop art, had stridently entered the domains of high art, yet a populist availability of elitist pursuits was more troubling in its disturbance of certain economic and semantic powers. These hybridizations of style and reference question the exclusive belonging of classical music to an intellectual few, something about which sociologist Pierre Bourdieu has much to say. Ken Roberts neatly summarizes Bourdieu's arguments about their underlying benefits:

> By patronising and consuming high culture, economic elites are able to present themselves simultaneously as benefactors, and as exceptionally cultured, refined people rather than simply privileged and wealthy. In return, cultural elites are given resources and influence—their views are heard by people with economic and political power. The *quid pro quo* is that they share their esteem with politicians and the business class. The outcome, Bourdieu contends, is a set of relationships which serves the interests of all the elites, and which is extremely difficult to break. He claims that high culture has played a crucial role in consolidating and sustaining the wider systems of economic and political stratification in the Western world.[67]

These very attitudes, their habitus, their modes of consumption, even their dress codes are all put in jeopardy by the movies' supposed contamination of classical music. Furthermore, the excess of Russell's depictions suggests quite forcefully that there is a tawdriness to Romanticism which taints the lofty values with which it is supposed to endow its safekeepers.

The films also formed part of a turning tide in higher education, which was crucial to the preparation of a broader range of culture and cultural workers in the circuits of postindustrial production and consumption. Robert Hewison maps out a tightly interconnected history of such scholarship in the United Kingdom:

> The University of Leicester established a Centre for Mass Communication Research in 1966, the same year that Leeds set up a Centre for Television Research. The first chair in film studies was established by London University in 1967. The University of Glasgow's Media Group was to follow in 1974; and in 1977 Cardiff became another centre for communications research and the Open University launched a course in mass communications and society. The most significant moves towards establishing cultural studies as a separate academic entity, however were at Birmingham.[68]

In all of these institutions, training was being offered via a different attitude toward culture, one that opened it up to a wider spectrum of contemporary life. Teaching in these institutions—and even writing well-regarded books, like Richard Hoggart's *The Uses of Literacy* (1957) and E. P. Thompson's *The Making of the English Working Class* (1963)—were academics who not only preached a more democratic attitude, but who were also in utterly new lines of work given their class backgrounds. Russell too was not from the typical home of an expert on classical music, and his oeuvre also aims to construct the avenues for more to follow into similar pursuits.

Such people were part of the expansion of the traditional working classes into middle-class professions, both in the boom years of the 1960s and during the more desperate postindustrial reconfigurations of profitable labor in the 1970s. As a consequence, there is an obvious bleeding across of tastes, one that was, as we have seen, heavily condemned by many critics. Roger Daltrey's accent reveals his working-class roots, and his Liszt decorates his house with the kind of nouveau-riche panache (soft furnishings with keyboard motifs) that affectionately betrays his arriviste "vulgarity." His lack of "restraint," however, comes across as something of a life force, a vitality that his screaming fans also display and that cannot be entirely thrown by the wayside. These characterizations are in sympathy with the connections that Robert Pattison makes in *The Triumph of Vulgarity: Rock Music in the Mirror of Romanticism:* "What separates elite from popular culture is its unwillingness to embrace the vulgarity inherent in its own premises. . . . Vulgarity is no better and no worse than the pantheism and the democracy out of which it grows."[69] On these occasions, a presence rather than an absence of culture signals itself insistently, proclaiming itself a value rather than a failure. Russell himself muses:

> It's strange that people can't reconcile vulgarity and artistry. They're the same thing to me. But don't get vulgarity mixed up with commercialism. By vulgarity I mean an exuberant over-the-top larger-than-life slightly bad taste red-blooded thing. And if that's not anything to do with Art let's have nothing to do with Art. Let's have more of *that*.[70]

Just as Romanticism witnessed the expansion of the middle classes and reflected its less cultivated, more melodramatic inclinations through opera and ballet (as Russell is keen to point out), so too do the characters in these films refuse to shy away from tastes that reveal a movement across social strata. They display an "unrefined" attitude toward consumption in doing so, but they also entirely reposition consumption according to the confusing status of production in the 1970s.

To frame this, as critics often seem happy to do, in languages of meritocracy was to elude the issue of access to privilege—cultural, educational, and, more nebulously, financial. But this opens up larger questions, ones to do with funding that have everything to do with both old systems of governance and their adaptation to the changing currents in labor practices.

Arts and Entertainment Funding:
The Dance of the Public and the Private

The "arts proper," like classical music, have long been favored by British government funding bodies and frequently in ways that pamper and prioritize the values of the ruling classes. Cinema, on the other hand, has largely been considered a commercial venture by the state, often backed and expanded by foreign (largely, by this point, disappearing American) investment.[71] The same could be said of popular music. In response to these kinds of discretionary boundaries and their impact, Russell railed at length:

> If *Tommy,* instead of *The Knot Garden,* was put on at Covent Garden and toured around, it would do a lot to shake up the music world, because I think at this present moment too many composers are being supported by the Arts Council and producing work which is really of no interest except to a very, very small minority of people in this country and to themselves. I met some Hells' Angels who said: "I'm glad you're making this rock film because at last we will have a film to go to that has got music in [it] that we like. We never hear music that we like." I said, "[W]hat do you do?" and one said: "Well, I've worked for seven years in a pottery. I work from seven in the morning to seven at night. I have half a day off a week, that's Saturday from one o'clock to six o'clock," and I said: "Where do you go then?" He said, "Nowhere," and it's for the nowhere people, maybe, that we should start thinking.[72]

But from where would the money for this come? Russell's movies were released in a period of transition for arts funding, one that directly traced his own move from a publicly financed BBC salary for work such as "Elgar" to the free-market currents carrying his feature film oeuvre. Paradoxically, state control, through both sponsorship and educational agendas, was elbowing the arts out of the public sphere and toward more market-driven objectives and activities. The Heath administration eagerly introduced commercial radio into the country, and Margaret Thatcher, then Secretary of State for Education, brought in a system of entry charges for all national museums, a policy that proved to be a financial failure.[73] Public spending cutbacks were perhaps inevitable given the economic crisis but were nurtured by a concomitant resistance to the "public good" consensus about culture and an increased marketization that was to gain in prominence during the Thatcher years. As usual, cinema was offered few financial shortcuts, especially as it was seen to be on the wane. The 1970–1974 government donated a meager £1 million to the National Film Finance Corporation, but only on the condition that £3 was found from the private sector for every £1 of public money.[74]

Without a healthier manual economy to help fund the state, it was rationalized, entertainment and the arts would have to either suffer or reinvent themselves as salable commodities. The (often implausible and defensive) nineteenth-century-derived assumption that high culture could stand at a remove from the crasser elements of commerce and could exist almost as Marxian unalienated labor was fighting to keep its head above water. While the three biopics present a body of compositions that are inextricable from "the self," they are keen to discuss how creative work is enabled, if stifled, by outside money and its own senses of "investment."

The Arts Council of which Russell seems so contemptuous had plummeted from a position of relative wealth under Harold Wilson's government to the hard times so common to many institutions in the 1970s recession. It is no wonder, then, that questions of patronage prevail with such forcefulness in the biopics' narratives; there is an explicit affinity between Romanticism's precarious, moneyless drift and the impoverished condition of artists in this more recent decade. By insisting upon the difficulties of survival in the marketplace, these films raise awareness of the privatization of this type of art and a decrease in funding opportunities.

However, the work of these selected composers from the Romantic era was also, conveniently, copyright-free, facilitating cheaper production costs. The labor had long since been paid for, adding a positive spin to Christopher Hudson of the *Spectator*'s jibe about Russell's "bargain basement introductions to the Classics."[75] In one sense, Russell's work also adopts the procedure of mergers, the cost-cutting measures that were sweeping the country. It aims to incorporate the most popular dimensions of two failing sectors, and it does so, as is often the case with synergy, by presenting a package that spins off several commodities, such as the soundtrack album or increased sales by linkage to Roger Daltrey's other work with The Who. It is not surprising that Stephen Farber of the more intellectual periodical *Film Comment* should have presumed at the time that "the casting of pop stars in both movies were [*sic*] made with an eye on the box office."[76] Tony Rose also remarked that "the subject [of *The Music Lovers*] certainly has plenty going for it on a commercial level. Of all classical music, Tchaikovsky's is almost certainly the most widely known and hummable."[77] How, then, do Russell's movies circumnavigate the new impositions and perhaps freer currents of the postindustrial turn? What lurked within them that caused such critical consternation in a time of unease about how and for whom exactly art was to be constituted—materially (or otherwise), politically, and ethically?

Ideas about matched funding drifted into policy making for other art forms just after *Lisztomania* was released,[78] but an ethos of thriftiness that erred toward conservative crowd pleasing had already been in the air for some time. Robert Hewison's *Culture and Consensus: England, Art and Politics since 1940* provides a fascinating and illuminating anecdote:

> [Arts minister Lord David] Eccles expressed [his distrust of theater] more judiciously in the House of Lords in February 1971 when he made public his disquiet about the use of public money to fund "works which affront the religious beliefs or outrage the sense of decency of a large body of taxpayers. . . . If the Arts Council could reach some understanding with their clients that takes into account the moral views of those who are putting up the money, I should be very glad" [House of Lords, 3 Feb. 1971, *Hansard,* 5th ser., vol. 314, col. 1210]. Eccles wanted the Arts Council to exercise censorship by withholding funds from offending companies, an idea that [Chairman of the Arts Council Lord Arnold] Goodman firmly resisted, though he passed on a general reminder to clients.[79]

Here, majority "morality" becomes synonymous with providing consumers with what they want. Not only is art positioned more as a money maker than as a money beneficiary, but its reformation must abide by codes similar to those which had previously policed that loaded term "vulgarity." While "art" might be on the move, the principles of investing in and hegemonically protecting it remained a constant concern.

Questions of mass appeal and the damage that it might bring in terms of artistic integrity are definitely at the forefront of these films' agendas. As experiences for sale, they not only commodify the process of art making and its end products, they also reflect back on this process. Toward the end of *The Music Lovers,* Tchaikovsky is prompted by his somewhat exploitative brother Modeste (Kenneth Colley) to resort to public performance and catchier compositions because his sexual preference has lost him his patronage. Money rains down on him as he conducts the *1812 Overture;* a gaudy spectacle with streamers and can-can dancers unfolds. Mahler's conversion is also highly cynical, and Liszt responds to the question "Writing a symphony?" with "Doing the accounts." He talks of box office takings and press clippings that even the pope has admired; his income is bestowed upon him by wealthy female lovers and the ticket revenues from the multitudes of screaming female fans. But these are the very same girls who later join Wagner's Nazi cult, implying the often sinister power of commercial artistic goods. Beneath the critics' contempt for these anachronisms perhaps dwells an anxiety about the extended history of exploitation and "misappropriation" through, by, and of art. Maybe music, like cinema, has been crafted by creative workers as a mass commodity for a longer period than those whom its ideals fortify would like to imagine.

Persuasive suggestions to this effect are also evident in the movies' treatment of advertising. Through citations of more direct forms of promotion and sales, bourgeois purchasing and its engagements with art are plunked unavoidably before our eyes. Both Russell and his producer, David Puttnam, had previously worked in advertising, with Russell providing campaigns, interestingly, for Black Magic, Horlicks, and Galaxy, short-lifespan, sweet food products with emphases on sensual ingestion. The visual repertoires for selling such goods are carried through into the erotic thrill that Madame von Meck somewhat absurdly achieves by biting into the half-finished peach that Tchaikovsky has carelessly left lying around. But these instances depicting gratification are then complicated by the scenes of carnivorous meal eating and, in the end, Nina's presentation of her body for oral sex to the inmates of the asylum.

The three movies refuse to see only the good in goods, a concern that matches Eisenstein's guardedness about the limitations of his methods and his sensitivity toward moments where the latent energy of dialecticism is needlessly dissipated.[80] For instance, Eisenstein mourns the lost potential of D. W. Griffith's juxtapositions, in particular his famous cross-cutting; estranged as they are from direct political reasoning, the end effect is one of mere comparison. In essence, this enables the trouble-free rendition of filmic elements into (or advertisements for) objects for procurement, a dilemma close to the ones I have identified as distressing so many classical music experts. For Eisenstein, these cinematic morsels "become mere playthings and an end in themselves. The better the shots, the closer the film comes to being a disjointed collection of beautiful phrases, a shop window of unrelated objects or an album of postage stamps with views."[81] In line with this, *The Music Lovers, Mahler,* and *Lisztomania* also insist that the compiled structure of cinema amounts to more than an array or taxonomy of (consumer) possibilities; it also begets a provocative set of interactions. Juxtaposition should not simply lead to comparison, but to the contemplation and extrication of what these "opposites" mean and how their interrelationships should/could be negotiated.

Thus, the *Piano Concerto in B-flat Minor* sequence in *The Music Lovers* is filled with imagery from cigarette commercials, Russell tells us, but not to glorify their merchandise or any other.[82] Tchaikovsky's friends and family are rendered in soft-focus, white, sunlit clothes, frolicking in meadows, daisy picking by a summer cottage and a lake with swans (prompting an impromptu ballet move or two in jokey reference to one of the composer's most famous works). This is a prolonged reminder of the worst excesses of Romantic pastoralism as well as the giddy sentimentality that music so easily provokes in its consumers, now just as much as then. In coming to grips with Tchaikovsky's sublimation of his emotions into art, Russell remarked, "I can only keep relating this to commercials. *They* are fantasies on life which promise a romantic solution but which can only lead to disillusionment, disappointment—death!"[83] He continued elsewhere, "The core of the film is the destructive force of dreams, particularly daydreams on reality. The television adman's trick of passing off his dream world as an attainable and desireable [sic] reality is to my mind the great tragedy of our age."[84] With these gestures, the films seem unwilling to unthinkingly equate "the masses" with "the consumer" to maintain a class system that sections off more "worthy" goods to create a social hierarchy. If history and art are to become salable as entertainment (or anything else), then the mobility of all of these factors, created by the energies they draw from each other, must be fed back into a critique of false differentiation and class distinction.

More often than not, the three films convey these ideas through comedy—the need to laugh in the face of bleak economic conditions from all sides, their problems, and their resolutions. The films' fluctuations between sincerity and reverence bear the markers of camp, a prime strategy for loving culture but also for communicating a detestation of its more noisome origins and outcomes. Tchaikovsky's attempted suicide is cut through with this sentiment. Accompanied by his own music, he hopes to drown himself by leaping into a canal, only to find that it is not deep enough. He must ignominiously climb out and is sniffed inquisitively by the Highland terrier of a strolling passerby. The joke is on the artist himself, but elsewhere mainstream cinema culture is targeted. Backstage in *Lisztomania,* we are emphatically introduced by name to Mendelssohn, Rossini, Brahms, Berlioz, Schumann, Chopin, Liszt, and Wagner in dazzlingly quick succession, just as a Hollywood biopic must heavily emphasize who its famous characters are for those without the necessary education. Camp like this, despite its affection, can also be snobbish and overly knowing too; as a strategy, camp finds its most comfortable home, after all, in the in-clubs of marginalized subcultures, particularly queer ones. It asks us to pass judgments when some of Russell's work instead leaves us with the kinds of ambivalence whose destruction (sometimes critical, sometimes Russell's own) is surely symptomatic of a conservative closing down of political possibilities.

Elsewhere, though, these biopics allow us in more. The polite distance from the maestro is disallowed by such composers' all-too-human qualities (which we can engage, if not identify with, at times), and we are encouraged, through a respect for the music that ties it to everyday life, to also associate ourselves with it more easily. This is not a comfortable connection to a bohemian rebel, but an invitation to involve ourselves in the production and commodification of culture and history with greater facility. *Because* the "musical" and the "cinematic" tracks are so dissimilar, we are forced to negotiate a place for ourselves, to *make* sense, as Nicholas Cook has advised in *Analysing Musical Multimedia.*[85] This is a generation rather than a replication of signification, some of it our own, some of it the films' creators. It seems that, when the artists are selfish or unreasonable, which they so often are, these biopics are also giving us warnings about the emotional extent of the creative economy as it spreads outward across society. But the answers, too, may lie in what is there for our consumption, if we linger in its ambivalence and watch out for the folly that besets the many music lovers on screen.

This is all for the best, given that, in the years to come, there was to be more privatization of the arts, more restrictions on industrial conflict, and more regulation of the entertainment images that discussed them. Within the mismatches both consciously amassed and critically leveled at *The Music Lovers, Mahler,* and *Lisztomania* lie a plethora of dialectical exchanges fed by, from, and into a profound renegotiation of work itself. Similar transactions characterize the period of my next case study, and comparable dialectical energies course through it. The marked difference between the two sets of material lies in how they have been treated in relation to why they "don't work." The movement from chapter 2 to this one could be described as postindustrialization's development from its wobbly, undirected baby steps into a sullen, depressed, angry, and confused adolescent, one who is hard to predict or control. The subsequent measures taken to tame and profit from postindustrialism were harsh, as the next chapter will testify.

◆ 4 ◆

Troubling Synthesis: The Horrific Sights
and Incompatible Sounds of "Video Nasties"

As Britain became more and more entrenched in "postindustrial" crisis, the efforts to suppress mismatches were stepped up. Ken Russell's movies, while draining to watch and perhaps irritatingly at variance with certain critics' quiet sensibilities, usually aimed toward rambunctious fun in the way they bundled up their audiences to whisk them away into the lives of famous composers. The voyages which my next film-music examples led and the localities to which they were seen to lure their audiences were felt to be distinctly less savory. When splayed out on the dissection table, these films—*Cannibal Holocaust* (Ruggero Deodato, 1979), *Inferno* (Dario Argento, 1980), *Cannibal Apocalypse* (Antonio Margheriti, 1980), *Cannibal Ferox* (Umberto Lenzi, 1981), *The Beyond* (Lucio Fulci, 1981), and *Tenebrae* (Dario Argento, 1982)[1]—all appear to share two things. They overlay a barrage of unflinchingly violent imagery with often smooth, mellifluous synthesizer scoring that refuses to comment negatively on the visual track. *The Beyond,* for instance, oozes, melts, and rips flesh on a regular basis; bodily fluids gush and eyeballs pop, but there is always a glossy, melodious synthesizer sound close at hand to confuse our responses to the cruelty and mutilation. Unsurprisingly, when these movies became available in the domestic format of the video cassette, every one of them was banned in the United Kingdom under the 1984 Video Recordings Act, making them, in colloquial terms, "video nasties."

Film censorship analyst Martin Barker believes that this name was first coined by the campaigner for "public decency" Mary Whitehouse in her attempts to demonize such material.[2] From there, the moniker spilled out across the press, into the public, and even through Parliament, becoming a toxic-substance label for many and a Barnum-esque sales pitch for certain producers and distributors.[3] Already there was a dialectical interplay at work in the "video nasty" label. By 1984, there can hardly have been a Briton who had not heard of video nasties, although precious few had actually seen one. The term set in motion a moral panic that demanded Parliament reappraise how film texts were classified in light of the increased penetration of video players into the private and thus less governable realms of the home. Before long, these movies were the subject of a public inquiry whose report defined "video nasties" as

> those feature films that contain scenes of such violence and sadism
> involving either human beings or animals that they would not be
> granted a certificate by the British Board of Film Censors (BBFC)
> for general release for public exhibition in Britain. Such films may
> be liable to prosecution by the Director of Public Prosecutions under
> the Obscene Publications Act 1959 Section 2.[4]

While this definition concentrates on content, alarm about the destination of these films—primarily the fear that video versions would fall into the hands of the young and innocent—propelled campaigners into a greater state of frenzy. The ensuing vigor was then rechanneled into outrage at the films' perceived refusal to condemn or morally justify their subject matter, and their soundtracks did much to convey this impression. In the cases of the six films considered in this chapter (and many more like them), outright prohibition through governmental intervention was the culminating action against the lack of clear-cut statements of repudiation coming from within these "mismatches."

Given the expeditious burial of the nasties, it is hardly unexpected that their resting place should have become something of a memorial site, a starting point for inquiries into the social construction of morality, the power of the press to stir up scandal, the government's (often opportunistic) implementation of censorship, and debates over viewers' rights in terms of access and interpretation.[5] What is usually lacking in these forays, however, is consideration of how the shift to "post-Fordist" rhythms and chains of command recast the very principles of censorship (legalistic and otherwise) in all of its multivalent forms. In the more precise terms of this chapter, how exactly did the *work* of entertainment, and film scoring in particular, agitate these movies' detractors' understanding of what labor should be and should mean? At which points on the taxing exodus from more manual to tertiary economies did these scores only serve to aggravate those struggling through the journey?

An insight into Thatcherism, that binding together of historical situation with political dogma, makes apparent the methods by which these pathways were constructed and, consequently, how video nasties were deemed impediments to the way British society might "progress." Thatcherism executed a willful obstruction of what it considered to be "the permissive society," leaving any supporters of these movies on the defensive. Thatcherism is simultaneously a byword for the massive government-led transfer of public assets and labor into the private sector. These actions were promoted as a means of maintaining economic viability in a postindustrial climate that, as chapter 3 explained, had left Britain at a distinct disadvantage. Newly exulted qualities like enterprise, deregulation, and competition were encouraged to storm ahead, making way for a distrust of protectionism in all forms of production and trading, as well as, of course, mass unemployment. Yet far from being rowdy outsiders heckling from the curb, the video nasty debates were integral threads to the very fabric of this route into a remodeled economy. The concerns they raised about how "free time" (through unemployment or otherwise) should be spent were part and parcel of a broader confusion about work at that time. In his *Economic and Social History of Britain, 1790–1990,* Trevor May somewhat anecdotally conveys the atmosphere at the time:

> Speaking in the House of Lords in November 1984, the Earl of Stockton (formerly [ex-Conservative prime minister] Harold Macmillan) was moved to speculate: "I foresee that in ten or fifteen years' time we shall never use the word 'unemployment.' We shall refer to the proper use of leisure and how to deploy it." . . . he was wide of the mark when he suggested that the unemployed would come to regard it as a "proper use of leisure." In the previous July, a Gallup poll had asked the question, "What would you say is the most urgent problem facing the country at the present time?," to which 60 per cent had responded, "unemployment" (it had been 80 per cent in July 1983, and was back up again to 79 per cent in 1985).[6]

These serious concerns about poverty were placed to one side as Macmillan's statement whipped up an optimistic, even utopian spin on how the country might readjust to the increasing extinction of standard blue-collar work.

But the legacy of past employment traditions was not to be so easily suppressed, nor were its replacements so readily apparent—conundrums that even erupted through the suspicion toward the formal conceits of the video nasties and the dialectical propositions they made about labor and leisure. In film-music terms, misgivings about synthesizers, before they had even reached the worlds of video nasty narratives, were riddled with anxieties about work. For the first few decades of its existence, electronic music had lived in the laboratories of the university research center and in the studio, the preserve of music producers with engineering-oriented competencies. This creative labor, in itself, had awkwardly interrogated the taxonomies of skill and performance that music had traditionally upheld, meaning that the concurrent aesthetic variations of, say, *Lisztomania*'s synthesizer sequences and Wendy Carlos's hit 1968 album *Switched-on Bach* were often picked out as "desecrations." By the late 1970s, innovations in transistors and, later, integrated circuit design bestowed synthesizers with greater affordability, user-friendliness, and accessibility. Somehow this caught up the synthesizer, and relatives like the drum machine, in contemporary battles about proficiency meritocracies and de-skilling that were hardly surprising given the high rates of unemployment and the pressure for workers to radically adjust their labor practices. If entertainment itself was hard to judge in terms of material input and output, then its moral dubiousness in a climate of short employment supply was immeasurably more troubling.

This is not to say that the video nasties' synthesizer soundtracks were uppermost as a contentious topic in their day, although occasional contemporary reviews voice disapproval of "often inappropriate"[7] or "pulverizing"[8] scores.[9] These discussions, though, were fairly sporadic, and I certainly do not wish to propose that synthesizer scoring played a central role in the banning of these videos. It is a major bone of contention for the defenders of the nasties that very few of the people involved in denouncing them had ever watched them,[10] let alone analyzed their soundtracks. Instead, I am drawn to how these scores become eerie echoes traveling to and fro across the fault lines created by post-industrialization. Undoubtedly, the music was meticulously designed in order to generate the very visceral shocks of which horror cinema is so proud, but any conclusive investigation of intention and effect is secondary to other political imperatives. Alternatively, if we open ourselves up with greater consciousness to the implications that synthesizers insert into the video nasties debate and survey them from a more open philosophical perspective (in this chapter, via the ideas of thinkers such as Gilles Deleuze, Félix Guattari, and Jacques Derrida), then we can unfurl a startling and revealing set of labor-related issues that are still deeply significant today.

The Connotations of the Synthesizer Score

By the 1980s, synthesizers had already charmed a disparate group of well-known performers from Herbie Hancock, Kraftwerk, Gary Numan, and Sun Ra to Led Zeppelin, Stevie Wonder, Yes, Linda McCartney, and ABBA. Nor was the synthesizer film soundtrack an unfamiliar creature: Vangelis's Oscar-winning electronic theme for *Chariots of Fire* (Hugh Hudson, 1981), for instance, was a widely recognized mainstay of popular culture. Given the breadth of these connotations, there is veracity in the conclusion of Philip Brophy, one of the few writers to deal sympathetically and thoughtfully with this type of music, that "synthesizers are no longer weird: they have become perversely futuristic, timbrally pornographic and radically dimensional."[11]

The synthesizer soundtrack's family tree stretches back longer than might be imagined and has deep roots in the science fiction genre. From early electronic scores like that of *Forbidden Planet* (Fred M. Wilcox, 1956) to the sound effects of *Star Wars* (George Lucas, 1977) and *Close Encounters of the Third Kind* (Steven Spielberg, 1977; where a synthesizer is diegetically employed to communicate to the alien spacecraft), the worlds of the genre are crafted from the instrument's soundscapes. With its airy, frictionless timbres, the synthesizer and its electronic precursor, the theremin, must have seemed entirely apt for the translation of extraterrestrial otherness and its unknown, perhaps even wraith-like materiality. It is no surprise, then, that the psychedelia of the Byrds and Pink Floyd, plus the Afro futurism of Sun Ra, should sense an out-of-body ambience within the synthesizer sound. The connection with the extraterrestrial was so strong that Robert Ashley recounted the Sonic Arts Union's late 1960s performance of *Night Train* as follows:

> The idea of the piece was that we were aliens and trying to make friends with the Earth people. . . . Somehow in the middle of the performance the audience kind of lost it and started attacking us. Of course, the way humans would attack aliens. They literally attacked us. They were throwing things.[12]

This early, and already the synthesizer was provoking somewhat overstated reactions. By the turn of the decade, Wendy Carlos's synthesizer reinterpretations of various classical favorites for *A Clockwork Orange*'s score (Stanley Kubrick, 1971; a film also long banned in the United Kingdom) had bound this *unheimlich* musical signifier to the misdemeanor of tampering with the classics in order to convey the protagonist, Alex's (Malcolm McDowell), twin "misuse" of both Beethoven and extreme aggression. Throughout the film, we are encouraged to read the synthesizer's humanly impossible regularity as overtly cold and distancing, something expressive of disenfranchisement and even a breakdown of traditional morality—an insinuation which becomes all the more upsetting when Beethoven's intensely emotional and tumultuous orchestral compositions are given the chillingly precise and staid synthesizer treatment. This sense of inappropriate detachment—which mirrors Alex's initial responses to his own actions—is heightened by a startlingly ironic deployment of familiar upbeat music (such as "Singin' in the Rain") during scenes of carnage, a technique which does much to usher into hermeneutic play, by association, this dialectical use of the synthesizer. A similar feeling of disconnection is conveyed in the synthesizer scores of other horror flicks, such as *The Exorcist* (William Friedkin, 1973), where we hear Mike Oldfield's delicate "Tubular Bells."

Traditionally, the lion's share of soundtracks to violence, including those attached to horror movies, deploy noises that are as close as possible to humans in pain: instruments like violins and even the voice that linguistically tag alongside the victim and, most pointedly, provoke our empathy. Music itself can also function as the perpetrator of brutality, so much so that assertive sonic spasms are commonly known in the scoring trade as "stabs." Dissonance rears its head frequently, although it does so mainly to tell us that things aren't quite right, to provoke an unease, certainly, but one which is in keeping with our sense of both moral and musical right and wrong. The famous shower scene in *Psycho* (Alfred Hitchcock, 1960) incorporates all of these techniques, leaving us suitably shocked, disoriented, and somewhat violated.

Conversely, a coldness inappropriate to such accompaniment is often attributed to the latest electronic music technologies, a historical trajectory which is expertly plotted in Andrew Goodwin's article "Sample and Hold: Pop Music in the Digital Age of Production." The synthesizer produces notes composed of much fewer overtones and so sounds "emptier" than more familiar instruments. This lack of depth—in all sorts of senses—complicates its position within horror scoring. Sonic flatness jars with the ways in which accompanying images might penetrate deep within the victims' bodies, rummaging around protractedly in their innermost recesses. The synthesizer's surface textures are too even to immediately evoke much rupture, emotion, or distress, and their workings and histories of technical achievement seem frostily scientific and futuristic rather than bohemian, artistic, and concerned with sensitivity toward human suffering. Critics of the day often concentrated on the synthesizer's preset predictability, the fact that no matter what the player did physically to a key, the note would still sound the same, and this, again, distanced the instrument from an association with compassionate human input. While a synthesizer may purport to provide a range of timbres, its various "voice" buttons (especially those on mass-produced 1980s models) produced at times laughably ersatz versions of the instruments they claimed to replicate. "Real" instruments, like "real" people, are less easy to pick out in this repertoire. These are cultural assumptions rather than truths necessarily, but such rationalistic resonances, along with the instrument's association with the nonhuman, did not and do not sit well with how music conventionally functions within the horror genre. As we shall see, this becomes all the more troubling when a film edges toward extreme obsessions like dismemberment, anthropophagy, and violence toward women, representations of which demand the most clear "justifications" for their very portrayal.

As the 1970s turned into the 1980s, musicians were beginning, as Carlos had done, to draw benefits from this typecasting. Tubeway Army's "Are 'Friends' Electric?" (from the album *Replicas*) and Kraftwerk's *The Man Machine* (1978) and *Computer World* (1981) were deliberate attempts to foreground mechanization, probe its "lifelessness," and ask some crucial questions about our proximity to the cyborg within a climate of fear over automated takeover. At the same time, the synthesizer's condensation of these ideas was increasingly contributing to the horror genre. John Carpenter's score for his movie *Halloween* (John Carpenter, 1978) calls upon the synthesizer to match the obsessive meticulousness of serial killer Michael's (Tony Moran) voyeurism and attack planning, which Dr. Loomis (Donald Pleasance) characterizes as "inhumanly patient." The synthesizer provides stabs and flutters to quicken the heart rate when required, but it is the power of the instrument in terms of "sustain," or unchanging resonance, that truly situates Michael in the realms of the incomprehensibly alien or mechanical.

Most of my six case-study films, contrastingly, use the synthesizer in a subtly different mode. Although it often identifies slaughter and its perpetrators, the synthesizer does not always succeed in maintaining the tradition of their castigation and thus sets in motion a dialectical investigation into the core dichotomies of horror. Like in *Halloween*, Fabio Frizzi's synthesizer tracks in *The Beyond* become directly associated with the horror that the film gradually reveals: that Liza's (Catriona MacColl) run-down hotel holds within it one of the seven gateways of hell. In the flashback delivered in the opening scenes, the synthesizer lurks in the background as the warlock's face is burned with acid. A synthesizer also readily accompanies Liza during her entry into the cursed room thirty-six, but in both instances the tone is encouragingly pacey and almost joyful. According to conventional logic, the more forceful synthesizer deployment is saved for the rendition of zombie attacks and their gruesome outcomes, while an elaborately flavored gumbo that mixes older musical styles and instrumentation from bass guitars, flutes, and violins evokes brief moments of "normality," such as when John (David Warbeck) and Liza meet up for a drink in a New Orleans jazz bar. So far, so typical, in terms of generic trickery, but the meeting of sealed musical and burst-open corporeal surfaces is something of a new development.

A comparable juxtaposition between musical safety and danger (this time, urban New York and the unpredictable Amazon basin) is concocted for *Cannibal Ferox*,[13] but, in this instance, the associations are rather more untoward. Perhaps the greatest musical jolt comes when we both see and hear a Salvation Army band as the movie cuts back to Manhattan immediately after the villain Mike's (Giovanni Lombardo Radice) castration. However, the film's other regular returns to "civilization" are more often bluntly marked by funky jazz-infused pieces on horns and bass guitars, which contrast with the unusual choice of representing nature (both bountiful and destructive) through the synthesizer. That the most technological instrumentation should stand in for the wilderness ultimately creates a sense of alienation rather than pity as we witness a variety of violent acts in this desolate space. We are left to wonder why this ambivalence has been devised, why a largely pop main theme—which does, admittedly, turn harmonically discordant at various intervals—should befriend such scenes of disorder, chaos, and inhumanity? Perhaps all of these sensibilities are closer than we imagine, and it is conceivable that this proposition (and others like it) helped to bring about the banning of the film.

Cannibal Holocaust fashions similar musical corollaries between its Amazon location and its score which was, interestingly, written and conducted by Riz Ortolani, the man behind *Mondo Cane*'s (Paolo Cavara, Gualtiero Jacopetti and Franco E. Posperi, 1962)[14] lilting and peaceful rejoinder to the film's various engagements with acts of brutality. The soundtrack is instrumentally, generically, and tonally complex, fusing synthesizer sounds with challenging modernist string arrangements[15] and a mawkishly dreamy acoustic guitar–led main theme which is, like *Mondo Cane*'s signature tune, somewhat out of place, considering the film's content. There is much to be said, of course, about how all of these components question not only the visual-narrative line but also each other's hermeneutic possibilities and points of stability. However, despite the score's hybridity, it is almost always the synthesizer—in either a wafting and ethereal mode or a jubilant, driving one—which we hear first during the many acts of savagery. Although other instruments are quick to participate in the commentary on the violence depicted, the initial shock of hearing a synthesizer at these moments is scarcely dampened when more typical instrumentation joins the fray. There are sections where we only hear synthesizers, for example, when the Amazonians commit their first act of cruelty and near-cannibalism by cutting off a monkey's head and eating its brains, but these are fairly rare.

Alexander Blonksteiner provides music for *Cannibal Apocalypse* which amounts to one of the least traditionally logical of the video nasty scores. Unlike in the other films, synthesizers roam the diegesis, freely combining and contrasting with a range of musical idioms to the point that they no longer seem to respect the border lines of music's ordained emotional and moral impact. A hospital doctor is attacked, he spits out his tongue and blood galore; the character Charles Bukowski's (Giovanni Lombardo Radice) stomach is blown through to create a visual framing device for the tunnel beyond him. All of this happens to melodic synthesizer lines accompanied by more menacing synthesizer surges whose dependable timbres still refuse to equate with the violent physical breaches on screen. Later on, however, a rotary saw meets its victim's flesh to the sounds of funk guitars and a saxophone, meaning that we cannot understand the synthesizer as the only accomplice in these acts.

There is something about this inconsistency (itself a betrayal of the synthesizer's methodical disposition) that threatens not to respect the moral codes that allow horror movies to be made. If certain villains are unwavering in their criminality and turpitude, then a soundtrack is expected to follow a similarly straight line in pursuing them to their just deserts. *Cannibal Apocalypse*'s equivocation finds its match in some similarly disjunctive elements of Keith Emerson's soundtrack for *Inferno*. As one might expect, Emerson's synthesizer prowess introduces us to perhaps the messiest corpse in the film—the one of John (Leopoldo Mastelloni), the servant, who is found with his eyeballs gouged out—through ethereal planes of synthesizer layering that seem oblivious to this stomach-churning tableau. But there is also a striking use of electronic music in the scene where Sara (Eleonora Giorgi), who is soon to be murdered, rides through the rain in a taxi. While nothing particularly dynamic is happening visually, we hear a complicated and ostentatious synthesizer reworking of Verdi's *Nabucco*, which has been the object of study in Sara's lecture earlier that day, positioned extremely high in the audio mix. Such sonic presences become slightly more tenable—but only slightly—when we later learn that the architect (who has designed the three hellish buildings the film explores) is forced to communicate through an electronic voice mechanism by whose cord he is eventually strangled.

In all of these examples, the codes of scoring *work* have not been obeyed. At times self-indulgent, at times lacking the patience to uphold a persistent and unambiguous message, these soundtracks seem somehow inappropriately fidgety and short of the requisite attention span. In a climate of unemployment, their methods are both a violation of the good faith of a contract and a warning of what lengths of time and lack of focus can lead to in one's conceptualization of violence. This seeming distraction is similarly evident in the placement of musical cues throughout all of these films. They frequently start and stop at the same volume rather than phasing subtly in and out as many standard sound-tracks tend to do, and this quick-fire launching and docking seem somewhat ridiculous if one is accustomed to the volume control of mainstream movies. Simple crafting conventions have been forsaken and, without them, the mean-ing of synthesizer scoring mutates dramatically.

The soundtrack for *Tenebrae,* composed by members of the reassembled band Goblin,[16] swerves in these ways disarmingly close to a most inappropriate mu-sical genre. Upbeat synthesizer music (the kind that easily seduces the body into dance-related movement) enters and exits loudly and abruptly without fail during the scenes of violence. As a shoplifter is repeatedly knifed in the neck and as pages of protagonist Peter Neil's (Anthony Franciosa) latest novel are shoved into her mouth, the music is utterly unfaltering in its sleek, laser-like melodies, its even rhythms and resonances. The tune's steady progress and the swift cut-outs of its sounds (particularly the hollow "drum" beats) do little to align us with the pain and penetration that is being forced upon this woman's body.

Something similar happens during the final scene of *Cannibal Holocaust.* One of the documentary crew is castrated, dismembered, decapitated, and devoured to a musical composition that is up-tempo and positively groovy, albeit infringed upon by the occasional discordant string surge. Nothing of the viscera spilling across the screen is captured by the soundtrack; the washes of the synthesizer resemble buzzing electrical currents rather than anything more corporeal. The soundtrack's signature sine-y "pow" noises also make a return visit. These flourishes, which are common to disco tracks like Kelly Marie's "Feel Like I'm in Love" (1980), erupt very much like little explosions of plea-sure, part of a disco firework display. Here, the score's pedigree is less that of horror or even "synth prog" (which was ever-present at the birth of these soundtracks).[17] At times like this, the music behaves more akin to the offspring of Giorgio Moroder–produced, orgasmically energized tracks like "I Feel Love" (1977) or even the popular proto-house track "I Need Love" (1982), written by *Tenebrae* co-composer Claudio Simonetti, under the pseudonym of Capri-corn. The obsessive ripping and piercing of flesh is disquietingly matched by high-sheen surface textures; as usual, wailing, pleading, and limbs torn asunder parallel a disinterest in pain evident in the synthesizer's spandex-like effortless-ness. The instrument's very name even recalls such high-tech artificial fibers. It is almost as if the soundtrack did not care about what it was watching and just wanted to carry on having a good time. Were these films wishing to proclaim the proximity of pleasure to pain, to unmask the menacing underbelly of disco hedonism? The fact that their scores sounded extremely similar to those of contemporary pornographic movies did nothing to extinguish a sense of inappropriate debauchery or a fundamental disrespect toward the evocation of horrific death. A suitable moral tone to comment upon debasement, rape, and torture was not to be found in the persistent clarity and tunefulness of the music. How far indeed these practices were from "the proper use of leisure" (or enforced unemployment) of which Harold Macmillan was soon to speak.

These film-music mismatches, then, these clashes in the semantics of working practices not only mangled a sense of how "labor" and "leisure" should be judiciously spent, but also spewed forth products that, it was argued, affronted common decency. "The message is clear," the psychiatrists' report which informed the creation of the Video Recordings Act stated, "there is glorification of evil acts of violent and perverse nature. There is frequently no end point where the offender (the 'bad figure') is defeated and justice prevails."[18] Might the moral and the fiscal be related here? Such cultural objects are often considered gratuitous, yet there is something paradoxical in invoking a word that implies free exchange when so many core elements of the national (and international) economy are implicated. What pragmatic shifts were being overshadowed by the dismissal of these films and their soundtracks as mismatches?

Generating Moral Outrage

The ostensible aim of the Video Recordings Act of 1984 was to institute "protection for children in home viewing,"[19] and the head of steam that propelled it was brought into being by a campaign stoked by various commercial British newspapers and financially fueled by their readerships. Although various studies into this particular moral panic and the resulting amendments to policy exist, there has rarely been much mention of how these crises can be understood in line with the Thatcherite move toward privatization and its attendant effects on the nature of work.

It was the *Times* and the *Sunday Times* that first picked up on the debates around child supervision and video content in 1982 in a series of articles which were followed by the more famous "Seduction of the Innocent" piece, written by David Holbrook and published early in 1983. In this, he describes "a feeling that we are powerless in such matters as though we were the slaves of our own technology,"[20] registering a wariness toward new electronic devices (something that is crucial to the contemporary fears of de-skilling that will be discussed later) and video in particular. It is worth contemplating at this juncture the fact that, in 1981, Rupert Murdoch's News International had acquired the two papers and then, a year later, an 80 percent share of Satellite Television UK (SATV). In return for Thatcher's awarding of this unparalleled share of private media ownership, the News International papers regularly and forcefully expressed a pro-Tory, pro-free-market line. In this instance, however, it is worth wondering whether the inconsistency of proposing a curtailment of consumer access via censorship could also be read as a deliberate assault upon satellite's future rival for home entertainment: video.

The *Daily Mail,* motivated by different agendas and backed by lobbyists like Mary Whitehouse of the National Viewers and Listeners' Association (NVLA), was even more vociferous and persistent in the crusade it dubbed "Ban the Sadist Videos," to which it even dedicated headline space.[21] It raged against the "rape of our children's minds"[22] and the adult viewer who "like the archetypal drug addict . . . is weaned on a 'soft' product. A typical trait among videoholics is that they soon lose all sense of perspective as to what makes suitable viewing for children."[23] The story of Martin Austin, a convicted rapist whose crimes were supposedly inspired by video nasties, received many a column inch.[24] In her careful study of the phenomenon, *Trash or Treasure? Censorship and the Changing Meanings of the Video Nasties,* Kate Egan astutely points out that, although the *Mail's* perspective mirrored the Thatcher government's on law and order, it was at odds with the Conservatives' favored decrease in business regulation, particularly in relation to small businesses like video shops.[25] Here, a rhetoric of child corruption through unmonitored consumption trumped the contemporary zeal to explore new markets, masking (as the castigation of mismatches frequently does) an inconsistency in government policy. Evidently, the broad fluctuations in production, distribution, and consumption were leaving their marks, often messy and contradictory, upon the postindustrial renegotiation of ethical values.

Originally, the government had hoped that the work of video classification would be handled, in favorably outsourced terms, by the usual nongovernmental organizations, the BBFC and the British Video Association (BVA), without resort to new legislation. Then, perhaps in response to the pace gathering behind the popular and print media movements, the *Conservative Election Manifesto* announced:

> We will also respond to the increasing public concern over obscenity and offences against public decency, which often have links with serious crime. We propose to introduce legislation to deal with the most serious of these problems, such as the dangerous spread of violent and obscene video cassettes.[26]

Whether or not this declaration had any sway in the Conservatives' landslide election victory in June 1983, it is significant that Graham Bright's Private Member's Bill on video nasties was introduced on 1 July 1983 and was soon (certainly sooner than usual) accelerated into action, prompting a research project which would investigate children's video-viewing patterns.

Amid all of the speechifying of the ensuing report, *Video Violence and Children,* and the parliamentary debates that led to the act's succession to the statute book in June 1984, much alarm about moral education, the practices of young viewers, and media influence can be found, but, tellingly, this is often inflected with perspectives on class and working practices (or lack thereof). *Video Violence and Children* stressed, "It may be of some significance that the majority of VCRs in British households are thought to be found among working class families,"[27] and "Working class children, especially those from large families, appear most at risk in watching the 'nasties.' There appear to be very few restrictions placed upon what children watch in most working class homes."[28] The follow-up report of 1985 states, "It is clear . . . that the lower the social class the more likely it is that children will have seen one or more, and four or more videos on the DPP's [Director of Public Prosecutions] list"[29] and that the highest penetration of video nasties among child viewers was in the rapidly deindustrializing areas of England's northwest.[30] In a House of Commons debate on the subject, Simon Hughes, the member for Southwark and Bermondsey, declared:

> I have talked to people not in the sylvan suburbs of Hampstead,
> which so far as I am aware I have never visited, but in the ordinary
> streets of Southwark and Bermondsey where Laura Ashley patterns
> and bean bags are fairly rare commodities. People in those areas find
> video control a difficult issue. Youngsters know that if something is
> made illegal it becomes more appealing. . . . That is true of alcohol
> and drugs and it is certainly true of video.[31]

Although it is not uncommon for censorship campaigns to bear the traces of class prejudice, what exactly were the ingredients blended to create this particular flavor in Britain in the first half of the 1980s?

Video Censorship, Redundancy, Unemployment, and the Decline of the Manual Economy

Linda Lee-Potter, the notorious *Daily Mail* journalist, plunged into the heart of the matter when she argued, "The video boom has meant that thousands of out-of-work, unstable teenagers are currently gorging themselves day-in-day-out on scenes of torture and depravity."[32] The unemployed youths were free to endlessly rewind the violent sections of these films and, conservatives argued, perhaps there was something in the fact that the 1978–1982 period had seen a rise in both violent crime and video player ownership.[33] A similar link between video viewing and a distaste and distrust of the unemployed was expressed in the Commons by Harry Greenway of Ealing North:

> I confirm with my own research and observation that the first thing that people with redundancy money buy is a video. . . . They are often a higher priority in the homes of people who are not particularly articulate, and who do not read books or listen to music very much. In some homes, videos even take priority over food and furniture. From my conversations with children in this situation, it is clear that many parents take no interest in what their children are watching. . . . Is it not appallingly serious that families are prepared to go without the necessities of life, like furniture, and sometimes even to restrict their diet, in order to have videos?[34]

VCR ownership and rental (ironically, the *Daily Mail* of the time was full of advertisements promoting this indulgence) was increasingly affordable, thanks, largely, to the cheap mass production taking place in industrial zones outside the United Kingdom that I detailed in the preceding chapter.[35] Similar advantages (in terms of cost cutting, at least) were also taken by many of the video nasties themselves, which were filmed in inexpensive regions like the Amazon basin by mostly Italian production companies. However, it is precisely moves such as these that helped to hasten the redundancies to which Greenway referred, and, in doing so, he and others like him had displaced the impact of broader economic shifts onto an inconsistently fewer number of their subsequent products, labeling them mismatches of a moral order.

Given this deflection, it is well worth redirecting the video nasty debates through another historical narrative: that of industrial relations. A Trade Union Research Unit report of 1984 situates job decreases amid the increasing pressure to "rationalise" and become more "flexible,"[36] measures aimed at combating Britain's decreasing competitiveness in the expanded global market, high inflation, and related professional insecurity. The reduced powers of the unions that I laid out in the previous chapter, along with stagflation and sustained reductions in unemployment benefits, exacerbated the situation for many citizens. By the year in which the Video Recordings Act was passed, unemployment was at 11.2 percent of the workforce (as compared to 1.1 percent in 1966 and only 2.2 percent in the crisis year of 1973).[37] Adrian Sinfield and Brian

Showler's contemporary research into the matter points out that a third of the redundancies made previously in 1979 were from more manual sectors: "mechanical engineering, the distributive trades and the construction industry, and many more from textiles, metal manufacturing, vehicles and electrical engineering."[38] As a consequence (largely unsuccessful) strikes were mounted within the industries of steel (1980), water (1983), and mining (1984–1985). As retaliation and as a buffer against such activity, trade union rights were systematically trimmed by the Employment Acts of 1980 and 1982, the Water Act of 1983, the Trade Union Act of 1984, and the brutal police violence that crushed the miners' strike. Again, authoritarian measures were exerted to ratify libertarian aims.

The rumblings of these disputes also rang through the topographies of cultural production. It is not hard to understand the amplified violence of the Italian video nasties as in tone with the strikes, unrest, and terrorism erupting from the attack on factory workers' rights in the late 1970s in that country. A nostalgia for and validation of more physical forms of production are also evident in the film texts themselves, as well as in their appreciation. Keith Emerson, the composer of *Inferno*'s score, is well known for attacking his synthesizer on stage with implements like knives in order to generate unusual sounds—a markedly aggressive and bodily approach to music making with an otherwise mechanized instrument. Horror fan magazines like *Shivers, Fangoria,* and *Cinefantastique* regularly commend the craftsmanship of the special effects in these movies.[39]

Despite Emerson's efforts, though, the synthesizer was hard to slot into this glorification of skilled and unskilled manual labor, the kind that was being knocked down at an increasing pace by snowballing postindustrialism. It bore with it none of the connotations of "man" battling with his instrument that, for instance, guitar legends had built up. A synthesizer cannot be easily wielded or posed with in the clichéd rock manner and requires little bodily vigor to play. A bodily attack does not make for a stronger sound; brute force does not have a sonic equivalent with a synthesizer. A range of sounds can be created by physically interacting with a guitar or violin in modes that vary significantly from the specific and predetermined sounds that the flick of a synthesizer switch can provide. Very little engaged corporeal struggle is involved in playing the latter, and the synthesizer's capabilities, such as arpeggiation and instant pitch clarity, dangerously erode the equation of physical dynamism with musical skill. Given the social implications of all this, the band Queen's disdain for the instrument in the famous liner note statement of "no synthesizers!" for their *A Night at the Opera* LP must have come as no surprise.

The synthesizer also pointed forward toward the disruptive turns that the British economy would increasingly adopt. In the scores of these six films, the emphasis is on studio production, rather than recording more rehearsed "live" performances. Technical know-how and more tertiary sector abilities rise above the physical effort and dexterity of traditional musical training. Most controversially, however, it was the synthesizer's potential for de-skilling (familiar from all-too-many introductions of new machinery) that really caught the tide of contemporary anxieties about work.

De-Skilling: The Fear of Replacement

An innovative technology will often arouse a series of concerns about how it might reorder the social landscape, and this was very much the case with the introduction of the video player as a home-viewing instrument. The government-sponsored reports on video, for instance, communicate the dread that "the power and impact of the school are being steadily eroded by that of the screen."[40] In addition, the vocabularies of technological change usually act to promote functional improvements, ones that advance beyond skill reliance or time-consuming working practices. The damaging upshot is that people who have invested in these particular ways of manufacturing are left adrift, superseded as valued producers. In music culture, this becomes increasingly significant in that instruments are much more than mere tools: they have specific, well-loved characters and capacities, their limitations create the space for mastery and exclusivity. Performer/composers such as Keith Emerson, Claudio Simonetti, and the other scorers of these movies had long been dabbling with the latest synthesizers, well before such gadgets had been mass produced, and were thought to intimidate particular hierarchies of competence. The extent of the threat that synthesizers posed is expressed in this 1985 tirade from Randall D. Larson's *Musique Fantastique: A Survey of Film Music in the Fantastic Cinema:*

> [Synthesizers are] fairly inexpensive for economy-minded producers— instead of paying vast sums for a large orchestra consisting of many musicians, it usually only requires one or two operators to compose and produce a score on synthesizers. (At the same time, they're also putting many musicians out of work.) Other disadvantages include the fact that, while synthesizers can create remarkable new sounds and very spacey effects, it is nearly impossible to achieve the emotional poignancy or warm coloration of a conventional symphony orchestra. Synthesizer scores have also been tediously abused in recent years, simply because they are so seemingly easy and cheap to pro-

duce. Anyone with access to a synthesizer and a recording device can shuffle together an assortment of menacing or atmospheric tonalities and call it a film score. Many have.[41]

The anger against synthesizers for financially undercutting skilled workers in order to assemble something that does not uphold traditional musical values (the very kind that generate the video nasties' mismatches) is palpable. Trevor Pinch and Frank Trocco's *Analog Days: The Invention and Impact of the Moog Synthesizer* draws on a longer history to point out that this is not a new occurrence:

> Whenever a new mechanical contrivance enters the field of music, it triggers the same set of concerns: is it a proper part of the musical domain, an instrument that can release musical talent, creativity, and art, or is it simply a mechanical device, a mere machine? This debate famously occurred when the piano forte replaced the harpsichord at the start of the eighteenth century. Much less well known is the similar debate that arose when mechanical levers were added to flutes in the mid-nineteenth century. The linked key mechanisms and valves that replaced the use of fingers over individual holes were found to be easy to operate and facilitated the production of much more uniform and cleaner tones.[42]

Within the context of the United Kingdom, all of this bears even greater significance. Britain is a country with a heritage of resistance to the new technologies that it is often so advanced in implementing (think, for example, of the case of the Luddites in the early nineteenth century). From a libertarian perspective, this is a type of, as Mancur Olson reasons, "institutional sclerosis,"[43] bound up in a long and specific history of economic stability and privileged protectionism.[44] From the Left, new technologies can be seen as Taylorism gone mad,[45] but, either way, their impact and reverberations through culture require scrutiny. Given the mobility of capital, widespread retraining in a range of sectors across the United Kingdom was not prioritized in the 1980s, resulting in impositions upon working practices that led to a number of industrial actions. One such dispute was conducted later, in 1986, by the print workers at Wapping in revolt against not only a threat to skilled worker wages brought about by the onslaught of new forms of mechanization, but also decreased union powers and flexible working conditions. Once again, as with the nasties media campaign, the perpetrators were Rupert Murdoch's News International and the Times Group, which were looking not only to rationalize, in a general sense, but also to recoup the costs of massive expenditures on this new portfolio of British investments.

Just as the unions mobilized their collective resources against this onslaught (unsuccessfully, in terms of newspaper production), so the music community strengthened its sense of what philosopher of performance Stan Godlovitch terms "the guild."[46] This is a set of criteria, preserved by various defensive bodies and meritocracies, that closes the fortress door to whom they see as outsiders looking to profit from their labor. The guild can be understood according to Gilles Deleuze and Félix Guattari's understanding of "the territory," where elements "cease to be directional, becoming dimensional instead,"[47] where differentiation becomes a marker of a border rather than a point of exchange. "Territories" can be distinguished, I would argue, as anything from appropriate technology to the very parameters of melody and harmony themselves. Professional music making's stance on the synthesizer is featured in a *Sunday Times* report that, interestingly, can be found in the same edition that asks for the director of public prosecutions to address the video nasties problem. The article recounts:

> When members of the Musicians' Union sat down in a recent conclave, it was to claim that Moog's brainchild [the synthesizer] has proved so successful that it threatens the very livelihood of its members. One man at the keyboards of a Moog can turn out synthetic sound on the scale of a full orchestra.... In an attempt to curb what they see as the creeping menace of electronically-made music, members of the union's London branch passed a motion seeking to prohibit, for the purposes of all recording and live performance, the use of any electronic device that imitates or simulates an existing musical instrument ... for reasons of economy in soundtracks, TV and film themes and commercials.[48]

This mirrors an earlier suspicion toward the capabilities of the synthesizer, which had led to its restriction by the American Federation of Musicians in 1969.[49]

For Deleuze and Guattari, though, the territory does have permeable boundaries, whether it likes it or not. A dialectic was at work within these synthesizer scores, one that endangered many people professionally. Synthesizer design, for instance, adopted a recognizable keyboard, which was scarcely technically necessary, purely in order to slip more smoothly into a particular and identifiable music-making tradition. And yet this give and take across designated categories and their semantics still does not account for the harm it caused, in this instance with regard to fears about replacement and redundancy (the "cuckoo in the nest" syndrome) and about loss of control through democratization (way too many cuckoos in the nest).

In terms of the former concern, the rules of warfare were being painfully redrawn: a victory might now be declared through results rather than musical skill. The technology of the synthesizer itself, with its ability, for example, to set extremely regular rhythms and pitches and to arpeggiate automatically, could displace hard-won human dexterity. The first popular public sortie into synthesizer prowess, Wendy Carlos's *Switched-on Bach* (1968), had hit hard right in the center of art music's territory with the reworking of well-loved material, something she continued with her treatment of Beethoven in the score for *A Clockwork Orange*.[50] The synthesizer, it was felt, was not just stealing ground, but razing much that had been built on it too, although, if one looks at the ideals of synthesizer pioneers this was hardly their intention.[51] Roy M. Prendergast, a soundtrack analyst, reveals the disdain that the music community could cast upon the instrument, particularly in terms of the types of labor that adapted well to it: "the synthesizer can be made to create sounds by just about anyone (engineer-types are especially enamoured of them), regardless of their creative gifts or dramatic sense for motion pictures, with understandably dull results."[52] As technology advanced apace, as hard disk editing, microprocessing, and screen-based interfaces developed over the turn of the decade, along with a greater variety of easily accessible "voices," whole new modes of composition burst forth. Within them, space was cleared for more autonomous forms of production, ones that could be lone endeavors rather than collaborations and that greatly decentralized musical creativity. And, just as crucially, these technologies were becoming cheaper and cheaper.

In the late 1960s, a complete synthesizer had cost up to $6,000. At this point, the Moog company was a small factory operating pretty much in response to specifications from individual orders. During this period, synthesizers required expert handling and were deemed too unpredictable for live performance, although *Inferno*'s scorer, Keith Emerson, pioneered this practice. The Moog company was bought in 1971, around the same time as the development of the Minimoog, which was simpler, more self-explanatory, and, crucially, available for the first time in shops. The outlay had also been pushed down, with the asking price for a Minimoog Model E settling at $1,195. The synthesizer might now venture out beyond the arsenal of the professional studio, perhaps even edge into educational or domestic spaces. Throughout the early 1980s, the developers of synthesizer technology concentrated on two areas: the top-of-the-range cutting-edge models (such as the $6,000 Synergy model with a sampler) and machines like the Yamaha DX-7 MIDI, which cost $2,000 and could also be programmed with samples. Cheaper still was 1984's Casio CZ-101, a four-voice model that cost under $500 and could be bought in nonspecialty department stores, bringing the instrument to a truly different market. Thus, over the period in which these soundtracks were created, the synthesizer mutated from a custom-manufactured machine into an easy-to-use, mass-produced one, from artisanal crafting to factory-line assembly. The expansion from purely professional to amateur usage that had greatly concerned the guild also extended the instrument's sphere of influence into another domain— the home—just as the video playback hardware had done for the nasty. What, however, was "the home" at this point? Who had influence over it, and to what, ultimately, did this amount in political terms?[53]

The Space of the Home: Unemployed Youths, Working Women, and the Changing Shape of the Private Sphere

Quite obviously, the alarm raised by the anti-nasties operation was a knee jerk triggered by the encroachment of a technology upon various specific types of family organization. John Myerscough paints the following picture from various data of the time:

> The British Market Research Bureau figures for the percentage of UK households with VCRs in the fourth quarter of each of the last five years are as follows: 2 per cent in 1980, 6 per cent in 1981, 16 per cent in 1982, 26 per cent in 1983 and 33 per cent in 1984. . . . There are notable differences in VCR penetration between demographic groups. The following additional figures have been supplied by the AGB: VCR ownership is highest among the C2 social class (38 per cent of C2 homes against only 14 per cent of DE homes). Penetration within age groups (age of housewife [sic]) varies from 45 per cent in the 35–44 year olds to only 3 per cent of 65+ households. Forty-six per cent of homes with children aged 6–15 possess a VCR while the figure for homes without children is 20 per cent.[54]

This more detailed statistical picture highlights two particular social groups, each bearing its own problems in relation to contemporary society: the "C2 class" of trained blue-collar workers and families with school-age children. An already vulnerable faction hit severely by postindustrialization and de-skilling, C2s were simultaneously hard pressed to preserve stable handed-down working traditions through the generations, since unemployment among eighteen- to twenty-four-year-olds totaled 266,928 between 18 and 24 July 1982, adding to a startlingly low and unprecedented overall employment rate of 55.5 percent.[55] Even in the darkest years of the early to mid-1970s, levels had never dipped below 60 percent.[56] What these families, and many others besides, were experiencing was an even more total shake-up of the domestic framework, its spaces, its interactions, its incomes, and its meanings, in both concrete compositional and more abstractly political-hegemonic terms.

In direct contrast to the broader picture of joblessness, by the early to mid-1980s, women (many of them mothers) were thriving in the sectors that were blossoming most in the postindustrial climate: services. Since these women were not conventionally employees within the downturning heavy industries and were now finding more and more opportunities in tertiary areas that had historically encouraged and often even preferred women workers, it is not hard to understand the talk of the "feminization of labor" at this time nor to observe its exploration in many cultural products. *Cannibal Apocalypse,* for example, acknowledges Jane (Elizabeth Turner) as a successful journalist, while most of the male protagonists are, in one way or another, redundant. Certainly, the vilification of the synthesizer—particularly in regard to the lack of physical effort its performance demanded—tallies with an uneasiness about these changes in working methods and their associated gendering. If the instrument's timbres conveyed a sense of corporeality at all, it was a smooth, "hairless" one that was more easily aligned with the stereotypes of womanhood. Alongside all of the trite clichés of male studio geeks, the synthesizer had also been firmly tied to all that the light, breathy female vocals of artists like Donna Summer (under the production of Giorgio Moroder) could mean. Then there was Wendy Carlos: "feminization of labor" incarnate who spent "his" profits from *Switched-on Bach* on gender realignment surgery.

Yet, if women appeared to be on the ascent—with the figures for working women rising steadily from 1971 onward, even through the recessions, and legislation seemingly backing them[57]—this escalation was mainly in the realms of part-time employment.[58] Might this have simply stepped up the country's rationalization process, undermining empowerment through forms of exploitation? This is one of the big questions asked of more recent postindustrial strategy and marks a maturation of postindustrialism that continues into the period covered in the next chapter. Part-time labor mostly comes at cut-rate prices, without the trappings for the employer of the many benefits or securities that make full-time work more costly. It is not surprising to hear from Jane Humphries and Jill Rubery, writing reflectively in 1988, that "female-intensive jobs have been remarkably resilient in the face of the economic restructuring in many advanced industrial economies in recent years."[59] The same was also true of the labor in the Free Industrial Zones, of which 70 percent was then completed by women.[60]

Greater numbers of women within the workforce also amounted to a greater variety in the types of women there. In *Myths at Work,* Harriet Bradley et al. observe, "Between 1981 and 1991 female employment among married and cohabiting couples rose by 16 per cent while for males it fell by 4 per cent," and "The increase has been particularly marked among married women."[61] Although often the least geographically mobile of all workers, married women, particularly mothers, were regularly in the firing line from a multitude of anxieties about their rising contribution to the economy and its impact (in terms of absence) upon their other familial "duties." In the nasties critiques, images abound of "extra busy mums"[62] whose "latch-key kids" gorge on horror flicks in their frequent periods alone. The first *Video Violence and Children* report observed:

Many children say they go straight home from school and watch video films when their parents are not in the house. They are often accompanied by other children in the neighbourhood who do not have videos or do not have similar free access to the "nasties" and they watch them together.[63]

The total picture of negligent parenthood is a double bind: unemployment and redundancy (presumably more for men) intensify the risk, so too does female employment, not to mention parents who lazily use video to babysit[64] or who have parted company from each other. In the second official report, single parenthood and single mothers in particular are assigned the most blame:

When we turn to the most powerful of the sociofamilial influences upon the development of behaviour we find the proportion of one-parent families to have been rising for decades. It continues to escalate. The prevalence of marital disruption and divorce also continues to show a steep upward trend. As the proportion of women who expect to find employment outside the home expands the number of latch-key children mounts each year. The influence of the family continues to be important. For example, as the surveys reported in this book have shown the viewing of "video nasties" by children correlates highly with the amount of viewing by their mothers.[65]

The "proof" to justify such conjecture evades the report itself, suggesting the hegemonic extent of normative motherhood at this time, a discursive formulation carried with great stamina by the anti-nasty newspapers, particularly the women-friendly *Daily Mail* and often its "Femail" women's section. Warnings were proffered there to mothers in the form of second-person address: "Could these be your children . . . and this your home?"[66] and "Do you know . . . do you *want* to know . . . what your children watch on it [your VCR] when you are out?"[67] If one's own home were safe, then there was always the worry of what was going on in other parentless houses.[68] Acting almost as a series of tip-offs, these statements can have only meant to encourage home working (paid or unpaid, and perhaps the most exploitative and unregulated form of employment) and a particular moral agenda to accompany it. Clifford Hill's conclusion to the second *Video Violence and Children* report sketches out a stark dichotomy that places brutality in opposition to "family values" and very much surpasses the information-gathering mandate of the document:

> Do we wish to convey the values of violent aggression as the norm
> for achieving the objects of ego desire including the use of torture,
> cruelty, sado-masochism and even the dismemberment of the human
> body as behavioural norms? Alternatively, do we wish to present the
> norms of harmonious interpersonal relationships, with marriage and
> stable family life as the model for child rearing, within the context of
> the ideals of a caring, sharing society?[69]

Throughout these portrayals of children in peril, then, and particularly those fed through the *Daily Mail,* there is an inconsistent approach to both work and consumption ethics as related to the Conservative dream of an ever-expanding marketplace. The sanctity of the family is under siege from "'gangsters' who peddle violence and pornography"[70] and even (and here we edge closer to the Thatcherite program) the National Union of Mineworkers and the Coal Board, which had, apparently, invested pension funds in a nasties distributor.[71]

"The home" here gives the illusion of "the territory," and the repeated utterances about child safety aim to cocoon citizens into a particular understanding of "the family." These reiterated notions function, to continue with Deleuze and Guattari's redolent terminology, as "a refrain," an easily assumed and repeated motif which the philosophers explicitly link with, fittingly (although with decidedly sexist overtones), the home, the housewife, and an allure of constancy which provides a feeling of predictability, mastery, and belonging. The desire for the refrain, the home, and such is motivated by a desire for enfranchisement, and with that comes a closure to the outside and any dialectical engagements with it. What these refrains achieved was the suppression of any serious contemplation of the conjecture encased within these mismatched films. While blocking certain associations, the contemporary moral assertions made about the movies also gorged on other meanings and agendas, swallowing them up and insisting upon the logical and organic wholeness of an essentially expansionist project—one which also made claims about safety, family, and surveillance. Such engulfing practices were only made possible because of the new status of film on cassette as a domestic object, allowing videos to now occupy a space that was heavily inscribed as a family environment, with all of its concomitant ethical trappings and its short shrifts for grey areas. The home is both utterly porous and penetrable on a conceptual level and, at the same time, neatly conveyed as a fortified (and to be fortified) *place*. By committing such actions in the name of child protection, the campaigners covered their backs with a raison d'être against which very few people were likely to want to argue. And under this guise, a host of other ideas furtively entered the political arena. As Martin Barker argues, "The video nasties issue allowed Thatcherism to become strong again, to present itself as unequivocally on the side of law and order."[72] During an all-important pre-election period, the ever-popular cause of child protection allowed the party to drum up mass support that then comfortably eased in the ensuing legislation.[73]

The confusion incited by a socioeconomic realignment and redefinition of the public and the private was also afflicting the country's understandings of the home, as is evident from the fear of filmic infringement adjoined to a desire for invasive legislation. Thatcher's famous 1987 claim that "[t]here is no such thing as society. There are only individual men and women, and there are families"[74] reframes her "rolling back of the state" in sociological, rather than economic terms. In the case of the video nasties, the powerful fantasy of security and stability within the private encourages modifications to the public. These were arrived at, despite Thatcher's often-draconian drive, through a consensus arrangement reached by the widely divergent needs of, to mention just a few such groups, the readers and journalists of the *Daily Mail* and members of Parliament.

Jane Humphries and Jill Rubery concisely summarize some of the agendas that hid behind the Thatcherite valorization of this smaller social grouping: "While collective responsibility and mutual aid have been denigrated as dependence, survival strategies based on the family, the marketplace and the individual have been elevated as self-reliance."[75] Even the British movie industry was forced to function according to some of these privatizing patterns with the 1985 Films Act terminating the old quota system entirely, leaving the country's cinema products floating without ballast amid global competition. Public media and cultural bodies (such as the BBC and the Arts Council) faced grant reductions and the pressure to reorganize along the managerial lines and financial rationalizations of the private sector. Furthermore, as Jo Littler's research into arts policy points out, all of this was accompanied by

> the extensive use of public money to privilege and support the private sector [which] took place through mechanisms such as Office of Arts and Libraries leaflets proclaiming that *The Arts are Your Business,* through the extension of such bodies as the Association for Business Sponsorship in the Arts (ABSA), and by the 1984 formation of the Business Sponsorship Incentive Scheme (BSIS).[76]

The buzzword here, and more generally, was "enterprise," which was not simply an economic strategy, but a new mode of existing, both culturally and socially. While there were cutbacks all across the public sector, enterprise was the recipient of advice and financial support (such as the enterprise allowance) and did all it could to foster competition, self-reliance, and, with them, risk that refused to cry out for a state-supplied safety net. This historical dimension is crucial to understanding how the video nasties' soundtracks didn't work.

Enterprise initiatives were slotted into a larger multipronged offensive of privatization that would, so the government argued, increase the United Kingdom's chances in the international marketplace. Large nationalized companies were sold off during this period, including British Petroleum (from 1979 onward), British Aerospace (1981), Cable and Wireless (1981 and 1983), Britoil (1982), Jaguar (1984), and British Telecom (a partial sale in 1984), culminating in $57 billion of public assets being resituated under private ownership. Even the regulation of employment was refashioned in a private-sector mold with job centers, as they were now called, taking up residence in commercial areas and mimicking shop fronts in their modes of presentation. This move is symbolic of a huge forced migration out of protected modes of work performance, ones that paid according to the going rate and were often supported by the state (30 percent of all employees had worked in the public sector in 1980)[77] and into the marketplace proper. As has been remarked upon already, the government of the time did its best to actualize such ideals unhindered by decreasing the rights of the trade unions, something which had an immediate reciprocal effect on working practices (of those actually working).

This rapid disassembly of the command economy did, inevitably, spark questions of self-management, ones that are also inherent in the debates about whether to deal with video nasties privately or governmentally. In all of this, the ban on videos seems a little contrary in that it strikes at one of the favored income generators of the time: the small-scale private enterprise as exemplified by the rental shop. But perhaps this was a small price to pay for the promotion of something that would help to wipe away the Keynesianism of old; the Video Recordings Act of 1984 can be seen as a sacrificial lamb slain by central control to catalyze more individual and familial responsibility. Its selection is impressive in that a (literally) familiar concern (the home) was used to push forward the more alien agenda of privatization and enterprise.

The acknowledgment of this paradox is all the more wounding when considered alongside the strictures against the ambivalence in the nasties' texts themselves. At the heart of the brutal legislation lay a positively laissez-faire way forward that, although economically liberal, was semantically conservative. "Freedom" here was essentially financial rather than social or political.

If, however, the Thatcher government, perhaps even "the moral majority" were capable of these sleights of hand, is there latitude to rethink the video nasties, to remove them from where such institutions placed them, and to unleash a similarly dialectical force from within them for other ends? Considering the force of the legislation exerted against these products, surely it is vital to conceptualize forms of resistance drawn from the kinds of work that went into them and the work that they continue to do.

The Allure of "the Beyond": The Scope for Recasting and Enabling the Video Nasties

On its own terms, the synthesizer—note the implications of its name—is a tool for combining unusual entities and invoking new states from their communion. If we do our best to bypass the obstructions erected by the Video Recordings Act, there is incredible dialectical dynamism to the synthesizer with its startling reinventions of "the human," "the domestic," labor, redundancy, and leisure— all subsequently positioned within a very unconventional pairing with horror cinema.

Deleuze and Guattari remark upon the potential of the synthesizer, although I imagine that their understanding of the machine was more abstract than the products for sale in the 1970s and 1980s. To their eyes:

> By assembling modules, source elements, and elements for treating sound (oscillators, generators, and transformers), by arranging micro-intervals, the synthesizer makes audible the sound process itself, the production of that process, and puts us in contact with still other elements beyond sound matter. It unites disparate elements in the material, and transposes the parameters from one formula to another.

The synthesizer, with its operation of consistency, has taken the place of the ground in a priori synthetic judgment: its synthesis is of the molecular and the cosmic, material and force, not form and matter, *Grund* and territory. Philosophy is no longer synthetic judgment; it is like a thought synthesizer functioning to make thought travel, make it mobile, make it a force of the Cosmos (in the same way as one makes sound travel).[78]

They also provocatively iterate:

A synthesizer places all of the parameters in continuous variation, gradually making "fundamentally heterogeneous elements end up turning into each other in some way." The moment this conjunction occurs there is a common matter. It is only at this point that one reaches the abstract machine, or the diagram of the assemblage. The synthesizer has replaced judgement, and matter has replaced the figure or formed substance. It is no longer even appropriate to group biological, physicochemical, and energetic intensities on the one hand, and mathematical, aesthetic, linguistic, informational, semiotic intensities, etc., on the other.[79]

It is worth testing these ideas on that key moment of synthesizer achievement: *Switched-on Bach*. The album makes so bold as to ignore anything ultimately "authentic" about Baroque instrumentation, thus pointing us to the implausibility of such verisimilitude in recorded sound anyway. By nevertheless adhering to the broader contrapuntal instructions of the music, it vaporizes them into a netherworld of purer electronic frequency, opening music to its core capabilities of sound production, a space where it more easily meets everything else that exists in such a present-yet-immaterial form. The album encourages us to contemplate a Bach who is even more mathematical and uniform than we presumed, and this is perhaps the album's downfall for many a listener: it is the human fallibility of irregularity and the struggle to achieve it that adds grist to a performance of Bach's oeuvre.

These more conventional renditions, then, are the acceptable face of varied categories coalescing which, ultimately, respect hierarchies: "the human" aspires and communes with the text of "the genius" or, for some, the near-divine. Perhaps, despite the exchange and unification of dichotomous elements, Bach is too solidly a territory. The same is evidently true of, to most witnesses, horror movie scores (and Deleuze and Guattari warn of the failure of synthesis through these rigid characteristics)—hence the extreme regulation of their territorial boundaries through criticism and more coercive measures. Yet what the synthesizer horror soundtrack threatens to do, precisely through its incessant recurrence in these films and more besides, is define the division between horror and synthesizer semantics as a membrane rather than a brick wall.

This particular relationship, however, has nothing to do with the ambitions of suture, where permeability is the objective, but, contrastingly, with an undemanding logic of compatibility that makes differentiation barely noticeable. Patricia MacCormack's examination of the role of Giovanni Lombardo Radice (who starred in both *Cannibal Ferox* and *Cannibal Apocalypse*) proposes another mode of engaging with cinema:

> We want to watch because watching extreme and impossible images is the true encounter of film—becoming open to worlds, textures, sounds, colours and intensities unable to be encountered in the "real" world. The sadistic gaze becomes the masochistic demand of the viewer upon the suffering body of the victim on-screen thus perverting the order of signs in film language and systems of images.[80]

The sheer incomprehensibility of the outer limits that the combination of synthesizer and horror meanings suggest both alarms and, for some, attracts and actualizes what is often considered "unthinkable." This aspiration is perpetuated by the claims, for instance, that *The Beyond* is "an Artaudian film."[81] Lucio Fulci upholds:

> [M]y idea was to make an *absolute* film, with all the horrors of our world. It's a plotless film: a house, people, and dead men coming from The Beyond. There's no logic to it, just a succession of images. It's true that all my films are terribly pessimistic. But humor and tragedy always join, anyway. If I emphasize the tragic side of things, it may have a comical effect.[82]

In this light, the film appears to both dismantle the very territory of filmic directness and also bring together the conventionally ostracized emotions triggered by tragedy and comedy.

Of course, situations like these, where cinematic matters become contested ground, are red flags to the bulls of the cult film fan world. In they leap (and continue to leap for decades afterward) to defend the subtlety, the intelligence, and, most important, the liberty of their cherished art form against a manipulative and sanctimonious conservative power structure.[83] It is these groups who strive hardest to open us up to such interpretations in their homage pieces published in magazines like *Fangoria* and *Shivers* and in their insistence upon the carefully planned outcomes of, for example, the Dario Argento–Goblin film-music collaboration.

Yet, although the general argument is that horror and fantasy cinema, along with their dabblings in jolting musical accompaniment, open us up to a more experimental approach to epistemology, fear, morality, and even life itself, there is often a simultaneous urge for inclusiveness. Peter Hutchings points out how defensive this body of debate is; so often, it pleads with us to make space within canons for this material.[84] While my sympathies lie more on the side of the fans than with the anti-nasties campaigners, I am not interested in validating or excusing these films outright. Fans who do this, I would argue, are often as unequivocal and unremitting as the protesters themselves, nearly as blinkered and control hungry and just as eager to territorialize—although, admittedly, their desired political end points are entirely different. The fascination in these films for me lies not in whether they are "good" or "bad," "trash" or "art," but in the fact that they are unresolved and nebulous, that they confound the strict notions of hermeneutics which are so easy to politically co-opt. While intriguing work is being done, mainly within the Bourdieu school of thought, on the hegemonic foundations of taste,[85] I am drawn less to the more rarefied stabilities that cult fandom (including the love of video nasties) offers and more to the wriggling chaos that remains if we refuse to neatly pack such films into preexisting pigeonholes, cutting off various of their organs in order that they might fit. The passages of history itself also allow this instability to continue its movements according to different trajectories and through different spaces, ones which preclude such compartmentalization, as is the case with the recurrent reworking of Bach of which Wendy Carlos's album is merely one moment.

In order to get a sense of the potency of such fidgetiness, it is worth turning to the writings of Jacques Derrida. Derrida claims that the constant reworking and repositioning of texts—and by this we should also infer all implied truths, histories, and social structures, as well as "films themselves"—are not something we inflict upon them in the academic laboratory, but an action that texts themselves carry out.[86]

This is exactly the case with this material and its ever-evolving meanings. Such thinking as Derrida's is ammunition in my struggle to cease the consignment of semantic disorder to the realms of more knowingly intellectual art (as fans often claim the nasties to be) and to move it into the ever-present flux of quotidian life. The nasties make overwrought recourse to easily graspable yet conventionally mutually exclusive symbols like the synthesizer's antihumanism and leisure allusions, and horror's extremities of torture. This then betrays the fabrication, rather than the consistency, of a world where they can coexist while also throwing open all number of questions about (the limitations of) our systems of difference and opposition.

Derrida's fascination lies in the action of texts rather than in acceptance of their supposedly predetermined descriptive functions. He does not deal with the practices of labor as such, but the liveliness of his thought has much to offer its analysis. In his earlier writings, he distinguishes between "constative" and "performative" language, the former insisting upon a kind of solidity, the latter embodying greater mobility and change. Here we can also perhaps fantasize about one of the central merits of deconstruction, one that is supported by what Derrida draws from the Greek word *poisesis* (from whence the root of "poetry" comes) and its linguistic implication of "something which makes one act." This is language that refuses to be self-revelatory and instead demands a creative response; the reader must thus perform, just as language does, and this is what I am hoping to encourage by exposing the vitality of these particular film-music arrangements and their refusal to contain and execute staid models of labor. Much of Derrida's oeuvre aims to reveal the performative dimensions that claim to be constative, and this speaks urgently to the desire to reincorporate video nasty ideals within a falsely presumed fixity of what is acceptable and esteemed.

One crucial aspect of this fluctuation is the constant deferral of meaning sustained by language, including instances when texts and the labors of their creation and continuation undo their own coherence. "Film," on account of the very particular amalgamating initiatives that fall within its constructed definitions (even in its most conventional guises), is an absorbing example of deconstruction in action.[87] When film-music analysts try to block out such interchanges by, for example, identifying film and what it "should be" in very rigid terms, an impossible stagnancy seems to be their ultimate, if unconscious, goal. This is the case with the abhorrence of the ethical suggestions of linking synthesizer meanings to the revelation of bodily harm. Although the soundtracks to these films are often distracting and might knock any confused audience members out of such a "detrimental" engrossment, the messages their music can relay, if read as constative rather than performative, are so wildly removed from the moral agenda of representational realism that the films seem even more detestable to those loyal to this aesthetic alone. Luckily, however, the concerted skittishness at the core of deconstruction, including that it not be constatively figured as a fixed apparatus, is shared by "cinema," whose very gaps and inconsistencies might be more productively considered as *aporia*. Derrida's adoption of the term *aporia* exemplifies his fascination with the "between," a state that acknowledges our current understandings of distinction and yet violates the rules that render texts separate. Derrida famously spins out the meanings of particular, chosen words—such as *différance*—so that we are confronted by their assertion of the manifold existence of the outside within the inside and vice versa. The value of this trope, for Derrida, lies in how it enables the possibilities of the center to be reworked and reinvested from the peripheries, from that which it presumes to have cast aside. If we follow a conventional constitution of "the center" as the narrative and its visual incarnations, and "the peripheries" as the soundtrack to these video nasties, then we can witness a messy reshuffling of the working methods and public perceptions of both entertainment industries, including a ceaseless reconceptualization of their processes of exploitation and agency. Music like this, for instance, can function according to what sound theorist Michel Chion calls *anempathetic* scoring, "a backdrop of indifference"[88] founded in the "uncaring" ambience of an accompaniment that is anathema to the role the soundtrack has traditionally been ascribed in more Fordist production lineages. Furthermore, this scoring not only destabilizes how we "ought" to receive such narrative material. It also, as Chion observes, exposes something quite morally frightening in relation to the topics of these movies:

> [We see] cinema's essence—its mechanical nature. For, indeed, all films proceed in the form of an indifferent and automatic unwinding, that of the projection, which on the screen and through the loudspeakers produces simulacra of movement and life—and this unwinding must hide itself and be forgotten. What does anempathetic music do, if not to unveil this reality of cinema, its robotic face?[89]

Instead of ethically enclosing the shock of these images or framing them within a consistent sense of three-dimensional depth where their comprehensibility might be pondered and assessed, the shallow quality of these soundtracks seems to be reminding the viewer of the fragile and ghostly presence of the flickering cinematic form.

A deconstructive eagerness seeps out of these plot lines too. *Cannibal Holocaust* follows an NYU research team into the Amazon basin to watch them make a documentary film. They fabricate all manner of horrific events in order to sensationalize not only the film they are making, but also the one we are watching.[90] Of note here is these movies' country of origin, Italy, especially if we are to consider it as pushed to the margins, its inheritance perhaps hidden within the contemporary center of a Conservative-governed United Kingdom of the 1980s. Italy is a place where the bewitchment by and interrogation of the codes of representational realism have been consistent philosophical threads leading from the development of Renaissance perspective through to

neorealism, the work of Federico Fellini, Pier Paolo Pasolini, and Mondo doc-
umentarists. These more recent cinematic engagements have definitely colored
the video nasties. For instance, Deodato (*Cannibal Holocaust*'s director) once
worked as an assistant producer for neorealist auteur Roberto Rossellini. And
the delight with which *Cannibal Holocaust* and *Cannibal Ferox* concoct lurid
fantasies about the non-Western world is not only a commentary on Mondo
movies, but also a continuation of the cinematic discussion of how to depict
violence and torture, which sees Pasolini's *Salò* (1975), itself a film with a long
history of prohibition, as its forebear. Other such self-aware qualities infuse
Cannibal Ferox, whose protagonist, Gloria (Lorraine De Selle), is a doctoral
candidate at Brown University intent on wielding what would now be called
postcolonial theory to disprove the existence of cannibalism. *Tenebrae* is the
story of a crime fiction writer embroiled in murderous situations that seem
inspired by his own books. All three of these films assemble a myriad of self-
reflexive plot devices and formal witticisms that alert us to how the media
manipulate realism. This ranges from *Cannibal Holocaust*'s jokey intertitle "For
the sake of authenticity, some scenes have been retained in their entirety" to
Deodato's contextualization of his film within a larger media environment: "At
the time on television we were always seeing death scenes, they were the years
of terrorism and my film was also a condemnation of a certain type of journal-
ism."[91] *The Beyond, Tenebrae,* and *Inferno,* in particular, are awash with irrational,
mystifying plot lines; their gore has more in common with spilled ice cream
splurted with ketchup than with the inner workings of an actual human being.
We are to marvel at the aesthetics of these mock-ups more than we are to believe in them. Perhaps the most rewarding, or troubling, characteristic of these
films is their confusion of fact and fiction, realism and fantasy—distinctions
that often support extremely delicate political propositions within the generic
domain of the horror film. This determination to tamper with semantic opposition, which is so much the darling of the defenders of these films, creates an
intellectual commentary on the role of the horror movie and its constriction
within contemporary society.

This, in itself, cannot be an end point. The activities upon which Derrida
draws reengage with the Marxian work that pre-dates them to elaborate a
greater urge within mainstream cinematic culture: that of effacing its labor (like
so many other good capitalist projects), of masking its hegemonic workings as
"entertainment" (including, in this case, its limitations), and of making all of its
deliberate and political aesthetic choices seem obvious, natural, and logical (or,
at the very least, traditional). This is the case with much of the so-called continuity system, narrative structuring, and, of course, the persistence of the sporadic late nineteenth-century-derived classical score. It would be disingenuous

to the Derridean methodology to crack open some sort of fallacious façade in order to attain "the truth"—and I do not hope to do so either—but his insights establish a generative schema for critiquing stultified modes of comprehension.

Might all these understandings promote political agitation in precisely that domain where anti-nasty activists so emphatically claimed these videos would harm audiences: the practices of identification? As noted above, Patricia Mac-Cormack has voiced concerns about the implication that viewing these videos is necessarily sadistic by illuminating the masochistic enjoyment of these excesses. This complicates the declared damage that is done to "young minds" and, more crucially, "society" by such texts. More perturbing, perhaps, is neither response: the sense that "cinema" is often, in this constant turning around of meaning, incapable of stimulating any such responses in direct terms, either as a straightforward cautioning against aggressive thoughts and behaviors or as an invitation to carry them out. In the most profound sense, it isn't working here, and we are left with a set of laborers (including parents) and potential laborers (children) who are not or, in the future, will not be able to derive necessarily clear pictures of "right" and "wrong" from within the strictures of employment regulation. Producers too are "working incorrectly" if the culture they set before us does not validate itself in terms of the related codes and allowances of creativity.

Argento's oeuvre especially can seem very much in contravention of these aims by instead creating a dialectical discussion with the worlds of fashion, interior design, architecture, and (interestingly, for a study of music) opera, realms where mutilation and murder are rendered with great abstraction and where art is less frequently asked to justify itself in the way that horror cinema is. Who are the audiences, the working subjects of these creative modes, and why are they allowed a different access to violence? These renditions of fantastical and almost ornamental violence did/do not sit well within the popular and distinctly more literal understanding of cinematic storytelling. Why? In order for the assumptions about the depravity of these films held by the anti-nasties lobbyists to stand firm and for greater numbers of troops to be gathered in support of their cause, particularly bland, unquestioning ideas about realism were projected and locked onto these movies. Experiencing them on a surface level of *what* can be seen (but not how and why it is shown) supposedly elicits facile revulsion, identification, and the dread fear of copy-cat behavior erupting out of society's most gullible and vulnerable viewers—or so the *Daily Mail* would lead us to believe.

The movies are not fulfilling an implied contract that requires them to *care* in particularly hegemonically limiting ways. It may be that, as Philip Brophy argues, they are "enraptured with [their] own stylisation"[92] and, in this sense, selfishly enjoy the layer upon layer of their own dense formalism, rather than trying to express a conventional moral agenda. In his essay "Spectacles of Death: Identification, Reflexivity and Contemporary Horror," Jeffrey Sconce proposes that horror fans often engage less with characters and more with the ingenuity of the mechanisms of artistic trickery, which they do not in the least "fall for."[93] Although this is the institution of a new form of territory, it is one that up-ends the hierarchies of expert knowledge—and thus work and its consumption—that gatekeep between art professionals and those who are supposed to learn from the messages of any given narrative flow. Certainly, none of this is alien to cultural commerce; our acknowledgment of skill is often part and parcel of why we buy. What might be novel about experiences like these, though, is that the accompanying message features so low on what is to be gained from the experience.

These paradoxically multiple engagements with both "finished" and delivered texts and their prior processes of manufacture can be politicized by Derrida's notion of "the trace." Here "the before" or "the other" are not in fact outside but a necessary constituent of the inside, integral to both its quality and existence. There is thus *potential* enacted by both the experiences of making film music *for* audiences (and their desires to simultaneously immerse themselves in it) and the prospect of understanding the processes of production. One does not humbly step into the shadows so as not to intrude on the other. In a more pervasive but seemingly abstract sense, this mobility between spheres of work and its consumption is an endeavor jointly assumed by the synthesizer scores that refuse such categories as "amateurish" or "professional," "work" or "leisure."

However, within Derrida's thought, any such questioning should not be an endeavor to replace an old regime with a new one, but a call for us to linger in these spaces of what he calls "undecidability," working with the multiplicities spawned from a lack of conventional resolution. He argues:

> [B]y analogy (I underline) I have called [these] undecidables, that is, unities of simulacrum, "false" verbal properties (nominal or semantic) that can no longer be included within philosophical (binary) opposition, but which, however, inhabit philosophical opposition, resisting and disorganizing it, *without ever* constituting a third term, without ever leaving room for a solution in the form of speculative dialectics (the *pharmakon* is neither remedy nor poison, neither good nor evil, neither the inside nor the outside, neither speech nor writing; the *supplement* is neither a plus nor a minus, neither an outside nor the complement of an inside, neither accident nor essence, etc.; the *hymen*

is neither confusion nor distinction, neither identity nor difference, neither consummation nor virginity, neither the veil nor unveiling, neither the inside nor the outside, etc.; the *gram* is neither a signifier nor a signified, neither a sign nor a thing, neither a presence nor an absence, neither a position nor a negation, etc.; *spacing* is neither space nor time; the *incision* is neither the incised integrity of a beginning, or of a simple cutting into, nor simple secondarity. Neither/nor, that is, *simultaneously* either *or;* the mark is also the *marginal* limit, the *march,* etc.).[94]

The indispensability of the undecidable's potential rests not only in how it complicates the factors within any kind of clash and refuses to engender them with a sense of opposition, but also in how it opens up deconstructive spaces or opportunities, sites where we might be able to constantly reimagine an understanding of labor or, as Patricia MacCormack urges us with Radice's movies, to "take pleasure in everything we cannot vindicate or explain."[95] Through our interactions *between* soundtrack and image, as well as video and social context, we are encouraged to question our need for an opposition of distanciation and the representation of death, or to unpack the allegiances among specific realist codes, humanist sympathy, and morality. Second, the urge to achieve a unified, spick-and-span conclusion about what the music, the image, and the narrative are trying to say *as a whole* (which often enters into a logic of conquest and eventual domination) can be exposed for failing to ask *why* such conflicts might have arisen in the first place. We can begin, at this point, to ask how producers and audiences might suffer from so uninquisitive a resolution, to wonder whether "the home" is really so insulated and how the economies of labor have become so restrictive. Perhaps we should also consider whether attributing or taking a stance over apparently opposed debates is always necessarily the most politically judicious action to take. Must we always *belong* (as cult fan academics are also often wont to do) to a coherent belief system?

Before such (anti)reasoning spirals beyond the realms of the possible, though, it is wise to return to some of Derrida's own cautions. For him, in spite of the potential richness of such confusion, attention to the linguistic structuring that situates and repositions these arrangements is of paramount importance. Derrida is far from declaring that any interpretation or determination is valid and instead emphasizes (based on Gödel's undecidability proof) the anomalous elements of most systems, saying that attempts to correct such irregularities severely limit the capacity of any such organization. This leaves us in a potentially tight spot. If we were to choose to watch the films at the level of deconstruction—enjoy the camp, remain detached and critical, or even *laugh,* which it is easy to do when confronted with the hyperbole of the synthesizers and the stylized gore—then viewers inclined toward the particular investments in realism and protection which were outlined earlier will find us repugnant. Such an unpredictable set of options, it would seem, was too dangerous for many Britons, who feared that the coin might land the wrong way up; these movies would have to be dealt with severely, kept out of harm's way, even destroyed. The ambivalence of the films became the pariah, something that just might coax the weak-minded toward an entwined Dark Side. Certainly, many cultural products delight in ambiguity and opacity, indeed derive their revenues from this, in part. However, the particular location of these films within a seemingly unsurveyable environment (on video, at home), being viewed by certain sections of the population who are habitually considered to be at risk, such as, to evoke the stereotype, poorly morally educated under-18s whose guardians are frequently out of the picture, meant that these films were inscribed as unsafe by a host of restless campaigners.

And so the delicate refusal of these texts to be forthright was left unreported by many tabloid news reports in favor of vehement claims that they embodied unmitigated, uncomplicated celebrations of evil and malice—which made them so much easier to outlaw. What became manifest for the great majority was neither the creation of new vocabularies which might incorporate such incoherence into a more widely acceptable understanding of logic, nor a ferreting among the ideological underpinnings of our old linguistic categories, but utter banishment under the 1984 Video Recordings Act. There is only the hope now that history, not just the future, but also the reworking of the past can find something of political potential in this incarceration, as is so often the case when one looks back to the composition of prior prison populations.

My next chapter is less concerned with such strict governmental rulings against the mismatch, perhaps because the project of decentralization grew more complete as time wore on and, as will become clear, self-regulation processes seemed increasingly dependable. During the following period, the 1990s to the present day, state policy has shifted its priorities from censoring the content of the media, to fully welcoming creative culture into how the economy is structured, both as a model of production and as a set of commodities. Postindustrialism, as the earlier chapters in this book have demonstrated, has been closely involved in and often inspired by the entertainment businesses' decentralization, employment insecurity, and small-scale adaptable manufacturing procedures. Chapter 5 charts how the media and postindustrialism have become even more deliberately and tightly interlocked, enforcing a proximity that seemed evocative in chapter 2, a possible but troublesome solution in chapter 3, and a necessary form of surveillance in this chapter.

◆ 5 ◆

Pop Stars Who Can't Act and the Limits of Celebrity "Flexibility"

Given all of the ruptures and permutations in the understandings and lived experiences of work in the last half-century, what can be gained from mulling over the pop star and, in particular, the lead singer who "can't act"? To start with, these cases often provoke overblown and vitriolic reactions from critics and the viewing public alike, telling us much about how we currently define the concepts and practices of labor—not just pop stars' acting dexterity, but also contemporary formations of work on a much broader scale.

Cross-over performers are by no means a new phenomenon. Bing Crosby, for instance, was one of the highest paid stars during and after the beginning of cinema's sound era. Since then, there have been hosts of successful artists crisscrossing between film and music: the "postindustrial" age has brought us Barbra Streisand, Ice Cube, Cher, Will Smith, and that indefatigable "brand" J-Lo (Jennifer Lopez), to name but a few. There are also movies in which famous singers with perhaps limited acting capabilities have been well used because their standard personas helpfully overlap with the film roles in which they have been cast or their individual performing talents ease them more naturally into certain roles. Think of David Bowie as an alien in *The Man Who Fell to Earth* (Nicholas Roeg, 1976), Bjork in the musical *Dancer in the Dark* (Lars von Trier, 2000), or Eminem in the more directly autobiographical *8 Mile* (Curtis Hanson, 2002).

Nevertheless, accusations of film-music alliances "not working" seem to erupt on a fairly regular basis when established pop stars try their luck in movies. There is evidently something compelling about seeing the mighty fall, a fact compounded by the host of celebrity magazines in the market, publications that glory in their photos of stars with cellulite, stars enduring bad hair days, or worse. The critique of cross-overs also flourishes in review writing and on fan Web sites, perhaps because of the tenuous positions that such writers (freelance journalists especially) hold in relation to the current cartography of careers and artistic labor. Accordingly, much of this chapter's anti-mismatch source material will be drawn from these quarters.[1]

As my preceding arguments have contended, the growing prominence of the media economy readily offers up film and music as both an accessible starting point for the discussion of work and as a set of objects and practices which themselves demand scrutiny through the lens of labor relations. If, as I shall outline, "creative" employment is on the rise, will more methodical means of judging and rewarding such work be required? Furthermore, where does the failed cross-over sit within the particular systems of professionalism that privilege flexibility and emotional labor, two fairly new, but significant, arrivals on the postindustrial scene? Might probing such cross-over mismatches also unmask various recent transformations of working time? These are the questions that occupy this chapter. To help answer them, *Freejack* (Geoff Murphy, 1992), starring Mick Jagger, and *Swept Away* (Guy Ritchie, 2002), a movie directed by Guy Ritchie and showcasing his wife, Madonna, seem especially apt follies to home in on. In both films, shrewd, enduring musical icons were thought by many to have been carried out of their depth, unable to battle the kinds of currents that they might have so adeptly navigated within music culture. What, or who, is not working?

Ah, *Freejack:* Mick Jagger's long-anticipated return to the silver screen after the lengthy hiatus since his notoriously embarrassing *Ned Kelly* (Tony Richardson, 1970), a severe disappointment after his luminous appearance in *Performance* (Donald Cammell and Nicholas Roeg, 1970). Sad to relate, Jagger hardly bristles with satanic majesty as the villain Vacendak in this somewhat hackneyed sci-fi picture. Rather ironically, the movie's narrative launches an attack on multinational corporations, precisely the kinds of entities that have promoted and distributed the film—and helped to disseminate contemporary models of labor.

A clash of working ideals scuppers Jagger's credibility in *Freejack* in contradistinction to the similar oppositions that are held in careful balance in his best-regarded feature film, *Performance.* If we position *Performance* as a discourse on work, although it is many other things besides, we see that its narrative is troubled by some fundamental questions: what is the connection between identity and performance? and how does this affect how we make money? Jagger plays a louche, retired musician (Turner) whose image, on the surface, seems very close to the star's own. Unlike Jagger, though, Turner is house-bound, enveloped in a world of the interior, spatial and psychological, that has both aided and hindered his creativity. His nemesis, with whom he ultimately merges, is Chas (James Fox), whose upward mobility has been dependent upon his status as a gangster until the moment when he is forced to flee his boss and hide out in Turner's house. Much of the film is propelled by the energy each character siphons from the other, while their conflicting relationships to (working) temporality—Chas is obsessed with time, while its passing is almost immaterial to Turner—provide an essential pivot for the diegesis. In its late 1960s moment, the film details the contemporary crises of labor as they related to class, the self, and from where creative inspiration might ultimately spring. Within all of this, Jagger-the-musician embodies a central point for the public discussion of such values. The film expertly mobilizes the alleged (but perhaps ill-conceived) assumptions that had been made about Jagger's supposedly decadent and debauched, yet still talent-driven and successful, mode of earning a living.

This instance of film-music working corroborates the definition of "charisma" to be found in Richard Dyer's *Stars.* For Dyer, charisma is a quality which bridges points that have been polarized by historical instabilities (dialectical play, I might add), and his perspective may well shed light on how shifts in working patterns are debated symbolically through our engagement with celebrity culture. As a 1960s icon, Jagger successfully encapsulated the libertarian indolence and raw working stamina that marked the two extremes of the postwar economic boom and its relationship to philosophies and practices of labor. Unfortunately, though, he seems not to have managed to bring together similarly divergent forces while completing his acting duties for *Freejack.*

Granted, there are other stylistic achievements (thoughtful cinematography, an evocative set) that swirl around and beautify Jagger's contribution to *Performance,* which are all too absent in *Freejack.* The latter movie's deficit of critical and audience acclaim could be equally attributable to a lackluster performance from costar Emilio Estevez and an uninspired script, editing, direction, and so on, but Jagger's reluctance or inability, as I shall demonstrate, to bow down to the working conventions of acting, as well as his commitment to the rules of pop stardom, hammer many nails into the film's coffin.

The critical responses to *Freejack,* from professionals and amateurs alike, linger morbidly on Jagger's performance: it is "corpse-like"[2] for *Sight and Sound's* Kim Newman. Making sure to shoehorn in references to the more successful aspects of Jagger's musical and cinematic career, Alan Jones's review for *Starburst* magazine professes, "it isn't a gas, gas, gas. It's a mess, mess, mess. . . . As for rad-dled Jagger, the audience at the preview I attended burst into laughter at his first deadpan line and never stopped. He waited 21 years to give this *Perfor-mance!*"[3] On amateur Web sites, we find the likes of "This is a must see for fans of Jaggers [*sic*] laughable acting talents and bad sci-fi. I giggled so incessantly upon viewing the video that I immediately rewound it and watched it again."[4] This is an example of the fascination with failure if ever there was one. Ad-mittedly, several reviewers interpret Jagger's acting style as one of clever, know-ing detachment from the film, an aloof response to a venture the star must have recognized as trifling.[5] However, the majority of writers presumed the per-formance to be what Mark Kermode and Trevor Johnston identify as "unin-tentionally hilarious."[6] As Janet Maslin of the *New York Times* dryly concludes, Jagger is "lucky to have other employment."[7] As usual in the vocabulary of crit-icism, the language of work is never too far away. However, might the facility with which people such as Jagger find work in the first place be exactly what breeds a considerable portion of the resentment toward cross-over artists?

Like Jagger, Madonna has enjoyed minor successes in cinema when her character overlaps sufficiently with her public image. *Desperately Seeking Susan* (Susan Seidelman, 1985) is perhaps the most apt example of this, but her con-tributions as a singer were also fairly warmly received in *Dick Tracy* (Warren Beatty, 1990) and *Evita* (Alan Parker, 1996). On the other hand, *Swept Away,* a remake of the more socialistically inclined Italian movie *Swept Away . . . by an Unusual Destiny in the Blue Sea of August* (Lina Wertmüller, 1974), was so loathed that it suffered the ignominy of skipping cinematic distribution in the United Kingdom and was released straight to domestic formats after it fared poorly at the American box office. The plot line follows Amber (Madonna), the spoiled and venomous wife of a millionaire (Bruce Greenwood). She is reluctantly par-taking of a Mediterranean cruise with her husband and friends when she is cast adrift with Guiseppe (Adriano Giannini), a crew member whom she had pre-viously singled out for idle persecution. The two are washed up on a deserted island and, with the tables turned, Amber has little choice but to indulge the somewhat sadistic urges of the only person on the land mass who is equipped with the necessary skills for survival. Work (the simple but crucial skills of sheltering and feeding oneself) is a central theme. In regards to this topic, the character of Amber is not positioned favorably to dampen any assumptions we might have about Madonna's ability to adapt under impoverishment, which, as will become clear, impacts upon the labor she completes as an actress.

The critical responses to the film have been almost unanimously vicious. *Newsday*'s John Anderson cautions us of this castaway narrative, "If Madonna is ever washed up on a beach near you, throw her back in,"[8] while Mick La Salle of the *San Francisco Chronicle* taunts: "They're stuck on a deserted island. What else are they going to do? Actually, that might explain Madonna's interest in the role—it's the one context in which she can be believable as a romantic lead: The guy can't get off the island."[9]

The belief that synergy will never simply function according to basic mathematics (addition, for the most part) resounds through all of these ripostes. Film-music convergences struggle with the complex habits of each industry; profit and coherence are never foregone conclusions of collaboration, despite the cost efficiency, cross-marketing potential, prior star familiarity, and horizontal integrations which enterprises like *Freejack* and *Swept Away* afford.[10] Beyond these general confusions that the mismatch creates, largely as a result of fragmented production procedures, how might the newer tactics that the sustained schema of postindustrialism has absorbed since the 1990s inflect the way these two movies "don't work"? At this point, as *Off Key* draws to a close, I want to answer this question by also summing up what my postindustrial periodization hopes to solicit: a better grasp of ongoing exploitation and monotony existing all the while in a climate of ingenuity and "progress," a situation that furthers fairly consistent capitalist aims. Stasis and movement coexisting? Dialectical politics can be found everywhere.

Contemporary Formations of Labor and the Role of the Celebrity

Catapulting onward from the contexts and developments delineated in the last three chapters, it would at first appear that the very geography of work has, again, altered. These days, we are now beholden to advanced communication systems, particularly the Internet, that enable an even freer flow of capital and an accelerated movement of manufacturing centers outside the so-called "developed" countries. This is a yet fuller realization of the decentralization project that this book has outlined.

Since the period covered in the last chapter, reduction in trade protectionism in the countries that made up the former Soviet Union, as well as the People's Republic of China and India, has opened up vast markets and resources, allowing for the expansion of Western capitalism in extraordinary new ways, including the increased influence of certain media conglomerates. The rise of multinational corporations (many of which disseminate these cultural products) has complicated the notion of a nation-state economy more than even chapter 3's context could have imagined. As Keith Grint confirms:

It is now clear that several of the largest MNCs have annual financial turnovers far in excess of several smaller nations. In fact, by the early 1990s about 37,000 MNCs controlled over a third of the world's private assets; and 359 MNCs account for 40 per cent of global trade, while of the largest hundred economies in the world, half are MNCs.[11]

This accelerated mobility of capital—aided, of course, by not only the wealth of communication systems, but also political pressures to favor free trade—means that costs can be slashed by moving production to where labor is the cheapest, often because benefits and wages have been shaved.[12] Concomitant with the firm grip the G8 nations hold upon flows of labor and wealth, the scope of work and the mobility of labor have been radically redefined in the last few decades, even in the richest of countries, the ones whose responses to *Freejack* and *Swept Away* are being detailed.[13]

As the previous chapters have attested, this shift in employment has progressed hand in hand with the rise in tertiary labor, and it has proved consistently worthwhile to consider entertainment within this trend. As early as 1986, Richard J. Badham, in his book *Theories of Industrial Society,* remarked upon

> a class structure characterized by the predominance of white collar and professional occupations (the major source of conflict lying between professionals and the populace at large); and a cultural system assigning increasing priority to self-expression, equality, participation and the general "quality of life."[14]

Amid all of this adaptation to the necessities of service and information labor, it comes as no surprise that the many social qualities associated with the performer have become so much more prized and subject to scrutiny. By the 1990s, the majority of UK and U.S. citizens maintained their steady relocation within services, with a drop from 1970 to 1990 in manufacturing from 38.7 percent to 22.5 percent (United Kingdom) and 59 percent to 17.5 percent (United States)[15] so that, by 1996, 57.3 percent of the U.S. labor force was white-collar workers,[16] and 21.4 million British people were employed in the country's largest sector: services,[17] which can include outsourced and externalized workers who might have borne other job descriptions in previous years, such as cleaning and catering staff.

It is now members of the middle class, perhaps traditionally one of the most secure strata of society, who feel threatened as greater numbers of workers flock into the somewhat limited spheres traditionally thought to be their preserve. Additionally, with the possibilities that contemporary freedoms of capital movement and accumulation allow, the sense of worker security within countries like Britain and the United States, which are now less competitive as sites of production, has diminished still further. Interestingly, journalists are among these ranks, and they are the most forthright and feisty in their public denunciations of arriviste labor in the form of the cross-over artist, perhaps because their positions as (often freelance) creative personnel are so precarious in the present situation. Reviewers' animosity toward these stars is perhaps symptomatic of the anxieties such workers endure from the unpredictability, fragmentation, and decentralization of these shifts and, thus, their jobs. Their subsequent desire to lay down particular meanings and values reveals much about this condition. Furthermore, in such situations of income uncertainty, it comes as no surprise that people of considerable wealth become fetishized, especially when they have reached their status by rising up from among the ranks of average folk—and this is exactly what many entertainment professionals have achieved.[18]

In order to contend with the more realistic situation on the ground and to counter the economic depressions and high unemployment that the last two chapters' time frames experienced, even the richer nation-states have had to assume much more volatile working practices, including impermanent, flexible, and short-term modes of employment. As we witnessed in chapter 4, there has been a massive push toward privatization and a growing sensibility that trade protectionism will decelerate export quotas. Consequently, social and institutional safeguarding is being reduced in countries where it was once more prominent and halted almost everywhere else. The resulting atomization is treated in sociohistorically particular ways, ones with which our discussions about cross-over artists allow us to grapple in a more sustained fashion than we might, at first, imagine. These mismatches cannot help but play out amid the pervasive mise-en-scène of the global decrease in unionization that was witnessed in the previous two chapters. As Keith Grint continues, "in the 1970s legal protection in Britain against unfair dismissal began after six months of continuous employment; by the 1990s this had increased to two years."[19] Since then, this has been furthered by yet more governmental and corporate intervention (sometimes coercion), the increasingly short-term and mobile nature of much employment, and the scattered, even illegal status of so many of the world's workers. As a consequence of all of this, and in addition to the rise in automation and working women that so troubled the subjects of chapter 4, vast overhauls have been inflicted on who works; when, how, and where they do so; what the opportunities are for change, development, and dismissal within employment; and how many jobs people might hold down.

A 1993 Labor Force Survey found that 38 percent of workers in the United Kingdom were not employed on a permanent, full-time basis (with 85 percent of them women); similar statistical surveys of the United States in 1992 found the figure there to be 25 percent.[20] Other analysts cite more extreme figures, claiming, "at least one quarter of men and one half of women of working age [hold] non-standard jobs," and the "structure of employment in the early 1990s looks very different from its appearance at the end of the 1970s."[21] Huw Beynon concludes, "[P]art-time work stands as the main source of employment growth in the 1980s and 1990s. In 1995 there were three and a half million fewer full time jobs [in the United Kingdom] than there were fifteen years earlier."[22] This modification in methods of employment shapes the trajectory of how we respond to the intermittent (essentially part-time) dabblings of musicians within cinema.

In addition, the "enterprise culture" so beloved of Thatcherism continues to blossom, propagating particular models of self-reliance within the frameworks of labor. Successive governments within the United States and Britain have advanced this ethic socially, and there are distinct overlaps between this mindset and certain ways of behaving that are familiar from media stardom. Interestingly, 1992 marked not only the release of *Freejack,* but also Britain's first attempt to record self-employment statistics. This documentation heralds an increasing realization that the economy is much more dependent of late on strategic alliances between big businesses and the largely unsupported workers to whom they assign short-term casual contracts and with whom they can relay so much through various communications networks. All of these arrangements allow for the more small-scale customized manufacturing that is typical of "post-Fordism," which is shared, significantly, by the typical means of album or film creation before they are mass reproduced. Mass production governed by centralized control and distinguished by multidivisional labor (the repetition of simple mechanical tasks) has, as we have observed, decreased of late, at least in the wealthier geographical spaces, and has been supported in Britain for quite some time by policy advice documents that urge "a shift towards smaller establishments and enterprises . . . a new kaleidoscope of careers . . . [and] a new accent on competitive performance."[23] Small and medium enterprises, enthuses Intellect, the trade association for the British high-tech industry, "are increasingly becoming the engine room of the UK economy as well as a critical source of innovation which enhances our competitiveness."[24] What is important to stress is that production of this nature is tailored to the needs of the marketplace and supported in varying degrees by the deregulation promoted by neoliberalized systems of government. It rarely, as we shall see, bends obediently to the concerns of employee welfare through social engineering, bureaucracy, benefit systems, or the more local interests of the nation-state.

Of note here is the fact that both the film and the music industries have functioned according to many of these principles for quite some time now. It is hardly surprising, as a consequence, that they are often regarded, whether knowingly or not by their fans, as models for understanding, even idolizing, the more successful operations of such a system. Irregular and unpredictable employment has, of course, been a constant within the entertainment industries. Hollywood, as was outlined in chapter 2, decreased its vertical integration and Fordist working methods early on when the numbers of long-term contracts shrank and freelance work became much more prominent. Musicians, although signed to labels, can just as easily be dropped, and the rates of failure to earn "sufficient" revenues can soar up to 90 percent. In both realms, one never knows when the next project or short-term contract will pop up. Performing in these areas means working at one of the more vicious ends of the Western free-market economy; one is a casual worker, rather than a regular employee. This set-up can also be extremely detrimental to the struggle for workers' rights within the entertainment industries. The huge numbers of aspirants guarantee that some hopefuls will be willing to undercut others in a variety of ways (including submitting to the casting couch), which places the inscription of acceptable working conditions squarely in the upper hands of the employers. Likewise, successful performers are kept in line by the fear that they might easily be superseded by a newcomer if they fall out of favor with their bosses. Even if unionized, performers will gain a low minimum wage, but very little else because competition is intense and there is always an overabundance of workers eager to assume the scarce number of jobs.

Although the majority of performers are poor and most cannot make a sufficient living from their craft, a small group clustered in the upper echelons earn such fabulous salaries that those at the bottom are hungry enough to continue to flood the employment market. Precisely because these workers are no longer held under long-term contracts, personnel in the movie business, for instance, now charge much higher rates for their services than they did under the studio system.[25] This, in turn, makes hiring more of a gamble and accelerates the practice of engaging nonpermanent staff, because corners need to be cut.

All of these correlations among film, music, and the postindustrial atmosphere are not simply cases of the entertainment business mirroring the broader economy in a one-way fashion: the multifaceted yearning for the creative worker ideal is integral to recent drives toward a redirection of production. As was observed in chapter 3, richer countries have been priced out of many markets by cheaper manufacturing zones. In order to survive financially, they have moved toward guaranteeing their actual employment, as opposed to their wealth (which is drawn from a much wider global reach and ownership of production), by specializing in management, services, and "informationalism."[26] More than ever before, this shift has become central to national legislation. The influential British white paper *Our Competitive Future: Building the Knowledge Driven Economy* of 1998 baldly laid out the fact that the "UK's distinctive capabilities are not raw materials, land or cheap labour. They must be our knowledge, skills and creativity."[27] Elsewhere, one of its authors, Charles Leadbeater argues:

> Most of us make our money from thin air: we produce nothing that can be weighed, touched or easily measured. Our output is not stockpiled at harbours, stored in warehouses or shipped in railway cars. Most of us earn our livings providing service, judgement, information and analysis, whether in a telephone call centre, a lawyer's office, a government department or a scientific laboratory. We are all in the thin-air business.[28]

These "thin-air" spheres are also now more central to our economies, with the creative industries in the United Kingdom currently earning more revenue than manufacturing ones[29] and enterprises like the British incarnation of Big Brother (Channel Four television) claiming annual profits of £769.5 million.[30] Such ventures have been supported and recast at the parliamentary level in a number of ways. In 1992 (the year of *Freejack's* release), a Ministry of Culture was instituted in Britain; by 1997, this had transmogrified into the Ministry of Culture, Media and Sport with the government now acknowledging the centrality of these entities to the economy. When the Labour Party regained power in 1997, Chris Smith, the ministry's head, announced in *Creative Britain,* his manifesto for the future of the country: "as a new government, we have recognized the importance of this whole industrial sector that no one hitherto has even conceived of as 'industry.'"[31] Theodor Adorno, of course, would beg to differ, but his politics were much less optimistic and capitalistic than Smith's. He would never have boasted the following in a speech delivered to an American audience:

> Increasingly, many people are seeing investment opportunities in British music. You may have read recently about the Bowie Bonds issued by Wall Street–based Nomura Securities, which enabled David Bowie to raise $55 million through their sale to Prudential Insurance. The bonds were guaranteed by the steady flow of royalty income David Bowie's songs and recordings still generate. Other top British

artists rumoured to be looking at similar deals include the Rolling Stones.[32]

Sustained institutional investment, encouragement, and governance of this kind have both prompted and adapted to noticeable demographic shifts. In his popular and influential study, *The Rise of the Creative Class . . . and How It's Transforming Work, Leisure, Community, and Everyday Life,* Richard Florida calculates:

> Over the twentieth century, the Creative Class grew from roughly 3 million workers to its current size, a tenfold-plus increase; since 1980 alone it has more than doubled. Roughly 15 million Americans, more than 12 percent of the workforce, compose the Super-Creative Core of this new class. . . . The Creative Class in the United States today is larger than the traditional Working Class—for instance those who work in manufacturing, construction and transportation industries.[33]

Florida also says, "The wealth generated by the creative sector is astounding: It accounts for nearly half [of] all wage and salary income in the United States, $1.7 trillion . . . , as much as the manufacturing and service sectors combined."[34] If larger and larger numbers of workers are entering the creative sector, then its means of justifying, valuing, educating, and exchanging not only the fruits of its labor but that labor itself must undoubtedly change.

Qualifying Creative Labor

In the move toward recasting culture as a supposedly dependable component of the postindustrial economy, we bang into a major dilemma: it is particularly tough to home in on what exactly creativity and artistry actually are (as the furor that Ken Russell's films provoked attest), let alone figure out how we might quantify or qualify the labor this production consumes. As Ann K. Peters and Muriel G. Cantor point out in one of the few analyses of acting-as-work, the standards by which competence is judged are hazy.[35] The same is true of popular music, which seems to deliberately uphold few stable scientific or objective means of determining quality through time. Obviously, there are various modes of training available in both music and acting and practice is all but essential, but none of these are as crucial to success as they are for, say, an architect or a nurse to engage in their professions; they are not necessary *qualifications* as they are for these other jobs. No wonder that performers often fall back on more recognizably respected ways of working, be it hard effort (like

Daniel Day-Lewis's involved and researched characterizations and James Brown's vigorous workouts) or moral and political activism (Bono and Sean Penn distinguish themselves in this regard). All of these people *earn* their status through an extension of their labor beyond the more nebulous meritocracies of performance.

But the love of (and consumer investment in) creativity is also often bound up in the belief that true art comes from somewhere intangible: from "above" or "within." What is more, this lack of clarity conveniently allows fans the scope to fantasize their own suitability for the job and to partake of the democratic insinuations embedded within these art forms, which is fine if this is the future of our economy, in production as well as consumption terms.[36] Creative skill can also be complicit in these ideals: technique is often obscured for the sake of creating an atmosphere of magic.

Frequently, and especially as far as the mismatch is concerned, the failure to erase this work is the point at which animosity can set in. The inappropriate cross-over stars make it baldly obvious that they cannot act, which undoes the spell that films purport to weave. The delirious mystery of magnetism for which so many audiences long, the kind that provokes the hagiographies dedicated to their musical oeuvre, fades away, and we see the bare machinery of entertainment hegemony incarnate in the badly constructed commodity. Here, we confront "the myth," as defined by Adorno and Horkheimer, unraveling. That we should see creativity attaining a lowlier level of accomplishment than its more euphoric upper possibilities is distressing or irritating to many audience members.

I would argue, then, that cross-over stars are popular figures of hate because they allow for a belief in the more transcendental elements of stardom that can, paradoxically, coexist with the need for laying down rules about quality of labor. By articulating standards in the negative, these judgments do not topple attainments in the higher realms of creativity. Without destroying the abstracted and fetishizable characteristics of artistic output (and I mean that in the Marxian sense most particularly), the *value* of successful creativity can be left suitably immeasurable so that it remains a viable ware in the competitive global marketplace. At the same time, as I have illuminated, there are moves afoot to expand this sphere, to train increasing amounts of producers according to specific postindustrial regimes.

In trying to ascertain how strategic growth without the loss of allure might be achieved and what the role of the cross-over mismatch might be in this equation, it seems pertinent to turn to the writing of Zygmunt Bauman, particularly his book *Modernity and Ambivalence*. A logical descendant of the dialectical tradition, but diverting from the possibilities Derrida presents with the "undecideable," Bauman focuses pessimistically on practices of semantic con-formity, the kind that fling performances such as Jagger's and Madonna's outside the realms of acceptable work. Bauman offers a model of analysis which is more apt for marking out how and why destructive operations are so frequently carried out on the dialectical forces of the mismatch. It is worth clarifying straight away that Bauman's case studies usually derive from investi-gations into Jewish history of the modern period, and they are thus, at first glance, dissimilar in character from my own musical and cinematic examples, their historical situation, and my fascination with practices of labor.[37] That said, there is much in the methodological premises of his book that can inform a reading of film-music that doesn't work.

Most important, the outcome of modernity's fragmentations and alienat-ing social structures (ones that are very much still in play), Bauman argues, is the urge to *identify* the resulting flotsam. He insists that, to do this, we draw upon language's function of setting things apart from one another, making them dis-tinct, and, ultimately, allowing them to assuage in us a sense of security through classification and semantic stability. Note the desire to peg Madonna's acting in these two reviews:

> Ah, a moral dilemma. How to describe the complete and utter
> wretchedness of Madonna's "Swept Away" without somehow imply-
> ing that it is somehow campy, ludicrous fun. It is not fun. It is, how-
> ever, bad. In fact, new ways of describing badness need to be invented
> to describe exactly how bad it is.[38]

> If it were only just a little worse, "Swept Away" could have been a
> so-bad-it's-good classic on the order of "Showgirls." But even camp
> status eludes this tepid and misguided picture, with Madonna as a
> nasty, rich control freak who gets her comeuppance when she is
> washed up on a deserted island with an Italian fisherman.[39]

The act of judgment evident in all of these journalistic offensives against *Freejack* and *Swept Away* is a means of staking out the limits of acceptability without truly engaging with the potential of "otherness" they embody. Instead, "new ways of describing badness need to be invented," a legacy of modern-age processes that seemingly linger in the postindustrial one. This tendency burrows into all manner of stratifications of labor, particularly the methods and markers of skill acquisition, in which creativity is evidently dangerously lacking. As Stan Godlovitch highlights in his philosophical investigations of performance:

[S]kill attributions are normative. Considered normatively, there has to be an acknowledged value or point in overcoming the challenge. Otherwise, no one would be prompted to praise let alone try to acquire any skill. To recognize that value, one need not accept it as one's own. Still, one must acknowledge that something is a challenge to those for whom overcoming hindrances to achieving it has positive interest.[40]

And what more authoritative voice to officially condone this compartmentalizing of artistic labor than that of government itself?

Muddying these fleetingly lucid waters of linguistic, critical, and commodity clarity, however, are actions that result in ambivalence, a state with which cross-over performances sometimes threaten us, precisely because, as we shall see, they leap straight in with a conflicting sense of how entertainment labor should be undertaken. Early in his book, Bauman draws attention to the origins, prevalence, and impact of this state:

Ambivalence, the possibility of assigning an object or an event to more than one category, is a language-specific disorder: a failure of the naming (segregating) function that language is meant to perform. The main symptom of disorder is the acute discomfort we feel when we are unable to read the situation properly and to choose between alternative actions. . . . The typically modern practice, the substance of modern politics, of modern intellect, of modern life, is the effort to exterminate ambivalence: an effort to define precisely—and . . . suppress or eliminate everything that could not or would not be precisely defined. Modern practice is not aimed at the conquest of foreign lands, but at the filling of the blank spots in the *compleat mappa mundi*. It is the modern practice, not nature, that truly suffers no void.[41]

Ambivalence, which is brought about by something falling into more than one category rather than none at all, has much to say about the split personality of the film-music mismatch. Ultimately, any such conflicted entity destabilizes our sense of steadfastness, creating splinters in the smooth and ordered domain of meaning. These, in turn, produce a type of instability and cultural anxiety aroused by a lack of taxonomic control, a condition anathema to the post-Enlightenment world, Bauman professes, although without recourse to how indescribably fabulous performances might exceed this matrix if it is *profitable* for them to do so.

Where Bauman's understanding of ambivalence parts company with similar strategies for the proliferation of meaning (ones such as polysemy and *aporia* or any of Derrida's notions of the "in between") is in its distinct sense of opposites existing together, rather than disassembling the construction of difference. It is in this dimension of his thinking that Bauman's ideas bear a thorough applicability to film-music alliances that don't work. The *ambi-* in ambivalence, after all, means *both,* each factor remaining to some extent discrete, pointing out or propping up an old order, the choice of action being paramount here. This is not a confusion or, more usually, a creation of something *unheimlich* or radically deconstructive, but a vacillation between coherent entities, such as those of two clearly identifiable entertainment industries or those of, say, the popular musical Madonna and the unwelcome cinematic one. Under these rubrics, and with two (at the very least) articulate and educated voices speaking at once—those of "film" and those of "music"—it is entirely possible that the semantics of the composite objects of my case studies might be jumbled and clashing, might tell us contradictory stories, might provoke a strange form of ambivalence that many find impossible not to inhibit. Labeling and classification still hold court and rule out any more diffused hermeneutic possibilities. Moreover, they do so in manners that unceasingly toe the line of various current modes of postindustrial work.

The Condemnation of Inflexibility

There is a lot to be drawn from Mark Kermode and Trevor Johnston's remark about Jagger's "unintentionally hilarious performance."[42] Here, they highlight the star's hubris, his inability to squeeze himself into the strict categories of being that Bauman feels are omnipresent or to adapt to his new environment. What is so displeasing about Jagger's inability to win over his audience in *Freejack* is that his supposedly abundant and dependable charisma is seen to be in shorter reserves than many viewers imagined and does not grant him indefinite immunity to mucking in with the *work* of acting. For me, responses like Kermode and Johnston's not only express broad disapproval of the performer's insufficient humility, they can also be seen to tap into current concerns about professional skill requirements or, rather, their management under the formulas of what are now dubbed "flexibility" and "multiskilling."

As has been noted, many corporations now outsource to smaller companies whose costs and profits they can squeeze in a climate of competition. In certain quarters of economic scholarship, "flexible specialization"[43] is beginning to replace the less exacting term post-Fordism. According to Michael Piore and Charles Sabel, who were some of the first authors to coin the term:

> Flexible specialization is a strategy of permanent innovation: accommodation to ceaseless change, rather than an effort to control it. This strategy is based on flexible—multi-use—equipment; skilled workers; and the creation, through politics, of an industrial community that restricts the forms of competition to those favoring innovation.[44]

Flexibility of these orders appears to be a prime means of coping with the openness of global market competition, where other workers will easily take your place (and for less money, often) and where there is little choice but to accept short-term and unreliable contracts because capital is, by and large, more mobile than the worker. In the eyes of its proponents, flexible specialization opens up opportunities for smaller companies to gain more significant positions within the market by producing effectively and profitably on smaller scales. Companies themselves must be flexible, in that, for instance, they must be able to find the appropriate "periphery" workers to complete whatever task is demanded for the price, and so too must workers. The general ethic is one of suppleness in every limb of production and the ability to imaginatively cut costs at short notice.[45]

Multitasking, then, is a necessary facility of many an employee living in the hope of maintaining work in the face of lean production, easy disposability, and global competition. With this mode of work dominating the public psyche, if not the totality of lived experience, the stress falls upon cultivating the ability to reorganize where, when, and how one works and acquiring the requisite new skills to keep abreast of the competition. Are these not the standards by which Mick Jagger and Madonna are judged? Again, Bauman's ambivalence is useful here because it lays the stress on how complicated and challenging to conventions it is to personify more than one value if they happen to mutually exclude each other. Ambivalence comes to the fore when close attention is paid to the acting techniques both musicians employ.

Most prominent in the factors that mean that Jagger's performance doesn't work is the slipping and sliding of his accent across the Atlantic: very rarely do natives of Kent say "asshole" without the British *r* as a second letter. Inaccurate accents are high on the checklist of how to spot inadequately realist acting: Keanu Reeves fell foul as an unconvincing Englishman in *Bram Stoker's Dracula* (Francis Ford Coppola, 1992),[46] while, at her peak, Meryl Streep received much praise for her acute sense of hearing and vocal precision. However, the mid-Atlantic accent does uphold conventions of pop delivery, so this is not purely an instance of technical inability, although, crucially, this is exactly how it comes across within the cinematic context. It is particularly common for British pop musicians to sing in American accents, a tradition which Jagger himself helped to establish and which is thus, in *Freejack,* another definite, if not deliberate, throwback to his pop identity. Likewise, his overemphatic diction throughout this film and many of his others is somewhat misplaced and distinctly more suited to the projection techniques that are vital to performing in stadiums.

On various fronts, one would not necessarily imagine that Madonna would struggle so as a film-music multitasker. The facility with which she has used Hollywood iconography as a template for loosening the shackles of musical star inscription, for adding an often-lost performativity to the work of musical creativity, would seem a fine recommendation to any casting agent. In her earlier career especially, we witnessed allusions to *Gentlemen Prefer Blondes* (Howard Hawks, 1953) in the "Material Girl" video and to *Metropolis* (Fritz Lang, 1927) in the "Express Yourself" one, while, throughout that period, critics and academics alike seemed keener to compare her to film stars, particularly Marilyn Monroe, and to discuss her visual presentation, rather than to engage with her music. However, where these filmic quotations deviate from cinema proper is in the fact that a sustained narrative is never truly invoked nor followed through and herein, perhaps, lie many of the "mistakes" that are made by the cross-over star.

The disjunction in working practices arises from the fact that popular music's ways of creating meaning are largely resistant to prolonged and teleological storytelling. Formal meaning within many musical genres is, for the most part, constructed out of A, B, and C units with A and B repeated at least once. Unlike film, the pop song does not conventionally travel down a one-way narrative path, and the acting style to which pop stars are the most accustomed is the type required for music videos. Digressing from the mainstays of narrative realism, promo performance techniques must withstand rapid-fire editing and thematic lurches (those that mark the shift from verse to chorus, for instance). Meanings, despite often invoking the filmic, are much more instantaneous and diffuse, rather than cumulative, and are cultivated in relation to the fact that videos are rarely shown in their entireties. Embodied and literalistic line delivery is uncommon nowadays, and the acting out of songs is considered outmoded and distinctly trite in comparison to the creation of a graspable persona that could plausibly span beyond and across a range of songs or lifestyle posturings. In *Performing Rites: Evaluating Popular Music,* Simon Frith points out:

> As video stars, pop performers have to play themselves. They are
> not acting out stories (videos are not operas). Video foregrounds the
> performance of music rather than the music itself. We don't take the

musicians to be interpreting the song; rather, our response is to interpret the musicians. Video performers are taken to be the authors of
what we see (videos are not watched as examples of either directors'
or songwriters' art [although this may have changed since the time of
Frith's writing]. . . . Pop videos, in short, foreground performance-as-
seduction and forestall performance-as-embarrassment. If nothing else
(and this relates to the long history of music photography, framing the
musician as pinup as well as stage star), video is now a key component
in our understanding of music as erotic.[47]

Given these conventions, Jagger's unwavering stares and almost pantomimic
movements are understandable. Yet, without the necessary editing rhythms to
chop up and vary such pose striking, a more sustained camera gaze gives Jagger's acting an unsubtle, hammy quality unsuited to the diversity and progression of a film's narrative. This is not to suggest that films are not pasted together
in a correspondingly, perhaps even more piecemeal fashion, but simply that the
spaces between the edits carry a different temporal mood. Similarly, the *New
York Times's* A. O. Scott argues of Madonna:

> In her concerts, music videos and recordings, Madonna has often
> been a mesmerizing performer, but she is still not much of an actress.
> Striking a pose is not the same as embodying a person, and a role like
> this one requires the surrender of emotional control, something
> Madonna seems constitutionally unable to achieve.[48]

The difference in performance styles has, as with so many other performers,
rendered Madonna accidentally impotent. Like Jagger, without the flickering
fluctuation of iconic images, her presentation quickly becomes flat and relent-
less in the framework of a cinematic narrative. In moments like these, and despite the fact that many of her "looks" are drawn from the world of film, her
poses reveal themselves to be high concepts, ideas, snapshots from publicity
flourishes, rather than displays of a mastery of characterization.

The specific nature of her usual mode of visual appearance (video), with
its quick, unexplained gear changes and about-faces, has, it appears, also been
drawn clumsily and without question into *Swept Away*. The movie's opening
mood is a parodic, almost slapstick rendition of Amber on the yacht. Once she
and Guiseppe are stranded on the island, the turn is toward a violent up-ending
of class roles, while the final act languishes in somewhat slushy romance. As a
consequence, and without the film's deliberate propping up of a multigeneric
formation, its evident short attention span is interpreted as a flaw.

Character continuity too is not something required of music videos, in fact it would seem rather unwelcome in a format that is designed to showcase several ideas in alternation. Yet at no point, as theorists such as Derrida or even Hegel would have wished, is there a breaking down of the criteria and value systems that separate these two art forms and that could make the mismatch creative or productive. Instead, a number of reviewers mention the "inevitable" interjection of a musical sequence: a lip-synched rendition of Rosemary Clooney's "Come On-a My House." Rather than enjoying this sequence, which opens with Madonna providing an amusing (some would say self-)parody of someone who really cannot sing, most journalists interpret this section as Madonna proving herself to be insignificantly qualified to stray too far from her regular profession. Similar concerns were leveled at her assumption of the title role in *Evita,* where the quality of her singing voice came under scrutiny. However, in that situation, meticulous vocal training—hard, quantifiable *work*— resulted in her surprising a good deal of the audience and critics with the caliber of her final accomplishments.

Variations like these between what does and doesn't work in both film and music lay bare, as Bauman would argue, just how closely guarded the perimeter fences encasing labor actually are within the two industries ("territories," Deleuze and Guattari would have called them). In refusing to conduct a modification in performance styles, Mick Jagger and Madonna are also clumsily tripping up amid the intricate nexus of specialization and adaptability that the cross-over star, as well as many everyday workers, must negotiate. They are both workers with proven abilities and evident commitment to hard graft (no one would call Madonna or Mick Jagger lazy or lacking in ambition), but they must sink or swim in unfamiliar waters like so many of the rest of us. Rather than opening the acceptable limits of film acting performance to incorporate these styles, an option outlined in Bauman's *Modernity and Ambivalence,* there is a need to shun the interloper in the established field of specialized knowledge. Furthermore, the acts of discrediting such mismatches are undertaken according to fairly specific standards about how to regulate "the self," and they very much tap into yet more of postindustrialism's core employment strategies.

"The Willingness to Surrender" as a Work Ethic and the Question of Emotional Labor

Freejack and *Swept Away* have been "ruined," it would appear, by unconvincing leads who swamp the team effort so crucial to enjoyable cinema, emphatically signaling the decentralized and fragmented nature of entertainment goods.

These shortcomings are rigorously inscribed, however, according to the language of individual blame. La Salle declares that Madonna "lacks the innocence of spirit, the willingness to surrender, that actors have."[49] Similarly, Ian Atkins of *Starburst* comments that, in *Freejack,* "Mick Jagger's principled bounty hunter . . . suffers mainly from being played by one of the most famous men on Earth,"[50] pointing out that he is too "Mick Jagger" to play Vacendak—or, rather, that Vacendak is not significantly "Jagger-ish" to usher all sorts of extratextual richness into the film's themes. Perhaps the most grating of these gestures is an eagerly repeated pouting mouth that is simultaneously too crass a facial shape to comply with the rules of big-screen acting and also the most obvious marker of "Mick Jagger" possible (which, elsewhere, has fortuitously enhanced his iconic visual presence).[51] In one of the few articles to address the musician-to-cinema cross-over, Ben Thompson observes, "A pop persona works in a different way from a film persona: it is *more* complete, which means it's harder to submerge and keeps popping up at the wrong moment."[52] Even popular music's most adamant chameleons (such as Lou Reed, but also Madonna) sustain their chosen colors too consistently and wholeheartedly to comply with the mutability required by realist acting, although such timing is perhaps essential for successful *musical* career building. Thus Madonna's inability to immerse herself in her character is routinely targeted, notably, like Jagger's, along the lines of whether or not we are receiving too much "Madonna" in her personification.

In addition, if at any point we were to forget that we were watching Mick Jagger in *Freejack,* then Jerry Hall (his wife at the time) is on hand to provide a knowing cameo as a TV presenter. Extratextual references like these are, of course, widespread in film acting of all types and, where musician/actors are concerned, they can often be woven into a narrative to great effect, as I have argued to be the case with *Performance.*[53] It is at moments like these that the self-contained product bursts outward into a network of other commodities, not only multiplying consumer potential, but adding greater meaning to "the film itself."[54]

The problem really lies, with *Freejack* and *Swept Away,* in the manner by which all of their errors can be understood to overwhelmingly favor *self-promotion* of a possibly egotistical bent.[55] Michael Atkinson calls *Swept Away* a "film that never asked to be made . . . an indulgent vehicle,"[56] thereby asserting the troubled response to star individualism. Here the strong notion of ego, so prized in musical stardom, is a distinct disadvantage. We are thus returned to so many of those questions, familiar from chapter 3, about what "the self" can actually be within, and how it interjects dialectically into, various forums of postindustrial professionalism. In order to grasp how various clashing conceptions of the (working) self lurk within the cross-over mismatch and to fathom why their cohabitation arouses such ire, the construction of musical personality and its relationship to work must be probed.

Mick Jagger and Madonna—however their personas might be industrially or managerially constructed—are public figures who are swathed in discourses about control, which is usually manipulated to "their" advantage and often extends into the marshaling of "their" more filmic dimensions.[57] This desire for consistency reveals how a work ethic might affirm power, but also morality.

Musical personas, especially within the more revered genres of popular music such as blues, jazz, rock, and hip-hop, are built upon philosophies of personal integrity, of staying close to one's roots, binding one's innermost feelings to one's work, and refusing to be party to anything which is thought to be untrue to oneself (which would also include such things as miming on stage). This ideal is central to the image of one of my two chosen cross-over stars, Mick Jagger: he is always "himself," regardless of the dictates of "appropriate" behavior for his age. Conversely, many successful actors work hard to point out the discrepancies between on-screen roles and off-screen self, precisely because such variance emphasizes the acting skills involved in morphing between the two. Certainly, there are pop stars who work in more collaborative or consciously "artificial" ways, but, so strong is the image of the "authentic artist" that musicians of this latter variant are constantly being asked to defend themselves against such accusations or to admit their inferiority as "manufactured" entities.

Jagger is not alone in his crafting of a public front. Since at least the 1960s, and this will come as no surprise considering the historical shifts I have outlined throughout this book, certain types of musicians have felt an even greater duty than screen stars to bond their performance personalities to their off-stage activities.[58] The Romantic ideal of artistic material perfectly corresponding to a unique personal creativity, preferably one which endures suffering, is a central bulwark to rock music stardom. This reflects the infusive properties of the rock (and Romantic) tradition familiar from chapter 3; one's oeuvre is less a body of artistic material and more a way of life than most mainstream cinema has ever dreamed of.[59]

It is not hard to see why this trope of artistry has remained prominent. Living in a world where there are no guarantees of permanent contracts, no routine company pensions or sick benefits, and very little sense of social protection, it is easy to understand how the musician has clung to her or his own isolated self, emboldening it, pitching it outward as marked by and as a marker of both art and the larger anxieties from which we all suffer, not least the sense of isolation from the greater social body. Workers are now, more than ever before within the postindustrial period, additionally decentralized in terms of career longevity. By 2001, the average American was switching jobs every 3.5 years, with workers in their twenties moving on every 1.1 years.[60] *The Corrosion of Character*, Richard Sennett's study of the emotional impact of the "new capitalism," clarifies, "Today, a young American with at least two years of college can expect to change jobs at least eleven times in the course of working, and change his or her skill base at least three times during those forty years of labor."[61] A sense of duty steering one's career has been more thoroughly replaced by a blurrier responsibility to earn the money to survive, in whatever field. The *vocation* has shrunk into the shadows to a certain extent.[62] Without this sense of purpose, this exceptional bond between employee and employment, it comes as little surprise that the role of an artist such as Mick Jagger is envied. Within this ideal, workers are driven by their crafts in seemingly positive, even socially beneficial ways; their identities are indelibly marked by what they do and vice versa.

Yet, in many an unsuccessful cross-over, these ideas are debilitated, parceled off as mismatches by the conventions of film acting. Castigation mutes any serious discussion of whether, in a growing creative economy, the Romantic stance is elitist, detrimental to the common good, or achievable on a mass scale. In addition, the ostracism of a supposedly more flexible acting persona from a "truer" musical one diminishes the political negotiations and expansions that a more dialectical interchange would afford. At what point can we distinguish the person from the machinery that helps shape the star and what might our fascination with solo figures, rather than apparatus, reveal about the stratification and fragmentation of labor according to the doctrines of individualism?

A musician's public personality cannot sincerely hold itself up to be some sort of coherent and unmediated essentialist self; it is surely as fabricated a role as any other and just as prone to external contributions, not least as a result of the corporate work undergone on it in order to create profit. Being, as well as acting, in the domain of entertainment is also heavily laced with what Marx would call the "effacement of labor." A divergence between these two actions, so often underplayed by the entertainment industries, is particularly glaring in the case of the lackluster cross-over star; the precariousness of human capital becomes apparent. In this instance, being is not enough, except for the most forgiving of fans.[63] In not having completed their expected actorly duties, the musician reminds us that, while watching movies, we are paying for a service, a job of work (albeit recorded), and a neatly packaged commodity fetish. These stars are definitely exuding effort, but their endeavors are incorrectly positioned within their new realm. Consequently, what they achieve comes across as either lazy or inept; neither of which, it seems, can be tolerated by audiences.

As a retort, cinema is often claimed to be staid. To appear in a movie (at least, a mainstream one) may even be tantamount to "selling out," and "selling" is central to this philosophy, which strangely sees music production as anti-capitalist and which mocks or pities musicians who dance between formats to the tune of a ringing cash register. The most precious case study and cautionary tale for advocates of such ideas is one that I have already sketched out: the artistically imprisoned Elvis Presley desperate to break free from the meaninglessness of movie making in order to do what really mattered, recording music.

While the mechanisms of both entertainment industries create questions of star control due to their fragmented means of production, music has a much more central history of critiquing such systems, even downplaying their existence. Indeed, open hostility to such modes of manufacture is pervasive in rock music, propounded not only in such things as interviews, but also in song lyrics themselves. This stance is regularly adopted regardless of the concurrent compatibility between consumer capitalism and the kinds of Romantic individualism that rock holds so dear, and perhaps as a validation of something that is strategic to and purposefully distracting from more macro-economic concerns. Ironically, corporations are well aware of the selling power of such ideals and have aided their inscription, including the struggle against that very same system in the rule books of rock. These negotiations are constantly being played out by our idols, whether the denouement is the success of a profitable and fulfilling set of public transactions or the psychological tragedy of a star's abject inability to accept such objectification (Kurt Cobain and Frances Farmer come to mind). In other words, those stars whom we hold in contempt for selling out reveal much about our own anxieties about managing our ethics and individual beliefs in the workplace. Mismatches disclose more fully, I would therefore argue, how musicians, like film stars, balance upon a knife edge between autonomy (they are seen as the primary site of what is produced in their name) and becoming commodities (selling out, compromising, essentially becoming something that is traded, rather than "just themselves").[64]

It is not hard to discern why shorter terms of employment, the resulting competition, the spatial fragmentation of workers, subcontracting practices, and the desperate need for the individual to network hoist a greater weight onto the concept of the self-as-commodity. Nor does it require a great leap of imagination to understand how the star provides a certain insight into this understanding of the self within what Charles Leadbeater has called the thin-air marketplace: he or she is both a worker and the simulacrum of, or intimate connection to, the created persona that is sold to us as a group of commodities. Here, the individual is factored into the rules of capitalist exchange in very particular and involved ways: the stars' constant touting of their own physical and psychological beings is an extreme variant of the selling of ourselves (including selling ourselves out) that is such a common feeling on the job market. The distance between identity and the commodity is distinctly muddled.

The separation between working and being in these instances and beyond is in no way a static arrangement. At present, such dilemmas can be seen to dovetail into certain corporate ploys for decreasing the particular sense of alienation provoked by the working conditions of postindustrialism. One of the more recent strategies, in some fields at least, is for bosses to niftily try to overcome the (unproductive) sense of dislocation experienced by workers by encouraging them to invest *at the level of personal development* in their company. Certain prevalent types of management coax from their workers more emotional investment, as well as more time, than was the norm in the Fordist environment by using the language of self-fulfillment and purpose.[65] Ultimately, desires for increased productivity exploit a deep psychological urge in many workers to belong, to be meaningful, to attain personal goals of many kinds, to be respected as individuals, and to see a greater correlation between what they do and who they "are." Again, the formation of this strange and fluctuating amalgam is clearly apparent in the working lives of entertainers. Sociologist Paul du Gay's *Consumption and Identity at Work* elucidates this fairly new shift in how the self has been reformatted within the workplace:

> [T]he effects of dislocation require constant "creativity," and the continuous construction of collective operational space that rests less on inherited objective forms (bureaucracy) and more on *cultural* reconstruction. Thus "new wave management" is concerned with changing people's values, norms and attitudes so that they make the "right" and necessary contribution to the success of the organization for which they work. To this end, excellence [a more specific reworking of the term with roots in Thatcherite enterprise initiatives] encourages managers to view the most effective and excellent organizations as those with "strong cultures"—patterns of meaning which enable all members of an organization to *identify* with the goals and objectives of the company for which they work. According to Deleuze, among others, the corporation only becomes "cultural"—develops a "soul"— once "the market" has achieved a position of pre-eminence. The discourse of excellence is therefore both symptom and effect of the increasing de-differentiation of economy and culture. As Jameson has argued, the colonization of culture by the market does not imply the

disappearance or extinction of the cultural; rather, it suggests a situation in which "the corporate is now at one with culture."[66]

Nikolas Rose in *Governing the Soul: The Shaping of the Private Self* adds another dimension to this:

> The worker is portrayed neither as an economic actor, rationally pursuing financial advantage, nor as a social creature seeking satisfaction of needs for solidarity and security. The worker is an individual in search of meaning, responsibility, a sense of personal achievement, a maximized "quality of life," and hence of work. Thus the individual is not to be emancipated *from* work, perceived as merely a task or a means to an end, but to be fulfilled *in* work, now construed as an activity through which we produce, discover, and experience ourselves.[67]

All of these developments must be understood in the light of a concomitant waning in the power of trade unions,[68] the rendition of unions into service providers rather than representative bodies, and the disincentives of expensive union membership for small and medium enterprises and more peripheral self-employed and part-time workers. It is becoming harder and harder to challenge job insecurity through collective industrial action. Arguably, the cause of these ills of alienation then offers itself as a placebo cure that has acknowledged benefits for many who take it, but not least those profiting from workers' labor.

Part and parcel of this renovated placement of the self is the encouragement toward "emotional labor," "the new industrial relations," and "human resource management."[69] Unlike the collective and social rhetoric of old-style unionism, the emphasis is individualist and psychological. The decline of the command economy opens up a greater need for self-regulation, even embodied and personally policed docility, which is then, in these instances, wrapped up in the languages of holism and emotive involvement.[70] Could "empowerment" and "fulfillment" have more complex undertones, with sensitivity functioning more as a commodity than as a route to ultimate employee well-being? The procedures of emotional labor are often not only central to how the service industries function, to the point where one does not only hide one's feelings in order to seem enthusiastic and caring, even when one is not that way inclined, but one is also encouraged to *believe* in the power structures and ideas that are embodied within and promote these sentiments.

Actors and musicians also share in these kinds of fabrications. Even if the experience they relay does not reflect the life of the performer, they make constant allusions to the extent to which they identify with how the type being played or how the audience (ordinary people at large, whom they do not know) feel. Unsuccessful cross-over stars, on the other hand, both fail to subsume their identities into their work and fall short of the upper limits of du Gay's understanding of corporate culture. They are just plainly and statically "themselves," having not embarked upon the journey of self-expansion that acting and contemporary management projects alike prescribe.

What is worse, they sometimes let slip more noisome versions of themselves. In the responses to *Swept Away,* the singer is upbraided for allowing the "wrong" Madonna to emerge and perhaps for endangering a more glowing general impression we might have of her. As Manohla Dargis argues in the *Los Angeles Times:*

> It seems no coincidence that the character comes across as an uglier version of the pop goddess, a kind of fantasy of what we all think we know about the star. It is, to put it mildly, a bewildering strategy. . . . she's done herself no favors with her choice of material. . . . the woman is debased from the start.[71]

In a comparable spirit, Mick La Salle continues:

> This might seem ideal casting for Madonna, who's known to be impatient and exacting, but in a comedy—which I think this is—it's usually better to have someone who's not the type play the type. That way, the actress has distance enough to understand what makes the type ridiculous. In "Swept Away," we know from the beginning that Amber is repellent, but we can never be sure whether the actress or the filmmaker know it. They may simply think that she's an attractive person who's just behaving badly.[72]

True to many caricatures of Madonna, Amber flies into a rage when she finds that the boat is not equipped with a gym. She is also drawn as a pampered wife, entirely dependent on her husband's wealth, arrogant about the poor, and, ultimately, indolent and unskilled.[73] In terms of Madonna's relationship to labor, the narrative reaffirms some of the more negative attributes that are projected onto successful entertainers. In the well-received *Desperately Seeking Susan,* Madonna helps to rescue the character of Roberta (Rosanna Arquette) from the tedium of such an unfulfilling moneyed life by enticing her into a more bohemian existence where one survives more off one's wits. Contrastingly, in this role, Madonna projects confusing information about her relationship to work and money. The idea that Madonna could not cope if marooned on a deserted island is not what many people, wary of her increased decadence over the years (at their expense), might wish to see, even in a fiction film.

As well as displaying aspects of "Madonna" that may graze too close to the bone, *Swept Away* also imbues her with characteristics that do not sit comfortably within her star persona. In the second act, Amber endures a great deal of violence, including near-rape, from the newly powerful Guiseppe. Furthermore, Ritchie's excited and amused commentary upon these scenes on the DVD extras package clearly indicates, to some degree, his enjoyment of this treatment of his wife. Displaced and artistically abstracted domestic violence, if we care to read it in this way, does not sit well with Madonna's usual construction as a strident and authoritative woman.[74] She is tied up in the double bind of having relinquished both not enough and too much control in the eyes of her public, a true dilemma for so many other workers whose individual creativity is their commodity these days, but who must yield to a larger organizational agenda.

The Working Day (and Night): Careers and Their Encroachment upon the Private Sphere

The recent managerial strategies that try to persuade us to discover ourselves through work as well as, and perhaps more important, to better ourselves as a by-product of heaping market value upon ourselves also abet the disintegration of the boundaries between work and off-duty periods, including free time. Such conditions similarly plague the self-employed worker, who must absorb the climate of competition by putting in more and more hours.[75] According to the June 2006 *Labour Market Trends,* Britons are now dedicating larger than ever amounts of time to their jobs.[76] Within the last few decades, the rise of flexible work has swallowed up much of what would have traditionally been described, at least in middle- and much working-class twentieth-century terms, as "time off." So too has the rise of career building in the cultural and leisure industries.

On one level, the musician who has not been formally trained to act, who has not had the *time* to sufficiently adapt to the new work environment, is effectively adopting the role of the uneasy freelancer many of us feel ourselves to be. Madonna's inability to come to grips with the right register of performance is, perhaps, a result of *Swept Away*'s brief shooting period of a mere five and a half weeks. This, it seems, was insufficient training time for a less prepared actor, and it also speaks of Madonna's busy schedule: she is punished for spreading herself too thinly, as are so many of life's multitaskers. On another level, though, she is reprimanded for upholding any such distinctions in how she administers herself across the working and being dichotomy. Here her disjointed performance impairs the clustering together and overlapping of culture, work (which, as Paul du Gay has pointed out, is often referred to as "work culture" in human-resources-speak), entertainment, and traditionally private-sphere thoughts, dreams, and activities.

A similar swamping of the work-leisure distinction is infringing upon many people's ordering of their time and is to their detriment, say, if their increased productivity is driven by anxiety over whether they will be reemployed. But much more glamorous variants of these circumstances can be spotted within the entertainment industries. This increasing intrusion of the working life into the so-called private one (the psyche and so on) functions most smoothly when "being oneself" is one's job, as it is, for instance, in the rock star myth, where self (as opposed to social) alienation is not thought to emerge so readily. The breach is at its worst when one feels one is flooded with work at all hours of the day and in every degree of one's conventionally private thoughts and actions, when the schism between self and estranging work is more fully apparent, as it is in the ill preparedness of these pop stars on screen.

Given the economic and demographic turn toward culture, it is imperative that we examine the management of *creative* time. Noting the impact of this state of affairs, Sylvère Lotringer, in his introduction to Paolo Virno's *A Grammar of the Multitude: For an Analysis of Contemporary Forms of Life,* argues that we are now complicit in a wholly different mode of production:

> In the post-Fordist economy, surplus value is no longer extracted
> from labor materialized in a product, it resides in the discrepancy between paid and unpaid work—the idle time of the mind that keeps
> enriching, unacknowledged, the fruits of immaterial labor. . . . The
> multitude is a force defined less by what it actually produces than by
> its virtuosity, its *potential* to produce *and* produce itself. So is it really a
> gain over what existed before? Workers used to work in servile conditions, leaving them just enough time to replenish. Now their entire
> life is live labor, an invisible and indivisible commodity.[77]

In collusion with this statement, modes of work like creativity are notoriously difficult to temporally quantify, so dependent are they on a diffuse set of activities such as experience and contemplation. Since (at least) the ideals of Romanticism were established, the work of the artist has been distinct from much other regulated, timed labors, ones which are now catching up with its tenets in their own way. The blurriness of this particular work input is treated with generosity. So long as artists are ingenious and excel at what they do, in the very vaguest of ever-changing terms, then they are often let loose to manage their time as they please, to "be themselves" more.

The consistency of, for example, the musician's persona highlights how relatively recent, and perhaps how linked to industrial capitalist inscriptions of labor and leisure, are the concepts of being on- and off-duty. While movie actors are often at pains to disentangle themselves from the limited, iconic values for which they stand on screen, musicians are under a certain amount of pressure to "be themselves," to live out their rock 'n' roll-ness beyond the realms of the 9-to-5. Although such jobs are residual legacies of all-encompassing vocations of the past, like the court composer or the wandering minstrel, they are also widely enviable in a current climate where there is, as Angela McRobbie observes, an "encroachment of work into every corner of everyday life, including 'flexible' working at home, 'sociable' working in cafés with plug-in points for laptops, and mobile working from indeterminate 'non-places.'"[78] That leisure and labor could be indistinguishable, that one would *choose* to be working hard because the job is so fulfilling in itself, is a common fantasy when overtime is more an inevitable encroachment of an increasingly unregulated postindustrial corporate buyers' market. To always be at work, but for those activities to incorporate decadence and creativity, is certainly central to why so many people dream of stardom.

A career in music is also much coveted perhaps because it is not always so explicitly concerned with money making. In *Making Popular Music: Musicians, Creativity and Institutions,* one of the few investigations of creative labor in this field, Jason Toynbee observes:

[The surfeit of labour in the music industry] also complicates the recruitment of musical labour. In popular music, unlike the other cultural industries, there is a field of production which remains unassimilable to the firm and its regularized disciplines of accumulation. Instead of being subsumed under corporate control, the development of new forms (that is, of popular music to come) takes place in a series of "proto-markets" which are poorly connected to the capital intensive sectors of packaging, distribution and the exploitation of rights. What distinguishes proto-markets is that they bring together performer and audience in arenas which are not fully commodified. . . . the defining

characteristic of the proto-market is that the level of activity cannot
be explained by economic factors alone. . . . there is a high degree of
ambivalence towards the industry. In many cases success is equated
with "selling out."[79]

Yet, bundled in with an understanding of self-management is the enforcement
of more dispersed incarnations of spatial, temporal, technological, and economic organization according to the flexible labor model. Technologies, for
those who can afford them, enable greater instances of "remote" labor, and this
goes for film and music making too. Working from home is on the rise again
after the twentieth century's shift toward centralized spaces of employment.
Like the entertainment industries, the pool of decentralized and self-employed
or itinerant contract workers is unimaginably vast and disposable, assuming,
at the same time, more of the burdens of self-preservation (like pensions, for
instance) itself. Mapping this outsourcing presents us with a reenergized model
of decentralization, one that takes full advantage of the privatized realm of the
worker's home—or the "dynamic work-live environment" as real estate agents
are often wont to term it—to shrivel its overhead. Again, the burden of cost is
placed upon the workers, who must frequently buy their own equipment or
at least pay their own utility bills, and, once more, it is easy to strike parallels
with the world of entertainment. Musicians, after all, cannot truly set up within
the profession without buying their own instruments or finding locations in
which to compose and rehearse, which are often bedrooms and other domestic spaces.

Again, we are presented with a model for acquiring expertise from entertainment culture that is gaining precedence elsewhere. Given the mobility of
capital and the global wealth of employees, there has been little incentive for
employers to train staff; instead, the onus is on workers to pay for reeducation
independently in terms of both time and money. This has been supported by
such schemes as Britain's individual learning accounts of the early 2000s, which
placed the responsibility for instruction, evolution, and even self-management
on the workers themselves. Certainly a more flexible approach to work allows
for such things as child care, yet, simultaneously, there has been a deleterious
impact in terms of a rise in anxiety-related health disorders.[80]

Divergences like these, where one subset of the service industry enjoys a
totally different relationship to time and working conditions from those of
another (media stardom), expose the utter inequality of postindustrial labor,
prompting many of the rancorous attitudes that are leveled against failed cross-
over artists.

Nepotism and Derision: Coping with the Injustices
of Creative and Postindustrial Labor

One of the most unmistakable sentiments in the criticism of these films is their disclosure of the corrupt working practices that afford enormous opportunities to only a relative few. The decentralized set-up of postindustrial employment here unveils its discriminatory character. The collaboration between the famous husband-and-wife team that brought *Swept Away* into being incited considerable amounts of negative press of a singularly personal nature, a healthy proportion of it incensed by Madonna's puffed-up self-belief, inflated by the opportunities opened up by her financial and marital status.[81] The possible nepotism—or, perhaps, arm twisting—of such an arrangement clearly irritated many viewers because similarly discriminating decisions are made to the detriment of the majority of us in our working lives, and our sense of fair play is upset when we see something similar happen in the world of entertainment. With films like *Swept Away,* there is something oddly fulfilling about the (admittedly very limited) democratic power that can be exercised by critics and ticket buyers to prove such performers wrong. As James Cameron-Wilson crowed in *Film Review:* "[Guy Ritchie] was heard to say that the combination of his talent and his wife's celebrity virtually guaranteed '£10 million worth of press.' Well, *Swept Away* has garnered plenty of press, but audiences have been staying away in droves, swept away by virulent reviews."[82] Not only is there a craving to see the cross-over star fail, but there is a distinct pleasure in being a willing participant in Madonna and Ritchie's momentary downfall. The uneasy tension between opportunity and bias becomes stark in these mismatches; the negotiations made by cross-over stars who fail in their roles illuminate the injustices of such set-ups.

Within the context of the competitive labor markets and uncomfortable projections of the self into the spaces of work that I have outlined, the ultimate frustrated question arises: why were *these* people hired in the first place? What sleights of selective hands glide through entertainment, and how might they ruin the chances of pure, bright talent coming to the fore from among the mass of hopefuls and capables? At the very least, and even this outrages many a viewer, market conservatism through its banking on known faces overrules professional standards.

The decision to hire figures like Jagger and Madonna undermines the classless wealth, the potential for access, that P. David Marshall in *Celebrity and Power: Fame in Contemporary Culture* observes as one of the draws of the star image.[83] While there is fabulous wealth for the few, and uncertainty, financial worry, and drudgery for the vast majority, the glamorous existence one could *potentially* assume makes the dream worth chasing. It is fruitful to lock this sensibility onto what media sociologist Angela McRobbie (inspired by Jock Young) terms a "lottery economy" because McRobbie sees this very same offsetting of inequality with "democracy" in an ever-increasing array of careers:

> As social groups and communities seem to disperse and give way to more atomized biographies, so also do individualized pathways become more culturally resonant. While in the past the idea of rags to riches was never anything more than a delicious popular fantasy, the very stuff of Hollywood dreams, now in what has been described as a lottery economy characterized by the "chaos of reward" (Young, [*The Exclusive Society*], 1999), the systemic features of class, gender and ethnicity, as they have become less stable, are pushed further into the political background as populist and "feelgood" ideas of chance, good or bad fortune, the contingency of occasion and the value of individual effort are taken to be more reliable indicators of achievement. These ideas pulsate through the entire cultural fabric, but they are so dispersed, without any apparent attachment to a central node, that their power and impact are easily overlooked.[84]

Jo Littler points out that this sense of meritocracy has particularly strong links to recent Bushite and Blairite policies where (in Britain) an old Left-style struggle for egalitarianism has all but been replaced by more vaporous promotions of "equal opportunities."[85] The aim is to convince us that there are no rules and that anyone can make it, but is this just a set of bywords masking a reluctance to institute such things as equality legislation, a handy disclaimer matched around the world by the mobilized and thus more elusive practices of so many commercial businesses in the face of hungry competition? Littler argues that these ideals simultaneously support competition and rely on neither the security of a welfare state, nor the massive investment in education and innovation that Charles Leadbeater has advocated to government as a means of achieving a functional thin-air economy.

Cross-over performers impair the ways in which these conflicting practices and beliefs can be brought into alignment without destroying each other; they discredit the skill of pure celebrity while also pointing out the injustices of film casting. The faith placed in the seemingly democratic structures of both entertainment professions is grossly undermined when we see stars shifting unfairly and effortlessly (although more effort would certainly be appreciated in their craft) from one art form to another. Perhaps most aggravating for the viewers who take up the critique is the fact that large amounts of money are shoveled into the hands of performers on whom we have problems pinning exact value.

Failed cross-overs, though, are a particularly conformist siphon for any ill feeling provoked by such machinations. Letdowns like cross-over stars allow for a forthright and indignant stance to be taken on something which is actually much more intricate and expansive. When lurid fascination is taken in their inferior work, a rather retrogressive division of labor is created in an arena where talent fluctuates, jobs' criteria cannot be pinned down, and ultimate worth is indistinct. The urge for exactitude, of which I have been wary throughout this book, reemerges in another guise: a particular understanding of merit is accepted, but only through the classification of what *doesn't* fit the bill. Ultimately, pop singers who "can't act" help to justify the salaries of big-name movie stars, leaving intact the ever-so-vague systems of value that allow riches to be drawn from an abstract thin-air economy. The modes of ascent are obscured, but the route downward is all too clearly marked. When musicians are incompetent within films and when actors who try to launch singing careers flop, they help to reinforce just enough of a comforting and explainable set of job descriptions to assuage the sense of uncertainty that Bauman has elucidated.

What is striking about the censure of the substandard cross-over performer is that it represents little action on the part of "the people" to initiate transformation from the ambivalent or dialectical positioning of film music or, more important, through it, to see the potential for change in the renegotiations that are constantly taking place within the worlds of work. Obviously, in contradiction to the haven of unity and wholeness that is promised by certain business cultures, there is a simultaneous emphasis in many jobs on competition, which is readily advocated in outsourced and freelance contract work, in corporations themselves, and, of course, in the hierarchies of entertainment labor. Such struggles and rivalries boost our enjoyment of failure. Furthermore, the general accent on *individual* achievement makes our own actions so highly accountable that we quickly learn how to spot such shortcomings in others, including those on screen. Ultimately, in an economic context that appears to be fragmenting workers and then validates this through a logic of personal development, it is illuminating that we recapitulate such estrangement by looking to individual figures as the markers of what is right and wrong.

But still there is something to the fact that the cross-over who "can't act" offers a series of focal points to discuss shifts in the everyday work being done within the G8 countries. *Freejack* and *Swept Away* coagulate in the sticky areas of multitasking and casualization. They allow us to reflect upon and evaluate older stratifications of employment; the projection of a certain, mediated working self; the difficulty of ascribing worth to labor that is not strictly understood as manual; and the dilemmas that arise from bewildering (often new) temporal and spatial relations within working spaces and practices.

Might there be the potential, as Bauman would hope, for a systematic expansion of the language system to include different paradigms of labor and collaboration? I want to close this book by dwelling on the scope that is offered by two factors that this chapter's analysis has made apparent. First, there is the multileveled *ubiquity* of entertainment culture within the postindustrial era that renders the mismatch so redolent a means of comprehending these matrices of work. And, second, there is the propagation of the idea that charisma and acting talent are too complex for any of us to scientifically ensure or classify (although we may buy all manner of products to help us try). The correlation between these two dynamics perpetuates a paradoxical set of responses. On the one hand, the aura burns so brightly that many wish not to investigate its chemistry. On the other, it acts as a beacon for the supposedly democratic properties of fame and fortune: in theory, a person from any background can make it. Such enticement encourages audiences to hold the fantasies that stardom offers close to their hearts (and purse strings), without minding too much that, beneath the radiance, an extremely strict and narrowly cast set of principles is also at work.

But might there still be something liberating in these very areas of creativity that have escaped rigid stratification? Given the sustained centrality of the media in postindustrial life and their dialectical interplay with the recent conditions of labor (despite the many attempts to thwart such exchanges), is there any prospect for the still-indistinct qualification of entertainment labor to formulate more equitable employment arrangements?

The Problems of Conclusion

Like many academic books, *Off Key* was driven by my urgency to maneuver crucial political debates into greater prominence within a particular discipline. For me, scrutinizing the outwardly aesthetic criteria that adjudicate whether film and music are "not working" together has facilitated a discussion of labor itself. "Postindustrial" developments in the United States and the United Kingdom have reconstituted employment according to methods and prerogatives that have significantly altered the status of the media as sites and modes of production, and as products themselves. Like many authors, the more I wrote, the more I noticed my central paradigm encircling and permeating me. Granted, this might have been a foregone conclusion: I am a teacher, "knowledge economy" staff, hired within a department of media studies. Like many universities today, mine has followed the paths charted throughout this book, weathering the transition out of almost total state support and into perhaps less economically predictable market forces. But the themes of the book penetrate further into my life than that. Akin to the workers to whom the previous chapter alluded, my "private" time and space appear to be more thoroughly invaded than ever before, despite, or rather because of, the light requirements to be in my office or classrooms. When I do travel to what might conventionally be called work proper (the campus itself), even the journey is distinguished by the embellishments and scars of postindustrialization.

I live in the East End of London. A multitude of reasons has attracted me here. I could say I enjoy involving myself in the mythology of the East End as promulgated by endless reams of historical and cultural narratives. The area also accommodates a fascinating, although definitely fraught, mix of people, many of whom would identify mismatches of all kinds within the community. Its inhabitants are here on account of many centuries' stultifications of and migrations for work, traditionally in the manual economies provided by the now-closed London docks, an imperial hub since transformed. I am also drawn here because it is one of the few places I can afford on my degraded, quasi–public sector salary, but I am far from the most unfortunate victim of the inflated house buying and rental prices in Britain's capital, a consequence of what I referred to in the last chapter (courtesy of Charles Leadbeater) as our thin-air economy—and also a contributor to it.

My journey to work proper often takes the form of a bicycle ride. It pains me to confess it, but I often rationalize it to myself in the languages of multitasking and time saving, of getting the exercise that my tertiary sector job does not demand of me while simultaneously traveling to the college. There is a weak environmentalism to my decision too, as if not consuming gasoline at that moment could halt the machinery of what I would choose to call "post-Fordist" overproduction. My route takes me along a canal that was once a core artery in the movement of goods from the docks. I am near the Bryant and May factory which, in 1888, witnessed one of the first press-supported instances of industrial action and which has now been converted into luxury gated housing. I move into the Docklands: its industrial infrastructure has been hollowed out or prettified to make way for a regenerated financial district concentrated around Canary Wharf. The whole borough's proximity to both these Docklands offices and the older trading centers of the Square Mile area has rendered this very landscape one of the many sites of struggle in the movement into the postindustrial era. Nearby Wapping, as we saw in chapter 4, was embroiled in violent clashes as the police tried to suppress striking print workers and their local supporters. Houses on its "quaint," narrow, cobbled streets, in the warehouses that once held goods from across Britain's exploited "dominions," now fetch astronomical prices.

I play a role in these changes that is neither blameless nor unique. This stretch of land, like so many others in the two countries I have investigated in *Off Key,* is bursting with similarly involved and implicated workers. Canary Wharf and Liverpool Street overspill with traders of thin air; their labor would seem utterly alien to their barrow boy or aristocratic great-grandfathers. Their offices are cleaned by contract staff, many of them migrants who can nowadays wire their meager salaries home to families in poorer countries. Then there are those made redundant by the drift of manual employment out of the area. Their long periods at home are often punctuated by communications from call-center employees in India, people who insist that their name is "Bertie" or some other Raj-redolent moniker rarely heard in contemporary Britain and who reach us through satellite communication systems to sell us better mobile phone contracts. These exchanges also interrupt the days of the many home-based laborers, from artists to illegal piece-work sewing-machine operators. This list could obviously have been spun out for longer, but the point is the extent to which postindustrial regimes shape our very geographies, our modes of connection, and our possibilities for being in the world in minute and profound ways.

What are the implications across these strata of a class system reorganized around immaterial labor, its elites, and the values embedded in symbolic commodities? Free-trade advocates are already on the scene. The World Trade Organization has enmeshed itself in the exchange of services and intellectual property with its Trade-Related Investment Measures (TRIMs), promoting and enforcing rules that favor a liberalism which is less accountable to local, elected legislators. Aggressive convergences in network systems like the Internet have seen even user-led sites like MySpace, YouTube, and eBay bought out by large corporations. Can the wishful sense of free-flowing, nonhierarchical organization which these sites seemed, for many, to exemplify be maintained? Were their structures perhaps merely postindustrially vanguardist and all-too-easily subsumed? The thin-air economy also has its own means of juggling supply and demand: a vast increase in consumer borrowing has helped to double bankruptcy in less than a decade.[1] Evidently, the distribution of wealth and opportunity is desperately uneven, a disequilibrium shaking through our wars, our religions, and so many other areas of life.

Off Key has drawn, on occasion, upon thinkers who have engaged with, even helped to conceptualize "postindustrialization" and who could never have dreamed of the fundamental problems that pepper my own descriptions. People like Krishan Kumar, Daniel Bell, and Michael Piore and Charles Sabel, writing twenty or more years ago, looked to the utopian dimensions of nonmanual, more small-scale, even craft-inclined production. It was not a foregone conclusion that decentralization would still function according to familiar systems of domination and injustice. Even more recently, Jeremy Rifkin has hoped for an "end of work" as the result of the rise in automation and intelligent technologies, although my last case study seems to indicate quite the opposite.

But it is pointless to solely and cynically speak of how optimistic visions of the future have soured. Instead, it is surely more fruitful to grapple with those which are now newly powerful—the media—and to assess their potential provision of different, more egalitarian structures of labor. I have stressed throughout this book that the media are more than an affected element caught up in the wake of postindustrialization. The media substantialize postindustrial priorities and contribute to their economic furtherance, both materially and ideologically. Things like film and music, their creators, their institutions, the companies that "own" them, and other such commodities do not simply harmonize with a general economy, they are increasingly essential to how it *works,* in the many permutations of what that can mean.

This trend, this investment in the cultural, preoccupies the political philosopher, activist, and author of *A Grammar of the Multitude,* Paolo Virno, whose writing seems an apt final addition to the roster of dialectical thinkers upon whom I have relied during my explorations. He postulates:"In the Post-Fordist environment, a decisive role is played by the infinite variety of concepts and logical schemes which cannot ever be set within fixed capital, being inseparable from the reiteration of a plurality of living subjects."[2] The greater reliance on these kinds of commodities, however, places an accent on collectivity and what he calls "the general intellect," the realms of communication where "[s]haring, in so far as it is a technical requirement, is opposed to the *division* of labor."[3] Not that this is some kind of Arcadia for Virno; he argues that the more cultural spheres are ruled by the motivations of capital, the less they can be "public" in a truly fair sense. By opening up to the logics of wage labor, the general intellect increasingly overcomes exploitation and division, he reasons.

Yet cultural items are never entirely reducible to rigid values either. The mismatch, I have established, embodies these tensions too: its definition rests on the fact that there are far from adequate numbers of objective markers by which to ethically or even financially peg the work of immaterial labor, especially now that a core doctrine of postindustrialization is flexibility, the insistence upon opportunistic change. The urge to be *categorical,* in both senses of the word, is somewhat of a sticking point in the flows of flexibility, and it speaks of a fervent contradictory desire to inaugurate some rules and meritocracies for assessing such work, both through and in the prominent media industries. Are critics of the mismatch looking for actual agreement on how to value and reward work, something that seems almost entirely impossible under the strategic and globally inconsistent fluctuations of contemporary capitalism? When the doling out of wages is dependent on such yardsticks, this could well be a practice that continues indefinitely.

At the same time, the yearning for fixity that the mismatch arouses is so pervasive that substantial profits can be made from it. The need to simultaneously ridicule and reaffirm courses through indulgences like "so bad it's good" nights out at the cinema, exposé magazine articles, and even the types of critical material that have shaped my chapters. Those who bother with these activities, and there are many of us, are, ultimately, *paying* for the privilege of judging, of assessing the potential for worthwhile craftsmanship without really demanding further knowledge of the debilitating systems that can perpetuate such conclusions.

Furthermore, mocking the confusing biopic or the ill-trained cross-over star has revealed itself to be just another form of labor-related self-governance projected onto and through our engagement with entertainment. Chapter 5 highlighted how rancorous responses to the mismatch are complicit with the part-time and casual labor norm; they betray an eagerness to see powerful people in unusually tenuous positions fall hard and get replaced. If individual competition diminishes mutual political ground, then we need to think long and hard about whether the media, especially when they "don't work," open up any loopholes that may lead to more egalitarian concepts and practices of work.

It is not the discussions of these film-music moments that, in and of themselves, lead to atrophy, it is the cauterization of the conduits that connect workers to each other. The need to be categorical—to make things fit, to bracket things off—ostracizes us, ironically, from understanding the alienation that production and consumption can prompt. As such, mismatch criticism surely forecloses some overwhelmingly common responses to and feelings about the globalized world, industrial and postindustrial alike.

After prolonged examination, the mismatch is an all-too-familiar outsider dwelling right in the heart of the system. Could it then draw us into a community? Could it, say, function according to the principles of camp: a nonconformist speaking to other nonconformists? Seemingly not. When failure and disintegration are believed to stem (as they often do when a preestablished film or music entity moves sideways into another line of entertainment) from a capitalist conservatism that is irreconcilable with liberationist agendas, the results seldom stir up a cult following. Mismatches often challenge vague but fundamental and widely held principles—"respect for genius" in relation to composer biographies or "democracy" in the case of nepotistic cross-over performances—meaning that they will rarely ever work for those who welcome challenging chaos or even random and unplanned political disruption.

No, the outwardly untenable tension that the mismatch nevertheless holds together has to be treated differently, as I have demonstrated. The way it exposes how certain reliable commodity strengths can be unexpectedly dissipated, how unaligned entertainment industry sectors can be, and how inequitable working conditions subsist are too important to dismiss. What is key to the mismatch is that it cannot adequately abstract its composite labor. However, a longing to judge, to place, and to sneer does not only reaffirm conservative models of employment, postindustrial or otherwise, nor does it simply block questions about the larger workings of contemporary labor. It also decreases the potential latent within ambivalence and disorder.

What a mismatch can allow us to do is to prize open the hegemonically regulated domain of professionalism to add to it the amateur, the off-the-wall, the differently skilled—none of which conform to increasingly narrow conscriptions of flexibility. Eisenstein, as we have seen, was consistently alert to and welcoming of this sensibility, while Derrida saw it as inescapably present and not an imposed action at all. At the very least, the mismatch challenges the standards upheld by authoritarian workplace specialization, which is still very much in play, even if greater numbers of specializations are demanded in the current climate. Mismatches, I have pointed out, inhabit an uncomfortable "in between," which Derrida finds so compelling. They are neither film nor music in the strictest sense of either's upper limits of expertise and, as such, can disassemble the smooth classification of creative professionalism. And yet they are not allowed to. So obsessively are they quashed that we have to wonder why exactly mismatches might be threatening. The confounding of the either-or binary for which Derrida longs—and, indeed, finds everywhere—is harshly denied by the majority of critics and audiences of these films, and the reasons for that are revealing. Bauman, as we have seen, notes the urge to distinguish and stratify, and to this I have added the sense of how difficult it is to apportion value, in financial terms, to such unfathomable yet symbolically redolent labor.

The lineage of dialecticism, as I have stressed throughout, is of tactical interest here, precisely because it foregrounds, even welcomes, the unresolved discrepancies and ubiquitous ruptures of life, rescuing them from ultimate suppression or polarization. Unrest lies in the very nuclei of these methodological propositions, rippling through history itself—something I have endeavored to maintain in my rendition of case studies from the past. The incongruities lying within or complicating schematizations of labor have risen to the surface time and time again in my analyses and, in celebrating the restlessness of dialecticism, it now seems treacherous to parcel up my thoughts in a tidy conclusion. Instead, I would like to highlight my often-jarring interdisciplinary conjunctions—scholarly mismatches, perhaps. Within a generically required framework of "coherence" (necessary, after all, for invoking anything like the general intellect), I would like to step away from this book admitting, as Marx would have wished, that there are perhaps Pyrrhic political motives to my selections of material, ideas, and histories. The unusual meetings that take place in given mismatches or in the pages of this book seem curtailed, in one sense, and limitless, in others: "so near, and yet so far from Paradise," as Presley sings from his prison cell in *Harum Scarum*. What the dialectical tradition I have followed advocates is an ethical responsibility that acknowledges its reasoning while ultimately believing in the power of dissolution.

This is not a contradiction. There is much political worth in defusing central oppositions within an understanding of work: calculable labor in relation to its thin-air equivalent; flexibility versus stability as it might delineate contracts, securities, or the temporalities of vocation; the core as distinct from the periphery. These dichotomies have ultimately exposed themselves to be arbitrary, artificial, and inseparable within my case studies. But it has only been possible to comprehend mismatches in this way because thinkers on dialecticism do not seek to wipe out either side of the equation; rather, they are committed to the airing of all voices, to polyphony rather than hierarchy. Dialecticism affords the potential to dismantle the distinctions that block laborers from meeting each other, discussing their common exploitation, or creating the kind of public domain that Virno has presented. To reiterate Adorno: "Total contradiction is nothing but the manifested untruth of total identification."[4] Opposition can only exist by refusing the incompleteness of the project of ordering and creating meaning.

In addition, dialectical theory reveals that, when constructed categories (arguments, histories, media synergies) run into each other, new formulations emerge. This has been the case, for instance, with the changing status of video nasties as time has worn on. The reliability that is sought at all costs in the debilitating labeling of mismatches is at odds with the machinations of (post-industrial) history, but very much haunted by the mindsets it conjures. The mismatch is an ever-mutating idea that, once grasped, can only be maintained through discourse, through time, through insistence. "Failure" is beholden to definitions that require ceaseless *work*.

All of these fluctuations have provided compelling reasons for me to lingeringly explore, rather than to carve up or expel, objects exuding indeterminacy. This is no hiatus, however, but a ride upon some particularly forceful political currents. Nor is this incongruity within our understanding of representation and entertainment culture exclusive to music and cinema research. In this book, I have delved into just one particular media locale—one, admittedly, where unity and clarity are often sought in all but the most avant-garde of spheres. However, there are many areas where such frictions could be surveyed—from computer games and karaoke clubs (if we stick to media experiences) to the nature of the cosmos (if we follow Hegel). I cannot even claim that the case studies represented in this book are particularly expansive in terms of my theory's applicability across the geography of film-music.[5] In the mismatch, then, what looks like something stultified by critical vocabularies is in fact also the very offspring of corporate capitalism prizing open the ground beneath its parent's feet, provoking tremors through its rules, principles, and definitions.

I want to turn again to Paolo Virno for some applicable ideas about how these cultural disjunctions might bring to trial certain imposed and unfeasible strictures of labor. For him, the activity of performance, which has been central to my arguments too, can draw upon dialecticism to refuse the utter exploitation of labor. Virno's protagonist here is the "virtuoso," a worker who initially looks like an inhabitant of a separate corner of the entertainment spectrum to the mismatch and whose activity

> *finds its own fulfilment (that is, its own purpose) in itself,* without objectifying itself into an end product, without settling into a "finished product," or into an object which would survive the performance.... it is *an activity which requires the presence of others,* which exists only in the presence of an audience.[6]

The surplus, uncommodified value that is generated mocks capital as it currently functions; it is not detachable and cruelly abstracted from the labor of creativity, and it speaks of the difficulty of totally monetarily or even ethically valuing this kind of work—indeed, any work. At the moment of performance, the audience members are also working. They are implicit in the act of creativity and meaning making and, as a whole, those present create a collective public space that can confuse the dichotomies of production and consumption.

This is a compelling ideal, but one that Virno insists is also highly monitored and controlled by capitalism; his concept of "the audience" is ultimately a poor approximation of his vision of "the public." Despite this, though, Virno cannot help but believe that the cultural sectors do allow for the vital questionings of labor. For me, this rests in the incapacity, despite its unstinting attempts, for mismatch criticism to finitely judge and quantify. The institution of cold mathematical systems grounded in commodification and capitalist regulation, and so ubiquitous in these condemnations, is ultimately doomed to fail. The supposed opposites, the virtuoso and the failure, both point out the shakiness of some of the pillars of contemporary postindustrial economics.

Returning to the mismatch, it is, as we have observed, first and foremost, *waste* in an environment which tries to rationalize (ruthlessly stamp out, all too frequently) any expensive clutter that snarls up the wheels of production. Post-Fordism must be as streamlined as possible, yet its aim is often to generate a huge glut of commodities littering the world to the point of strangulation. The mismatch links these two overarching priorities and makes us realize the paradox and the hypocrisy of this "balance." If disposability is so important to contemporary life, then why does the mismatch cause such consternation? In a rationalized environment, we need to look at waste, the lost potential, the time-stealing elements that I have identified in the mismatch more than ever. Rationalization gets rid of mismatches, but many other things besides: valuable proposals and narratives of the past, as I have maintained throughout this book, are swept away too. In the ravenousness to pile as many commodities as possible into one supposedly containable entity and in not succeeding, an inability to control productivity and profit becomes manifest. This was the case, for example, in the surprisingly antiracist suggestions that exploded out of the heavily loaded rock 'n' roll movies that featured Fats Domino (such as *The Girl Can't Help It; Shake, Rattle and Rock!* and *Jamboree*), whether or not their semantics were intended by all involved. More broadly speaking, if given particular attention, the sprouting of certain seeds of capitalist ruination becomes apparent in the (often commercial) failure of mismatches.

My presentation of these suggestions has not been shaped by a desire to up-end hierarchies so that waste now takes on a lauded position that absolutely contradicts its traditional status. Any such will to stymie only replicates the destructive inclinations behind mismatch classification. Instead, the arguments that I have developed have foregrounded the often inevitable swamping of supposedly discrete categories. In this way, post-Fordism's darling, flexibility—the privileging of risk, change, and unpredictability, *but only of a certain strain*—must necessarily open itself up to political sensibilities, including revolutionary dialecticism, which have conventionally been banished from its heartlands.[7]

Obviously, these models of infestation are not perfect; the divisions forced upon the world encourage many of us to behave toward them through direct retorts to and complications of social and economic taxonomy. Dialecticism cannot be a partially adopted ideal: concepts and practices like "violence" do not cease either, nor even stand still. Yet realizing the often torturous material conditions of labor stratification, as I have hoped to demonstrate, is fundamental to drawing greater energies into labor reform. If we cannot totally halt a mismatch from congealing into a (wasted) commodity, we do not have to stop short at unveiling the motivations for this. Dialectical interchange, I have emphasized, provides rejoinders to a model exclusively dedicated to profit and exploitation, clearing a space for the communal discussion of labor's injustices, as well as its benefits.

Creativity, so central to the current economies, weaves its way under the steam of and through dialecticism too. It can also use its newfound socioeconomic power and its residual hermeneutic nebulousness to expansively bond labor practices to each other and to refuse certain systems of banishment and hierarchy, the kinds that keep mismatches' propositions at bay. What dialecticism like this can reveal is that my chosen mismatches, and all of the others besides, cannot be excluded from work, nor can their efforts, their toil in whatever form, be denied so easily. My examples of what "doesn't work" are, in fact, working extremely hard, and will continue to do so. What we have to recognize is that the definition of "work" is under constant political renegotiation, regardless of whether people wish to stabilize its meanings for particular "ends."

Notes

Overture

1. See, for example, the fan damnations of *Harum Scarum* on "Just One Mistake" and "*Harum Scarum*," *Recex Films.* Simpson's "What Was Elvis' Worst Film?" assesses the film's election to "worst ever" status on the *Elvis Information Network* (http://www.elvisinfonet .com), while *Washington Post* critic David Segal contributes his professional opinion on *Harum Scarum*'s worthiness for this title in "Elvis: One for the Money."

2. Presley had previously made *Jailhouse Rock* (Richard Thorpe, 1957) for MGM, before working variously for Twentieth Century Fox and Paramount. In 1963, he returned to MGM, the studio that is widely thought to have exploited him the most, and he remained there under several different contracts for ten years.

3. Eames, *The MGM Story,* 311, 317.

4. Vellenga with Farren, *Elvis and the Colonel,* 119.

5. *Harum Scarum* was the eleventh-highest box office grosser in its opening week, after which its popularity gradually slumped. The album of the soundtrack reached number eight on the charts and remained there for twenty-three weeks.

6. This is a case made by Dyer's *Stars* in his examination of various film stars' careers, popularity, and symbolic power.

7. See, for example, Marcus, *Dead Elvis;* Guralnick, *Careless Love;* and Graham, *Framing the South.*

8. Zmijewsky and Zmijewsky, *Elvis,* 32–34, provide an in-depth breakdown of key figures and movements that opposed everything for which Presley supposedly stood.

9. Graham, *Framing the South,* 127–128.

10. There are repeated recorded instances of Presley's gentlemanliness, his kindness to others (particularly his mother), his unwillingness to be thought of as destructive or harmful because of his creative output, his willingness to learn, and his abhorrence of street drugs (it was only later that knowledge of his addiction to prescription drugs became widespread). As Zmijewsky and Zmijewsky argue, "[C]ontrary to his rebellious image, he was fairly conservative in his views. He looked upon himself only as an entertainer. 'For me a stage is a place where I go to work and sing—not where I talk about the things of life'" (Zmijewsky and Zmijewsky, *Elvis,* 38).

11. Graham, *Framing the South,* 127.

12. Lewis fell out of favor for bigamously marrying his thirteen-year-old cousin, while Berry had been imprisoned for transporting a minor across a state line.

13. Presley's complacency about the content of his contracts is corroborated by his ex-wife (Presley with Harmon, *Elvis and Me,* 188).

14. Guralnick, *Careless Love,* 74.

15. Presley has, of course, been the subject of countless critical and academic treatments. What seems, to me, missing in these accounts, however, is a prolonged engagement with why his "bad" films create such a negative response not just by interrogating his biography, but by looking into the formations of the entertainment industries.

Chapter 1

1. Reay, *Music in Film,* is another book that explores horizontal integration in this fashion.

2. Mary Ann Doane, "The Voice in the Cinema: The Articulation of Body and Space," in Altman, *Yale French Studies,* 33–50; Silverman, *The Acoustic Mirror;* and Chion, *Audio-Vision,* all contribute to this line of inquiry, although in examinations of the voice, rather than music, in cinema. Like Gorbman, they are inspired, in large part, by the psychoanalytical writings of Guy Rosolato, but also by key figures from within apparatus theory, a branch of 1970s film studies, whose most renowned examples could be considered to be Baudry, "Ideological Effects"; Metz, "The Imaginary Signifier"; and Baudry, "The Apparatus"; with Mulvey, "Visual Pleasure and Narrative Cinema," also adding considerable political weight to the theorization of seamless but ideologically framed audience engagement with the media text.

3. David Raksin, uncited quotation from Prendergast, *Film Music,* 213.

4. Aaron Copeland, uncited quotation from Prendergast, *Film Music,* 213.

5. Davis, *A Complete Guide to Film Scoring,* 10.

6. Bazelon, *Knowing the Score,* 46.

7. Evans, *Soundtrack,* 11.

8. As writers like Smith in *The Sounds of Commerce* argue, synergy has been with us since the inauguration of the moving pictures.

9. Based on a novella by Prosper Mérimée, the Carmen story did not become famous until the staging of Bizet's opera in 1875. Nearly forty Carmen films were made in the silent era, most notably, perhaps, Cecil B. DeMille's 1915 version, starring Theda Bara.

10. Cook, *Analysing Musical Multimedia,* deals with this confusion in more detail.

11. Cook, *Analysing Musical Multimedia,* 86.

12. Flinn also argues, as I do, that aesthetic traditions are knitted into the conditions of production. Her book is dedicated to understanding why Romanticism was such a popular trope in classical era film scoring, and, for her, such urges originate in the specific circumstances of industrialization, the situation that also brought about Romanticism. Flinn argues that, by invoking this style—one emblematic of (often thwarted) struggle—composers working in the U.S. studio system were voicing their concerns about career insecurity and the diminishment of their artistic autonomy within this industrialized framework. What is significant about both their adaptation to this world and the critical response to scoring that sees it as "beyond words" is that transcendence and/or the return to a hazy and now lost past are simultaneously conveyed as the (impossible) solution. However heartfelt this need to escape may have been and may continue to be, it is si-multaneously packaged into the movie and sold as removal from the rigors of everyday life in a manner that does not seek to offer any solutions or ideas for change. The cruel irony of Flinn's chosen examples (as she seems well aware) is that their methods became standard(ized) and their nostalgic aims are divorced from any viable potential for anti-capitalist struggle, so reinscribed are they in the capitalist product itself. This is short-term relief we pay for, rather than criticism of the larger system itself.

13. Aside from various how-to manuals, this is also evident in books such as Mac-Donald, *The Invisible Art of Film Music,* where we see a tendency to promote "good prac-tice" through a "great works" tradition, with subchapters dedicated to single films and their soundtrack's auteur/composer's methods. Even fine, critically informed books, such as Brown's *Overtones and Undertones,* still work within the convention of exemplars, a re-affirmation of canon that is not endemic to film studies in its other dimensions. In this regard, Brown is not significantly removed from the groups of more practice-focused writers, such as Bazelon, whose basic aim has been to ameliorate the scoring tradition to the point where it merits a place alongside the European concert music stalwarts and thus, by association, to upgrade the beleaguered position of the movie scorer. Even within the works of more academic writers, ones who bear little sustained commitment to improv-ing the craft, the traces of this pattern of thinking are still marked. Writings from Kalinak, *Settling the Score,* to Neumeyer, David and James Buhler, "Analytical and Interpretive Ap-proaches to Film Music (I): Analysing the Music," in Donnelly, *Film Music,* 16–38, which is anything but a rule book for generating commendable soundtracks, still train their at-tentions on these same standard or ideal practices.

14. As expressed by, for example, Bazelon, *Knowing the Score;* and Evans, *Soundtrack,* or the interviews of composers in Timm, *The Soul of Cinema;* or Hagen, *Scoring for Films.*

15. Adorno and Eisler, *Composing for the Films,* 74.

16. Flinn, *Strains of Utopia,* 11.

17. Adorno and Eisler, *Composing for the Films,* xiv.

18. Even before the introduction of synchronized sound, experimental directors dabbled in unusual image-music juxtapositions. For instance, the premiere of *Un chien Andalou* (Luis Buñuel and Salvador Dali, 1928) featured a soundtrack (provided by a gramophone) that alternated between popular tangos and Wagner. However, this type of assembly "works well" in terms of both generating shock value in particular, selected audiences and in maintaining a coherence with the film's overall ideas.

19. Numerous accounts, such as Brown, *Overtones and Undertones;* Flinn, *The New German Cinema;* and Davison, *Hollywood Theory, Non-Hollywood Practice,* have approached the discordant interrelationship of music and cinema within this type of material, where disjunction is often the ultimate aim of the works in question, but where the mismatching is, in the end, closer to a model of coherence than one of incompatibility. Similarly, authors who attend to the atonality or unnerving juxtapositions of horror scoring (such as Link, "Sympathy with the Devil?") are working with material that is accepting of the traditions of a genre which is *meant* to discomfort and isolate us.

20. Watson, *Sociology, Work and Industry,* 112.

21. Sennett, *The Corrosion of Character,* 137.

22. May, *An Economic and Social History of Britain,* 468.

23. Blackburn et al., *Technology, Economic Growth and the Labour Process,* 55; Watson, *Sociology, Work and Industry,* 343; and Brown, "Introduction: Work and Employment in the 1990s," in Brown, *The Changing Shape of Work,* 11, provide fuller summaries of these characteristics of postindustrialism.

24. Grint, *The Sociology of Work,* 289.

25. Huw Beynon, "The Changing Practices of Work," in Brown, *The Changing Shape of Work,* 29–30.

26. Florida, *The Rise of the Creative Class,* 74.

27. Flinn pertinently attacks similar responses to the shock of modernity (such as those conceived by Walter Benjamin) by comparing them to the ingestion of homeopathic pills to coach our bodies into an acceptance of the effects of contemporary living. There are more productive ways to utilize this knowledge than as a means of acclimatization, she stresses; Flinn, "The Legacy of Modernism," 182.

28. Godlovitch, *Musical Performance,* 5.

29. Virno, *A Grammar of the Multitude,* 58.

30. Richard Dyer's foundational article "Entertainment and Utopia," for instance, focuses on how the discrepancies between everyday and fantasy life are bridged by musicals according to the tenets of capitalist preservation. Jane Feuer's *The Hollywood Musical* examines the commingling of binary opposites such as work and entertainment, "high" and "low" art, utopia and reality within the genre, while Rick Altman's *The American Film Musical* reiterates Dyer's concerns, stressing that escapism is firmly held within the constraints of the musical number and is never allowed to pervade the more realist dimensions of a film. Given their interest in schisms, though, it is intriguing that attention is rarely warranted in this group of books to the immensely jarring experience that countless audience

members feel when a character bursts into song in a musical—a crucial formal element of the genre and one that is constantly at risk of revealing the chasm lying between two entertainment industries and their codes of performance. What is unusual here, given the convictions of writers like Dyer, Altman, and Feuer, is that they scarcely acknowledge the mismatches inherent, for many, in their chosen genre. Instead, this body of literature interrogates the longing for balance through an exposure of the formal instability of certain films; there is an inclination within all of this work to understand not only why particular inconsistencies are brushed under the carpet, but what specific types of brush and carpet are involved. In this way, writers on the musical are often guided by a conceit of their genre: they become more absorbed by the ultimate resolution of opposites and their political foundations that so insistently conclude such movies.

31. Gabbard's various writings on jazz in cinema deal with specific instances when different visual and musical modes of display, sexuality, and "racialized" patterns of behavior and performance are found to have difficulties cohabiting. Similarly, Knight in *Disintegrating the Musical: Black Performance and American Musical Film* thinks through different models of "integration" (including the filmic and the sonic) in relation to Hollywood musicals starring African Americans. Gabbard and Knight are both engrossed in the musical's assumption and formal translation of the various difficult integrations—social and industrial—that clouded particular moments in history. These writers are motivated, as am I, to ascertain what is gained, what is lost, even what may and may not be debated when the two species of film and music come together in any given time and space.

32. During this period, perhaps some of the most diverse and engaging thinking about the interaction of sound and film materialized, and it is enormously worthwhile to absorb ourselves in it, especially as a means of coming to terms with the fact that what constitutes a movie text has been consistently reworked in relation to the sonic dimension. In the vanguard of the opposition to naturalistic sound, of course, rides Sergei Eisenstein, perhaps the most vociferous proponent of disjunctive film praxis and a vital ally to me in the work I wish to pursue. Even before the arrival of sound, he, Vsevolod Pudovkin, and Grigori Alexandrov penned a treatise against the possible tendency of filmmakers to employ sound to "back up" a visual idea, to allow sound to slip into an unchallenging naturalism that merely mirrors whatever is going on visually. For them, "Sound is a double-edged invention and its most probable application will be along the line of least resistance, i.e., in the field of the *satisfaction of simple curiosity*" (Eisenstein, Pudovkin, and Alexandrov, "Statement on Sound," in Eisenstein, *S. M. Eisenstein Selected Works,* 1:113). Instead, sound should be endowed with a more autonomous semantic power: "*Only the contrapuntal use* of sound vis-à-vis the visual fragment of montage will open up new possibilities for the development and perfection of montage.... *The first experiments in sound must aim at a sharp discord with the visual images*" (Eisenstein et al., in *S. M. Eisenstein Selected Works,* 1:113). If sound were to unquestioningly synchronize itself with the image, then individual units of film would not stand out more independently from others, thus denying them the capacity of debate through juxtaposition. This dialogue (tussle, sometimes) between competing film elements and the concomitant thought processes and political realizations that

are enticed from the audience are essential to Eisenstein's understanding of montage, itself a response to the Marxian dialectic—something I will explore in more detail in chapter 2 and, in particular, chapter 3. "Statement on Sound" continues by expounding:

> Sound, treated as a new element of montage (as an independent variable combined with the visual image), cannot fail to provide new and enormously powerful means of expressing and resolving the most complex problems, which have been depressing us with their insurmountability using the imperfect methods of a cinema operating only in visual images. (Eisenstein et al., in *S. M. Eisenstein Selected Works*, 1:114)

Writing independently of Eisenstein and Alexandrov, Pudovkin worried about the "superficial copying" that sound would add to the more abstracted experimentation of silent cinema (Pudovkin, "Asynchronism as a Principle of Sound Film" [originally 1929], in Weis and Belton, *Film Sound*, 86), while René Clair stressed, "It is the *alternate*, not the simultaneous, use of the visual subject and of the sound produced by it that creates the best effects" (Clair, "The Art of Sound," in Weis and Belton, *Film Sound*, 94). From more occularcentric perspectives, writers such as Béla Balázs, Siegfried Kracauer, Jean Epstein, and Rudolf Arnheim—although they scarcely deal with music—were deeply apprehensive about how sound might infringe upon the more subtly evocative and artful allusions that cinema fostered. A superfluity of sound, whose communicative methods might be too evident and literal, was to be avoided at all costs.

33. For Marx, this is the result of economic determinism; for Hegel, the dialecticism exists a priori.

34. Hegel, *Science of Logic*, 66–67.

35. This sense of mobility infuses all of Hegel's responses to philosophy. For example, in *Phenomenology of Spirit*, he is drawn to skepticism on account of its cynicism toward objective reality, yet he feels he must remain highly critical of how this guiding principle of disbelief then becomes just as solid and unassailable as other propositions about reality. For him:

> What vanishes is the determinate element, or the moment of difference, which, whatever its mode of being and whatever its source, sets itself up as something fixed and immutable. It contains no permanent element, and must vanish before thought, because the "different" is just this, not to be in possession of itself, but to have its essential being only in an other. Thinking, however, is the insight into this nature of the "different," it is the negative essence, as simple. . . . In Scepticism, consciousness truly experiences itself as internally contradictory. From this experience emerges a *new form* of consciousness which brings together the two thoughts which Scepticism holds apart. Scepticism's lack of thought about itself must vanish, because it is in fact *one* consciousness which contains within itself these two modes. This new form is, therefore, one which *knows* that it is the dual consciousness of itself, as self-liberating, unchangeable, and self-identical, and as self-bewildering and self-perverting, and it is the

awareness of this self-contradictory nature of itself. (Hegel, *Phenomenology of Spirit,* 124–126)

36. Hegel, *Phenomenology of Spirit,* 121.

37. Hegel, *Phenomenology of Spirit,* 124–126.

38. According to Howard Williams, the term *Aufheben* encapsulated for Hegel the means by which being functions:

> As is pointed out in Cassell's *German English Dictionary* the word may signify either: to keep; preserve; store away; provide for; reserve; or: to abolish; suspend; repeal; annul; invalidate; break up. . . . the term *Aufheben* . . . catches the true nature of Being. Being, in Hegel's view, is not one unchanged, eternal state of affairs. It is the continual transition of Being into nothing and nothing into Being. (Williams, *Hegel, Heraclitus and Marx's Dialectic,* 118–119)

39. This is, for example, how Hegel's master-slave dialectic resolves its inequalities. The slaves become increasingly self-aware of the part they play in the manufacture of reality, and thus the master's dependence upon them ultimately renders the master less liberated than the slaves.

40. In her biography, *Elvis and Me,* Presley's ex-wife, Priscilla, recounts the following information:

> He was eagerly looking forward to one particular film, *Harum Scarum,* seeing it as a chance to create a genuinely interesting character. He identified his role with Rudolph Valentino's in *The Sheik.* At last, he thought, a part he could sink his teeth into. He saw a physical resemblance between himself and Valentino, especially in profile. During preproduction, he came home darkened with makeup, dressed in white harem pants and a white turban. . . . Night after night he kept his makeup and the turban on all through dinner and up until bedtime. (Presley with Harmon, *Elvis and Me,* 211–212)

41. He expounds upon this dynamic of improvement in *Science of Logic:*

> [W]hat results [from the dialectical process], the negation, is a *definite* negation, it has a *content.* It is a new concept, but a higher richer concept than that which preceded; for it has been enriched by the negation or opposite of that preceding concept, and thus contains it, but contains also more than it, and is the unity of it and its opposite. . . . The Method is no-ways different from its object and content;—for it is the content in itself, *the Dialectic which it has in itself,* that moves it on. (Hegel, *Science of Logic,* 65)

Chapter 2

1. "The Music Goes On & On & On," *Look,* 13 June 1956, 51 and 58.

2. See, for example, Martin and Segrave, *Anti-Rock;* Modell, *Into One's Own;* Denisoff and Romanowski, *Risky Business;* Palladino, *Teenagers;* Ward, *Just My Soul Responding;*

Lawson, *Civil Rights Crossroads;* and Barry Keith Grant, "1956: Movies and the Crack of Doom," in Pomerance, *American Cinema of the 1950s,* for some of these discussions.

3. The weekly industry stalwart *Variety,* for instance, reported in detail on the unfolding social reception of rock 'n' roll as both a musical and a filmic phenomenon. These articles range from coverage of the opposition to the genre ("Rumpus Halts Rock," 28 Mar. 1956, 1; "R&R Bettered 'n' Badgered, Riots Sparking New Crackdown," 18 July 1956, 41; "Katzman Hurrying New Film on Rock 'n' Roll; First Banned in England," 26 Sept. 1956, 3; "Cardinal Stritch Would Ban R&R 'Tribal Rhythm,'" 5 Mar. 1957, 1; "Making House Guilty if Kids 'Loiter': Newest Crank Proposal in Albany," 5 Mar. 1957, 15) to musings on whether the lucrative returns for rock 'n' roll on film are worth all of the damage and police involvement ("Rock 'n' Roll B.O. 'Dynamite,' Biz Big but So Are Kids' Riots," 11 Apr. 1956, 1; "Teenage Biz vs. Repair Bills, Paradox in New 'Best Audience,'" 19 Dec. 1956, 1) and even the revelation that there was nothing really to be feared from the craze ("Genteel Conduct: Theaters Were Fearful of Elvis Presley's Admirers," 16 Jan. 1957, 3).

4. Other writers with similar objectives include Keightley, "Manufacturing Authenticity," and Medovoi, *Rebels.*

5. Review of *Don't Knock the Rock, Motion Picture Herald* 205/11 (15 Dec. 1956): 186.

6. Review of *Rock, Rock, Rock, Motion Picture Herald* 205/11 (15 Dec. 1956): 187.

7. The press book produced for the re-release of *Rock, Rock, Rock* by Rearguard Productions as part of Dynamite Entertainment Inc.

8. Review of *Mister Rock and Roll, Variety,* 23 Oct. 1957, 18.

9. Review of *Jamboree, Variety,* 27 Nov. 1957, 6.

10. Review of *Mister Rock and Roll, Variety,* 23 Oct. 1957, 18.

11. In his chorus-like introduction *The Girl Can't Help It* (Frank Tashlin, 1956), Tom (Tom Ewell) claims, "The motion picture you're about to see is a story of music."

12. Kumar, *Prophecy and Progress,* 201.

13. American Film Institute, *American Film Institute Catalog,* xiii.

14. These early examples include Ellington's performances as himself in *Check and Double Check* (Melville Brown, 1930) and *Murder at the Vanities* (Mitchell Leisen, 1934), and Calloway's in *The Big Broadcast* (Frank Tuttle, 1932), *International House* (Edward Sutherland, 1933), and *Manhattan Merry-Go-Round* (Charles F. Reisner, 1937).

15. Eric Avila, "Dark City: White Flight and the Urban Science Fiction Film in Postwar America," in Bernardi, *Classic Hollywood, Classic Whiteness,* 56–57.

16. Rifkin, *The End of Work,* 71–72.

17. See Lipsitz, *The Possessive Investment in Whiteness,* 5, for details about white privilege, and Honey, *Southern Labor and Black Civil Rights,* for a fuller investigation of the actions of trade unions during this period.

18. They were also self-reflexive, as shown in the quotation used in the heading for this section, which is a line from *Rock, Rock, Rock* (Will Price, 1956).

19. See, for instance, the *Variety* report "Summer Peculiarities? Take Cheapest Terms Regardless on Certain Drive-In Nights," *Variety,* 18 July 1956, 19.

20. According to "'Come Early for Radio Disc Jockey': New Biz Gimmick for Drive-In," *Variety,* 27 June 1956, 19.

21. Speaking more generally about this trend, Storper and Christopherson write: "Since the late 1940s, the industry has been shifting away from a mass production format (the studio system) to a project-by-project format in which most of the work is done by subcontractors" (Storper and Christopherson, *The Changing Organization and Location of the Motion Picture Industry*, 4).

22. Fuller analyses of this dispute are available in Martin and Segrave, *Anti-Rock*, 85–102; Ward, *Just My Soul Responding*, 117–121; and Lawson, *Civil Rights Crossroads*, 246–248. Throughout the decade, *Variety*'s pages were liberally dosed with articles on ASCAP versus BMI and the consequences for other sectors in the industry (see, for example, "ASCAP Concern over BMI Surge," *Variety*, 6 Mar. 1957, 1).

23. Arthur L. Mayer, "Dissent with Consent Decree," *Variety*, 9 Jan. 1957, 25.

24. *Variety*, 5 Dec. 1956, 4.

25. *Variety*, 5 Dec. 1956, 7.

26. Doherty, *Teenagers and Teenpics*, 17–18.

27. "'B' (for Budget) Films Return," *Variety*, 6 Feb. 1957, 5 and 22.

28. See, for example, "Rock 'n' Roll Fevers Foreigners; Nearly Dozen Juve-Aimed Films Spread New Jazz Convulsion," *Variety*, 5 Dec. 1956, 5.

29. For further details, see, for instance, "Major Diskeries Pulling Out of R&B Competition as Indies Hold On," *Variety*, 8 Aug. 1956, 43.

30. Marx, *The Poverty of Philosophy*, 1:178–179, 187.

31. Review of *Mister Rock and Roll, Variety*, 23 Oct. 1957, 6.

32. According to *Variety*, 14 Aug. 1957, 12.

33. Denisoff and Romanowski, *Risky Business*, 44–48, details some of these industrial alliances while articles such as "Ram Bucks for Film Status: Manager-Songwriter Ties Up with Pic Co. as Outlet for R 'n' R Roster," *Variety*, 14 Nov. 1956, 54, chart the deals that were struck between composers and film production companies.

34. Review of the TV shows *Rock 'n' Roll Review* (WABC, New York) and *Rock 'n' Rally* (KPIX, San Francisco), *Variety*, 8 May 1957, 31.

35. Jackson, *Big Beat Heat*, 152.

36. Marx, *Economic and Philosophic Manuscripts of 1844*, 108.

37. Marx, *Economic and Philosophic Manuscripts of 1844*, 102.

38. See, for example, the review of *Rock, Rock, Rock* published in *Variety*, 12 Dec. 1956, 6, which damns everything from the script to the lip-synching.

39. "Increased Flow of 'B' Indie Films No Cure for Biz—Say 'A' Distribs," *Variety*, 15 Aug. 1956, 7.

40. This myth is maintained even in more recently written material such as Betrock, *The I Was a Teenage Juvenile Delinquent Rock 'n' Roll Horror Beach Party Movie Book*, 30.

41. Mitch Miller quoted in Richard Schickel, "The Big Revolution in Records," *Look* 15 (Apr. 1958): 28 (cited in Keightley, "Manufacturing Authenticity," 165).

42. See, for example, the scathing commentary on Elvis Presley's acting in *Variety*'s review of *Love Me Tender* (21 Nov. 1956, 6) and its later condemnation of the performances in *Mister Rock and Roll* (*Variety*, 23 Oct. 1957, 18).

43. Ward, *Just My Soul Responding*, 48.

44. Lawson, *Civil Rights Crossroads*, 259.

45. In an interview, AIP boss Arkoff claimed, "None of our pictures have any stars. . . . It's well worth it to avoid big names and put the saving into a little extra production" ("Action-and-Horror Staple Stuff; 20,000,000 Thrill-Seekers (12–25) Backbone of Exploitation Pix," *Variety*, 5 Mar. 1957, 20).

46. According to Jackson, *Big Beat Heat*, 148.

47. As published in *Variety*, 5 Dec. 1956, 26.

48. According to Betrock, *The I Was a Teenage Juvenile Delinquent Rock 'n' Roll Horror Beach Party Movie Book*, 29, the budgets ran between $50,000 and $100,000, but a *Variety* interview with AIP head James H. Nicholson cites the top figure as $200,000 ("'War Babies' Now Big B.O. Factor," *Variety*, 17 Oct. 1956, 1).

49. As testified by producer Sam Katzman in an interview in *Variety* ("Katzman Hurrying New Film on Rock 'n' Roll; First Banned in England," *Variety*, 26 Sept. 1956, 3) and in "20th's 'Tender' Rush Job to Make Hay on Presley," *Variety*, 5 Sept. 1956, 3.

50. Lhamon, *Deliberate Speed*, 8.

51. This is something that Daniel Bell's *The End of Ideology* noted shortly after the end of the decade.

52. Latham, *Consuming Youth*, 14.

53. Keightley's "Manufacturing Authenticity" makes a similar claim, although his argument is propelled by a slightly different agenda:

> The stories told by these films matter a great deal, insofar as they consistently proffer a cutting critique of the culture industries—a critique that subsequently becomes foundational for rock culture. These films portray the music industry in such critical terms that they effectively "manufacture authenticity" for audiences; by consistently representing the antitheses of authenticity (alienation, fraud, manipulation, phoniness, corruption, etc.) as evils to be avoided, these films contributed to the ideological foundation of rock culture in the mid-1960s. (Keightley, "Manufacturing Authenticity," 16)

54. Hine, *The Rise and Fall of the American Teenager*, 139, 171.

55. Landis, *Understanding Teen-Agers*, 3–4.

56. Figure provided by the Bureau of Advertising of the American Newspaper Publishers Association and related in "How Big Is Teenage Audience? $9,000,000,000 in Pocket Money!" *Variety*, 24 Oct. 1956, 22; and "Newspapers Hammer Their Value; Call Point-of-Sale Ads Best Way to Reach Show-Crazy Teeners," *Variety*, 5 Mar. 1957, 5.

57. Palladino, *Teenagers*, 129.

58. *Variety*, 13 Mar. 1957, 43.

59. Hy Hollinger, "H'Wood's 'Age of the Teens' Need Stars with Coke-Set Draw," *Variety*, 22 Aug. 1956, 3.

60. Review of *Rock, Pretty Baby*, *Variety*, 21 Nov. 1956, 6.

61. Review of *Rock Around the Clock*, *Variety*, 21 Mar. 1956, 6.

62. Review of *Mister Rock and Roll*, *Variety*, 23 Oct. 1957, 6.

63. Review of *Untamed Youth*, *Variety*, 27 Mar. 1957, 6.

64. Review of *Rock, Rock, Rock, Variety,* 12 Dec. 1956, 6.

65. *Rock, Pretty Baby* advertisement published in *Variety,* 5 Dec. 1956.

66. Palladino, *Teenagers,* 97–115, provides a useful summary of the female youth market in these terms from the end of World War Two.

67. Latham, *Consuming Youth,* 14.

68. Review of *The Girl Can't Help It, Motion Picture Herald* 205/12 (22 Dec. 1956): 193.

69. Review of *The Girl Can't Help It, Variety,* 19 Dec. 1956, 7.

70. The telethon sequences in *Jamboree* have a markedly gimmicky feel to them that accurately depicts the television revue tastes of the day, and a good number of Presley's songs in *Jailhouse Rock* are restrained ballads.

71. Kathy M. Newman, "The Forgotten Fifteen Million: Black Radio, Radicalism, and the Construction of the 'Negro Market,'" in Squier, *Communities of the Air,* 109–110. Such propositions are also attested by Ward's *Radio and the Struggle for Civil Rights in the South* and various *Variety* articles of the time, such as "Era of Specialization Pays Off for New York Indies WLIB, WWRL," 29 Aug. 1956, 38; "WOV's 48% Gain in Negro Audience," 30 Jan. 1957, 27; "N.Y. Negro Market as Radio Potential Big City in Itself," 17 Apr. 1957, 24.

72. Kathy M. Newman, "The Forgotten Fifteen Million: Black Radio, Radicalism, and the Construction of the 'Negro Market,'" in Squier, *Communities of the Air,* 110.

73. Gomery, *Shared Pleasures,* 164.

74. Dan Streible, "The Harlem Theatre: Black Film Exhibition in Austin, Texas: 1920–1973," in Waller, *Moviegoing in America,* 274.

75. So claims "Rock 'n' Rollers No Flash-in-the-Pan; They're 1-Nite Goldmine in-the-Flesh," *Variety,* 19 June 1957, 57.

76. Ward, *Just My Soul Responding,* 26.

77. Jones, *Blues People,* ix–x.

78. Lhamon, *Deliberate Speed,* 80.

79. They were the largest, in fact, of the suburb-bound groups, according to Tilly, "Race and Migration to the American City," 143.

80. For further details, see Jackson, *Crabgrass Frontier,* 213–215, 241–242; and Lipsitz, *The Possessive Investment in Whiteness,* 5–6.

81. Marx, *The Poverty of Philosophy,* 89–92.

82. Jackson, *Crabgrass Frontier,* 249.

83. The survey is analyzed in detail in "Justice Dept.'s Own Analysis: Films Crimped by Three Facts (1) Video (2) Drive-Ins (3) Suburbs," *Variety,* 13 June 1956, 3, although it must be noted that *Variety's* own agendas probably shine forth from this interpretation.

84. "Too Many Ozone Parks So Soon?" *Variety,* 17 Apr. 1957, 13; and Frank J. Taylor, "Big Boom in Outdoor Movies" (1956), in Waller, *Moviegoing in America,* 247.

85. As warned at the time by Fred Hift, "Films' B.O. Rainbow in Suburbs, Pix Slow to End Downtown Kick," *Variety,* 1 Aug. 1956, 1.

86. "Par Skips Broadway with Presley; Seek[s] Teenagers via 90 Nabes," *Variety,* 26 June 1957, 5.

87. Jackson notes that the mid-1950s saw an upturn in businesses moving out of city centers (Jackson, *Crabgrass Frontier,* 268).

88. For the particular populations involved in this lobby, the commercial and the civic, see Jackson, *Crabgrass Frontier*, 248–249.

89. This was documented at the time in articles such as "Outland Spots Woo Producers," *Variety*, 14 Nov. 1956, 3; and in Barry Keith Grant's more recent essay "1956: Movies and the Crack of Doom," in Pomerance, *American Cinema of the 1950s*, 157.

90. "People Don't Talk about, Care about Radio—They Just Listen," *Variety*, 15 May 1957, 32.

91. Piore and Sabel, *The Second Industrial Divide*, 89.

92. Jackson, *Crabgrass Frontier*, 250.

93. Lipsitz, *The Possessive Investment in Whiteness*, 6.

94. Ward, *Radio and the Struggle for Civil Rights in the South*, 14.

95. "Are People Too Well Off?" *Variety*, 4 July 1956, 4.

96. See Lipsitz, *The Possessive Investment in Whiteness*, 6, for an analysis of the racist logic that destroyed many more houses in African-American neighborhoods than in white ones to make way for "improvements."

97. Hoover and Vernon, *Anatomy of a Metropolis*, 70, 191, and 196.

98. *Variety* picked up on this trend in "Rock 'n' Roll Niteries Spring Up for Teeners," *Variety*, 18 July 1956, 2, and Abel Green, "Presley, No. 1 Music Biz Phenomenon, Rides Crest of the Rock 'n' Roll Rage," *Variety*, 9 Jan. 1957, 235.

99. A similar argument is extrapolated by Medovoi in *Rebels*.

100. On this last point, see Lipsitz, *The Possessive Investment in Whiteness*, 34.

101. Adorno, *Negative Dialectics*, 5.

102. Marx argues, "The same men who establish social relations conformably with their material productivity, produce also the principles, the ideas, the categories, conformably with their social relations. Thus these ideas, these categories, are not more eternal than the relations which they express. They are *historical and transitory products*" (Marx, *Capital*, 1:38).

103. Adorno, *Negative Dialectics*, 11.

104. So claims "Near-Riot in Houston as Police Nix Dancing by Negroes at R&R'er," *Variety*, 15 Aug. 1956, 1, and "Is It 'Worm 'n' Wiggle?'" *Variety*, 9 Jan. 1957, 235.

105. Baldwin, *The Devil Finds Work*, 112.

106. Marx, *Capital*, 1:154.

107. Cited in Ward, *Just My Soul Responding*, 105.

108. Relevant articles include "Alabama Rp. Summerlin Sees Belafonte's 'Sun' Pic as Commie 'Propaganda,'" *Variety*, 17 Aug. 1956, 1; "No Dates for 'Edge of City,'" *Variety*, 20 Feb. 1957, 7; "South Carolinian Stirs Race Rap vs. 'Island' Film," *Variety*, 24 Apr. 1957, 7; "Producers Risk Dixie Boycott," *Variety*, 8 May 1957, 3; "Nothing Could Be Fiercer in Carolina than Belafonte; Zanuck Offer Passed By," *Variety*, 15 May 1957, 1; "Theatre, Library Shut Out Negroes; Pastor Petitions Woner (City) to Change," *Variety*, 29 May 1957, 24; "Racial Romance in 'Sun' Upsets the Neighbors," *Variety*, 5 June 1957, 1.

109. "State Senators' Credo: Don't Want White Kids Seeing Negro Acts Mixing," *Variety*, 13 June 1956, 1.

110. Massey and Denton argue, "Among northern cities, the average level of black spatial isolation more than doubled between 1930 and 1970, going from 32% to nearly 74%" (Massey and Denton, *American Apartheid*, 43).

111. Anecdotes to this effect are recounted by Valentine, *The Show Starts on the Sidewalk*, 170; Dan Streible, "The Harlem Theatre: Black Film Exhibition in Austin, Texas: 1920–1973," in Waller, *Moviegoing in America*, 275; and Sanders and Sanders, *The American Drive-In Movie Theater*, 55.

112. The NAACP spoke out in issues of *Variety* on 21 Nov. 1956, 2, and 26 Dec. 1956, 18, while the actors were interviewed in the journal on 1 May 1957, 3, and 24 July 1957, 1.

113. "Urge Negroes to Boycott '10 Commandments' under Segregated N.C. Set-up," *Variety*, 8 May 1957, 3; and "Negroes Boycott Columbus Station in Rogers Axing," *Variety*, 14 Mar. 1956, 29.

114. This kind of argument is leveled against Hollywood by Barry Keith Grant, "1956: Movies and the Crack of Doom," in Pomerance, *American Cinema of the 1950s*, 156–157.

115. The heading for this section, "Rock 'n' Roll Is a River of Music Which Has Absorbed Many Streams," is from that Alan Freed speech in *Rock, Rock, Rock* (Will Price, 1956).

Chapter 3

1. Tom Lupton and Robert Hamilton, "The Status of the Industrial Worker," in Robertson and Hunter, *Labour Market Issues in the 1970s*, 151.

2. "Elgar" (first broadcast on 11 November 1962) was, as John Gardiner notes, "repeated four times during the 1960s, won a higher audience reaction index than any other 'Monitor' documentary yet made, and was voted Britain's second most popular television program of the decade" (Gardiner, "Variations on a Theme of Elgar," 197). For further discussion of Russell's television composer biopics, see Dickinson, "'The Very New Can Only Come from the Very Old.'"

3. Elgar apparently disliked the lyrics that E. F. Benson had concocted for "Land of Hope and Glory" (see Kennedy, *Portrait of Elgar* for a more detailed biographical study of Elgar's objections).

4. Later in his life, however (when Stalin's shadow was bearing down on him), Eisenstein was considerably more insistent upon highlighting a quieter reconciliation between oppositions. In effect, he was being uncomfortably swamped (to the point of feeling that his life was under threat) by the effacing coherence of contemporary socialist realism, and a concentration upon disparity and messy procedures became less blatant in his publicly available work. This change in approach is especially marked in his *Towards a Theory of Montage*.

5. That said, Eisenstein is never entirely preoccupied with clashes. In the essay "An Unexpected Juncture," he fawns over Kabuki theater's contrapuntal sparseness yet also points out that, at moments of extreme drama, Kabuki combines elements (as montage does) in order to create a heightened effect.

6. Eisenstein, "The Dramaturgy of Film Form (The Dialectical Approach to Film Form)," in Eisenstein, *S. M. Eisenstein Selected Works,* 1:161. Similar ideas are also expressed in, for example, "Perspectives," in Eisenstein, *S. M. Eisenstein Selected Works,* 1:156.

7. Eisenstein, "Our *October:* Beyond the Played and the Non-Played," in Eisenstein, *S. M. Eisenstein Selected Works,* 1:104.

8. John Coleman, "Transfer Liszt," *New Statesman* 90 (14 Dec. 1975): 622–623 (cited in Rosenfeldt, *Ken Russell,* 90).

9. David Robinson, "Liszt in the Burlesque Tradition," *Times,* 15 Nov. 1975, 61–62 (cited in Rosenfeldt, *Ken Russell,* 110).

10. John Simon, "Mahler," *Esquire* 83 (Apr. 1975): 58 (cited in Rosenfeldt, *Ken Russell,* 112).

11. Peter G. Davis in the *New York Times* (uncited in "Lisztomania," on *The Creative Fire of Ken Russell*). See also Pauline Kael, "Genius," *New Yorker* 46 (30 Jan. 1971): 76–79 (cited in Rosenfeldt, *Ken Russell,* 64); and Pauline Kael, "*Lisztomania,*" *New Yorker* 51 (24 Nov. 1975) (cited in Rosenfeldt, *Ken Russell,* 105).

12. Walker, *National Heroes,* 83.

13. Dempsey, "Ken Russell, Again," 20.

14. Murphy, "Lisztomania," 26; and Castell, "Lisztomania," 100–101.

15. Bilbow, "Mahler," 16.

16. Russell interviewed in Jaehne, "Wormania," 54.

17. Brzezinski, *Between Two Ages,* 3.

18. However, this was not fully agreed upon by national referendum until 1975, and the move provoked much consternation among the population.

19. Storper and Christopherson, *The Changing Organization and Location of the Motion Picture Industry,* 49; Park, *British Cinema,* 126–128; and Street, *British National Cinema,* 15.

20. Walker, *National Heroes,* 273.

21. Walker, *National Heroes,* 275–276.

22. Harrod, *Power, Production and the Unprotected Worker,* 209–210.

23. Piore and Sabel, *The Second Industrial Divide,* 178.

24. Hinton, *Labour and Socialism,* 181.

25. Cronin, *Labour and Society in Britain,* 194.

26. Piore and Sabel, *The Second Industrial Divide,* 195.

27. Street, *British National Cinema,* 17.

28. Stuart Laing, "Institutional Change in the 1970s," in Moore-Gilbert, *The Arts in the 1970s,* 34.

29. The following trade press articles predicted good box office returns in selected theaters: Bilbow, "Mahler," 16 (*Mahler*); Murphy, "Lisztomania," 26; and Bilbow, "Lisztomania," 14 (both *Lisztomania*).

30. Myerscough, *Facts about the Arts 2,* 256.

31. Rosen, *The Romantic Generation,* 50.

32. Rosen, *The Romantic Generation,* 48.

33. Jay Cocks, "Hardly Classical," *Time* 107 (17 May 1976): 74 (cited in Rosenfeldt, *Ken Russell*, 117).

34. This formal declaration took place at the Labour Party Conference of 1976. For more details, see More, *The Industrial Age*, 266–267; and Richard Brown, "Flexibility and Security: Contradictions in the Contemporary Labour Market," in Brown, *The Changing Shape of Work*, 70.

35. May, *An Economic and Social History of Britain*, 458–459.

36. Grint, *The Sociology of Work*, 162.

37. Birchill, *Labour Relations*, 42–43.

38. Walker, *National Heroes*, 276.

39. Heath, *Music*, 122–123.

40. Bart Moore-Gilbert, "Introduction: Cultural Closure or Post-Avantgardism?" in Moore-Gilbert, *The Arts in the 1970s*, 2.

41. Rosenfeldt's *Ken Russell* provides a lengthy collection of such responses to Russell's films in published reviews.

42. Richard Schickel, "Rock Bottom," *Time* 106 (20 Oct. 1975): 61–62 (cited in Rosenfeldt, *Ken Russell*, 111).

43. Cronin, *Labour and Society in Britain*, 198–199.

44. Cited in Walker, *National Heroes*, 84.

45. See, for example, the constant recourse to this word in Gillett, "The Music Lovers," 108–109, and Richard Schickel, "Rock Bottom," *Time* 106 (20 Oct. 1975): 61–62 (cited in Rosenfeldt, *Ken Russell*, 111).

46. Kumar, *Prophecy and Progress*, 201–203. Kumar points out that the United States, in contrast, maintained a fairly strong manufacturing sector in the 1970s with the bulk of job reduction happening in agriculture.

47. Bourdieu, *Distinction*, 310–311.

48. Russell cited in Baxter, *An Appalling Talent*, 183.

49. Paul, "Letter," 4.

50. Stuart Laing notes that a restructuring of the newspaper market during this period meant that Britain was left with a tabloid-broadsheet polarization as never before (Laing, "Institutional Change in the 1970s," in Moore-Gilbert, *The Arts in the 1970s*, 35–36).

51. According to Rose, "Other Peoples [*sic*] Pictures," 301.

52. Russell interviewed in Jaehne, "Wormania," 54.

53. For a fuller argument along these lines, see Jackson's *Tchaikovsky*.

54. Armes, *A Critical History of British Cinema*, 305.

55. Rosenstone, *Visions of the Past*, 46.

56. Kolker, "Ken Russell's Biopics," 42.

57. Russell quoted in Phillips, "Fact, Fantasy, and the Films of Ken Russell," 200.

58. Pattison's *The Triumph of Vulgarity* offers a fuller exploration of the affinity between rock and Romanticism, particularly in relation to their understandings of democracy and pantheism.

59. Eisenstein, "Dickens, Griffith and Film Today," in Eisenstein, *Film Form,* 254.

60. Russell's claim, "I'm doing Franz Liszt meets Richard Wagner. It's going to be rather like Frankenstein meets Godzilla," humorously invokes the dialecticism between high and popular culture that sustainedly reiterates throughout all three films (Russell, interviewed by Previn, "André Previn Meets Ken Russell," 367).

61. Lack, *Twenty Four Frames Under,* 302.

62. Richard Mallett, "Music Lovers," *Punch* 35 (3 Mar. 1971): 129 (cited in Rosenfeldt, *Ken Russell,* 66).

63. Dempsey, "Ken Russell, Again," 24.

64. Thor, of course, was taken up as a character by the comic book producer Marvel.

65. This idea was found in Russell's contribution to the film's press packet.

66. Dempsey, "Ken Russell, Again," 20.

67. Roberts, *The Leisure Industries,* 187.

68. Hewison, *Culture and Consensus,* 184.

69. Pattison, *The Triumph of Vulgarity,* ix–x.

70. Russell quoted in Baxter, *An Appalling Talent,* 131.

71. McGuigan, *Culture and the Public Sphere,* 58.

72. Russell cited in interviewed by Previn, "André Previn Meets Ken Russell," 367.

73. See Hewison, *Culture and Consensus,* 171, for further details.

74. Walker, *National Heroes,* 274; and Andrew Higson, "Renewing British Cinema in the 1970s," in Moore-Gilbert, *The Arts in the 1970s,* 226.

75. Christopher Hudson, "Mauling Mahler," *Spectator* 232 (13 Apr. 1974): 456 (cited in Rosenfeldt, *Ken Russell,* 90).

76. Farber, "Russellmania," 46.

77. Rose, "Other Peoples [*sic*] Pictures," 300.

78. Bart Moore-Gilbert points out:

> [T]he Redcliffe-Maud report of 1976, *Support for the Arts in England and Wales,* prodded local authorities to make further provisions for cultural pursuits. The report was an important step in introducing the principle of "matching funds," whereby central support for the arts was made dependent on raising equivalent sums from other sources such as local government or business sponsorship. Private patronage was increasingly co-ordinated by the Association for Business Sponsorship of the Arts (ABSA), founded in 1976. ABSA estimated that such support grew from £600,000 in 1976 to £4 million in 1979—and £25 million by 1986. But support for these developments was not unqualified. Some anticipated a trend towards more conservative programming in bodies supported by ABSA, while others interpreted the principle of "matching funds" as demonstrating that the Arts were becoming a less important priority for central government than had been the case in the 1960s. (Moore-Gilbert, "Introduction: Cultural Closure or Post-Avantgardism?" in Moore-Gilbert, *The Arts in the 1970s,* 14–15)

79. Hewison, *Culture and Consensus,* 172.

80. This is conveyed most compellingly by two essays, "Dickens, Griffith and Film Today" and "'Eh!' On the Purity of Film Language." The former is found in Eisenstein, *Film Form,* the latter in Eisenstein, *S. M. Eisenstein Selected Works,* volume 1.

81. Eisenstein, "'Eh!' On the Purity of Film Language," in Eisenstein, *S. M. Eisenstein Selected Works,* 1:287.

82. Russell in an interview with Guy Flatley, "I'm Surprised My Films Shock People," *New York Times,* 15 Oct. 1972, Arts and Leisure Section: 15 (quoted in Gomez, "*Mahler* and the Methods of Ken Russell's Films on Composers," 48); and Russell quoted in Baxter, *An Appalling Talent,* 187.

83. Russell quoted in Baxter, *An Appalling Talent,* 192.

84. Russell in an interview with Guy Flatley, "I'm Surprised My Films Shock People," *New York Times,* 15 Oct. 1972, Arts and Leisure Section: 15 (quoted in Gomez, "*Mahler* and the Methods of Ken Russell's Films on Composers," 48); and Russell quoted in Baxter, *An Appalling Talent,* 187.

85. Cook, *Analysing Musical Multimedia,* 70–71.

Chapter 4

1. In English, *Inferno* is also known as *Horror Infernal; Cannibal Apocalypse* as *Cannibals Are in the Streets, Invasion of the Flesh Hunters, Savage Apocalypse, Slaughterers,* and *Cannibals in the City; Cannibal Ferox* as *Make Them Die Slowly, Let Them Die Slowly,* and *Woman from Deep River; The Beyond* as *Seven Doors of Death;* and *Tenebrae* as *Unsane* and *Shadow.*

2. Martin Barker, "Nasty Politics or Video Nasties?" in Barker, *The Video Nasties,* 10.

3. Egan, *Trash or Treasure?* 47–77. John Martin observes, "'Nobody had heard of CANNIBAL HOLOCAUST . . . ,' boasted its British distributor, '. . . till I wrote to Mary Whitehouse complaining about it. Once she got in on the act I couldn't run off enough copies to meet the demand'" (Martin, *The Seduction of the Gullible,* 45).

4. See appendix 1 of Barlow and Hill, *Video Violence and Children* (n.p.), and an elaboration of the statement made in part 1 of this report (Hill, *Video Violence and Children, Part 1,* 1).

5. The case is often mentioned in studies of British censorship history and is the subject of various book-length investigation, such as Barker, *The Video Nasties;* Martin, *The Seduction of the Gullible;* and Egan, *Trash or Treasure?*

6. May, *An Economic and Social History of Britain,* 474.

7. Petley, "The Beyond," 38.

8. Jones, "Inferno," 45.

9. Commentaries about these scores have slowly mounted with the increased fan attention that these films now attract, and they range from the reviling to the reverent. Of *Cannibal Apocalypse,* for instance, we hear, "This movie has maybe the worst score ever. Whenever any sort of action or gore breaks out, this ultra-upbeat disco beat kicks in high gear. It's really really strange watching a Vietnam firefight and listening to this disco hustle bullshit. Takes me right out of the mood every time" ("Cannibal Apocalypse," in *My Movie*

Journal Is Better than Yours, n.p.). On the other hand, Goblin (the band behind several Argento-directed features) enjoys many tribute Web sites, and *Cannibal Holocaust* is congratulated by Randall D. Larson for its

> brutal beauty...almost completely crafted by Ortolani's musical score, which provides the disturbing film with its compassionate edge....The score's main theme sounds like anything but horror film music. Its melody is a disarmingly sweet composition for violins and synth that stands in great contrast to the substantial violence depicted on the screen. The beauty of the music makes the brutal terrors encountered by the expedition all the more unexpected and horrific in contrast. (Larson, "Riz Ortolani," 71)

10. This is made clear by the writers of the government-sponsored report on the phenomenon, such as Hill, *Video Violence and Children, Part 1,* appendix 3 (n.p.).

11. Brophy, "Cinematic Electronica. Part 1: Reverberant Oscillators in Outer Space" (originally published in *Wire* 160 [1997]), in Brophy, *The Secret History of Film Music,* n.p.

12. Robert Ashley, "Autobiographie"; *Musiktexte* quoted in Holmes, *Electronic and Experimental Music,* 197.

13. The music in this film was composed by Budy Maglione and arranged by Carlo Cordio.

14. This is a film which, as we shall see, like *Cannibal Holocaust,* plays cat-and-mouse with the standard propositions of documentary filmmaking.

15. It is worth noting here that modernist recourses to atonality are themselves often gestures toward redefining semantics. "Consonant" and "dissonant" musical arrangements meet on an equal footing in the work of composers like Arnold Schoenberg, who refused to adhere to hierarchies which tell us which combinations of notes "sound right." However, to ears that have been tutored according to age-old notions of harmony (and this applies to most of us), these pieces sound confusing, even "wrong." Just like video nasties, then, certain strains of modernist music interrogate cultural oppositions and logics.

16. Goblin was a band that focused mainly on producing soundtracks, most famously for the director Dario Argento, and that attained a large amount of album chart success in Italy for its work. Its line-up changed from time to time, but this score brought together Massimo Morante, Fabio Pignatelli, and Agostino Marangolo.

17. Dario Argento, in particular, is known to be a fan of Yes and King Crimson, and, of course, he commissioned Keith Emerson to score *Inferno.*

18. Andrew Sims and Graham Melville-Thomas, "Psychiatrists' Survey," in Barlow and Hill, *Video Violence and Children,* 89.

19. Clifford Hill, "Conclusion," in Barlow and Hill, *Video Violence and Children,* 168.

20. Holbrook, "Opinion," 14.

21. For example, on 28 June and 1 July 1983.

22. "Rape of Our Children's Minds," 6.

23. Neighbour, "Hooking of the Video Junkies," 6.

24. The most prominent of these is Miles, "Fury over the Video Rapist."

25. Egan, *Trash or Treasure?* 81–82.

26. *Conservative Election Manifesto,* 34, as cited in Barker, "Nasty Politics or Video Nasties?" in Barker, *The Video Nasties,* 10.

27. Hill, *Video Violence and Children, Part 1,* 2.

28. Hill, *Video Violence and Children, Part 1,* 15–16.

29. Geoffrey K. Nelson, "The Findings of the National Viewers' Survey," in Barlow and Hill, *Video Violence and Children,* 48.

30. Nelson, "The Findings of the National Viewers' Survey," in Barlow and Hill, *Video Violence and Children,* 37.

31. Simon Hughes quoted in *Parliamentary Debates: Commons* 48:569.

32. Lee-Potter, "Switch Off the Nasties," 7.

33. So claims Hill, *Video Violence and Children, Part 1,* 2.

34. Harry Greenway quoted in *Parliamentary Debates: Commons* 56:624–625.

35. According to John Myerscough:

> [A]t least three-quarters of the VCRs imported into Britain came from Japan. According to the British Radio and Electronic Equipment Manufacturers' Association the numbers of VCRs imported into the UK market in the three years 1982 to 1984 were as follows: . . . 2,235, 2,160, 1,411 (thousands). According to the Henley Centre for Forecasting (*Leisure Futures,* 1983) between 1977 and 1982 spending on equipment, rental, purchase and tapes grew from around £11 million per annum to £1,200 million. The rate of increase of households with a VCR decelerated in 1984, but whereas in 1981, rental accounted for about half the VCRs in UK households, in 1985 it accounts for little more than a third. . . . The Federation Against Copyright Theft claim[s] that pirated product accounts for some 20 per cent of the market. (Myerscough, *Facts about the Arts 2,* 269)

36. Trade Union Research Unit, *Labour Market Issues,* 1.

37. Birchill, *Labour Relations,* 33.

38. Adrian Sinfield and Brian Showler, "Unemployment and the Unemployed in 1980," in Showler and Sinfield, *The Workless State,* 7.

39. See, for instance, Curci with Gingold, "One Step Beyond"; and Waddell, "*Cannibal Holocaust.*"

40. Martin Roth, "Introduction," in Barlow and Hill, *Video Violence and Children,* 5.

41. Larson, *Musique Fantastique,* 266.

42. Pinch and Trocco, *Analog Days,* 306–307.

43. Olson, *The Rise and Decline of Nations,* 78.

44. See, for example, Fox, *History and Heritage,* 383, for a full analysis of the United Kingdom's exceptionally low acceptance of technological change in the workplace.

45. Braverman in *Labor and Monopoly Capital* argues in such a manner.

46. Godlovitch, *Musical Performance,* 61.

47. Deleuze and Guattari, *A Thousand Plateaus,* 315.

48. Brown, "War over Moog Sound of Music," 4.

49. Pinch and Trocco, *Analog Days,* 148–149.

50. For these arguments, see Lack, *Twenty Four Frames Under,* 313; and Brophy, "Cinematic Electronica. Part 2: Schizo Scherzos & Psycho Synths" (originally published in *Wire* 160 [1997]), in Brophy, *The Secret History of Film Music.*

51. For example, Robert Moog argues:

> A[t] the beginning, I think everybody outside of the electronic music field thought that synthesizers were supposed to imitate traditional instruments. The people who were inside electronic music wanted to used [*sic*] the synthesizer to make completely new sounds. If you listen to the early records, especially *Switched on Bach,* you don't hear anything like traditional sounds. Nonetheless, people just made this assumption that synthesis was about imitation. (quoted in Shapiro, *Modulations,* 207)

52. Prendergast, *Film Music,* 304.

53. Questions like these understandably preoccupy many scholars in the field of television studies, given that the technology under examination is largely interpreted as domestic. Silverstone's *Television and Everyday Life* uncovers how "the home" is cast semantically and politically, while Morley's *Family Television,* Lull's *Inside Family Viewing,* and Gray's *Video Playtime* engage in complex sociologies and ethnographies of how televisions and VCRs are used in the domestic sphere. My work differs from theirs, however, in that its focus is both historical and more absorbed by how the home is governed from outside, rather than from within.

54. Myerscough, *Facts about the Arts 2,* 270.

55. As cited by Wilsher, "The Wasting Generation," 14.

56. The Equal Pay Act of 1970 (implemented in 1975) did much to level the pay differentials between women and men. Although another Equal Pay Act was passing through Parliament as the video nasties debates reached their climax and, again, helped women to claim equal pay for work of equal value, the differences in labor divisions according to gender often made it difficult to argue for parity.

57. Jane Humphries and Jill Rubery, "Recession and Exploitation: British Women in a Changing Workplace, 1979–85," in Jenson et al., *Feminization of the Labour Force,* 85–105, verify this claim through recourse to various censuses of the period. See also Adrian Sinfield and Brian Showler, "Unemployment and the Unemployed in 1980," in Showler and Sinfield, *The Workless State,* 6; Richard Brown, "Work: Past, Present and Future," in Thompson, *Work, Employment and Unemployment,* 267; and Grint, *The Sociology of Work,* 209.

58. Jane Humphries and Jill Rubery, "Recession and Exploitation: British Women in a Changing Workplace, 1979–85," in Jenson et al., *Feminization of the Labour Force,* 86.

59. Fröbel et al., *The New International Division of Labour,* 344 (this percentage is based on a lot of statistical analysis on the part of the authors).

60. Bradley et al., *Myths at Work,* 74.

61. Pat Wynnejones, "Educationalists' Report," in Barlow and Hill, *Video Violence and Children,* 143.

62. Hill, *Video Violence and Children, Part 1,* 16.

63. This was an argument presented by the head of the inquiry, Clifford Hill, in Miles, "Rape of Young Minds," 11.

64. Martin Roth, "Introduction," in Barlow and Hill, *Video Violence and Children*, 5.

65. Renowden, "The Secret Video Show," 12.

66. "Video Sadists and Respectable Dupes," 6.

67. See, for example, the article in the *Times* which claims, "Even those parents who are careful about what is shown in their own homes may find their small children coming home with the horrors from a friend's after seeing *Jaws*, or something much worse" ("Video Violence," 9).

68. Clifford Hill, "Conclusion," in Barlow and Hill, *Video Violence and Children*, 169.

69. Miles, "The Men Who Grow Rich on Bloodlust," 14.

70. Payne and Carter, "Video Shares Shock," 2.

71. Barker, "Nasty Politics or Video Nasties?" in Barker, *The Video Nasties*, 11.

72. Barker, "Nasty Politics or Video Nasties?" in Barker, *The Video Nasties*, 9–10.

73. Jane Humphries and Jill Rubery, "Recession and Exploitation: British Women in a Changing Workplace, 1979–85," in Jenson et al, *Feminization of the Labour Force*, 88.

74. Jo Littler, "Creative Accounting: Consumer Culture, the 'Creative Economy' and the Cultural Policies of New Labour," in Bewes and Gilbert, *Cultural Capitalism*, 210–211.

75. May, *An Economic and Social History of Britain*, 473.

76. Deleuze and Guattari, *A Thousand Plateaus*, 343.

77. Deleuze and Guattari, *A Thousand Plateaus*, 109.

78. MacCormack, "Masochistic Cinesexuality," 116.

79. Dardano Sacchetti, the screenwriter for *The Beyond*, points out that this is how Lucio Fulci, its director, referred to the movie in an interview by Curci with Gingold, "One Step Beyond," 64.

80. An uncited interview with Lucio Fulci from *Starburst/ L'Ecran Fantastique*, quoted in Connolly, "Two More Departed," 42.

81. Sconce's "'Trashing' the Academy" and Hawkins's *Cutting Edge* offer particularly subtle analyses of the formation of "taste cultures" such as these, including also a sense of what it means to protest them. More related to this chapter's focus, Peter Hutchings, "The Argento Effect," in Jancovich et al., *Defining Cult Movies*, 127–141, is an astute study of how Italian horror fans defend such interpretations.

82. Peter Hutchings, "The Argento Effect," in Jancovich et al., *Defining Cult Movies*, 127–141.

83. This is a sizable area of scholarship with key studies such as Jenkins, *Textual Poachers;* Sconce, "'Trashing' the Academy"; and Thornton, *Club Cultures*, using Bourdieu in their respective analyses of the cult texts of television, film, and music. Hills, *Fan Cultures*, offers a rigorous overview, critique, and development of these theories.

84. As Derrida himself points out, "Deconstruction is neither a theory nor a philosophy. It is neither a school nor a method. It is not even a discourse, nor an act, nor a practice. It is what happens, what is happening today in what is called society, politics, diplomacy, economics, historical reality, and so on and so forth" (Jacques Derrida, "Some Statements and Truisms about Neo-Logisms, Newisms, Postisms, Parasitisms and Other

Small Seismisms," in *The States of 'Theory': History, Art and Critical Discourse,* ed. Anne Tomiche (New York: Columbia University Press, 1990), 85, cited in Royle, "What Is Deconstruction?" in Royle, *Deconstruction,* 10.

85. A detailed Derridean exploration of cinema (although not one that deals with music particularly) is offered by Brunette and Wills, *Screen/Play.* They do, however, draw some compelling ideas out of the practice of sound bridging which, for them, "always opens at least a small breach, a breach (which when the technique first appeared must have seemed even greater) sutured by means of the visual cut, leaving little but the memory of a momentary *frisson* of uncertainty. . . . this disunity must be recognized as a constitutive structure of any sound film" (Brunette and Wills, *Screen/Play,* 63).

86. Chion, *Audio-Vision,* 8.

87. Chion, *Audio-Vision,* 8–9.

88. This story line resurfaced in the form of *The Blair Witch Project* (Daniel Myrick and Eduardo Sànchez, 1999), another film which plays with the formal conventions of vérité documentary, updated by the integration of that contemporary "truth-exuding" and immediate technology, the hand-held digital camera.

89. Interview with Deodato by Gian Luca Castoldi in Fenton et al., *Cannibal Holocaust and the Savage Cinema of Ruggero Deodato,* 19.

90. Brophy, "Between Song and Score. Part 1: Rock Operas of Violence" (originally published in *Wire* 170 [1998]), in Brophy, *The Secret History of Film Music.*

91. Sconce, "Spectacles of Death," 111–117.

92. Derrida, *Positions,* 42–43.

93. MacCormack, "Masochistic Cinesexuality," 113.

Chapter 5

1. Naturally, there are hosts of viewers who beg to differ about the quality of such acting performances, and these are usually the die-hard devotees of the musician qua musician, people who can affirm their loyalty and the strength of their fan identity by blindly loving these performances regardless of their quality—and, of course, by willingly buying the augmented range of media products that such cross-overs generate. In my study of musicians-turned-ineffective-actors, however, I do not wish to linger to listen to these outspoken lone voices nor to prioritize a study of the proliferating means by which cross-over products are invented, marketed, and consumed, although this aspect must necessarily be considered.

2. Newman, "Freejack," 50.

3. Jones, "Freejack," 31.

4. Shives, "Jumping Freejack Flash, It's a Gas, Gas, Gas . . . ," n.p.

5. Hal Hinson claims, "Only Jagger, whose flesh hangs as if it were stretched over a skeleton of coat hanger wire, strikes the proper note of ironic indifference. He's delicious" (Hinson, "Freejack," n.p.), while an unnamed author on *Ziggy's Video Realm* insists, "Jagger's utterly detached performance is that of a man who 'gets it'; he knows the movie's

cheese, but he's determined that he's going to have a good time of it anyway" ("Freejack," *Ziggy's Video Realm*).

6. Kermode and Johnston, "Freejack," 66.

7. Maslin, "Scurrying Back in Time in Search of a Healthy Body," n.p.

8. Anderson, "Swept Away," n.p.

9. La Salle, "*Swept Away* Goes Way Off Course," n.p.

10. While *Freejack* was independently produced by Morgan Creek International and then distributed by Warner Brothers, and the Rolling Stones' current and back catalog belongs to Decca and Virgin, many of the songs that we hear on the soundtrack come from Warner-affiliated acts such as Little Feat, Ministry, and Jane Child. Jagger himself has been involved in film production, including a contribution to *Enigma* (Michael Apted, 2001), so an involvement in another dimension of cinema—acting—at the very least puts him forward as someone who is serious about this art form. Similarly, *Swept Away* was financed by Screen Gems, a Sony Pictures Entertainment Company, while Madonna's music comes out on Maverick/Warner Brothers Records. On a smaller scale, however, the film was produced by Matthew Vaughn, a consistent collaborator with the movie's director, Guy Ritchie, who is also Madonna's husband.

11. Grint, *The Sociology of Work,* 311–312.

12. Again, this is not new—it is, of course, integral to how imperialism works—it is just that a different construction of global exchange has emerged from these historical developments.

13. G8 stands for Group of Eight, an international forum for the governments of the world's richest nations: Canada, France, Germany, Italy, Japan, Russia, the United Kingdom, and the United States.

14. Badham, *Theories of Industrial Society,* 72–73.

15. Castells, *The Rise of the Network Society,* 209.

16. Castells, *The Rise of the Network Society,* 218–219.

17. May, *An Economic and Social History of Britain,* 471–472.

18. Phil Powrie's essay "The Sting in the Tale," in Inglis, *Popular Music and Film,* 39–59, for instance, draws comparisons between Sting's class dislocation and the promise of classlessness offered by popular film stars, an allure that is more broadly pointed out by analyses of stardom such as Dyer's *Stars.*

19. Grint, *The Sociology of Work,* 317.

20. Castells, *The Rise of the Network Society,* 265–266.

21. Shirley Dex and Andrew McCulloch, *Flexible Employment: The Future of Britain's Jobs* (Basingstoke, England: Macmillan), 173, cited in Bradley et al., *Myths at Work,* 53–54.

22. Huw Beynon, "The Changing Practices of Work," in Brown, *The Changing Shape of Work,* 33.

23. Fogarty with Brooks, *Trade Unions and British Industrial Development,* 169.

24. Intellect, *Progress Towards a Knowledge Driven Economy,* 12.

25. For further details of this practice, see Storper and Christopherson, *The Changing Organization and Location of the Motion Picture Industry,* 101–108.

26. See Castells, *The Rise of the Network Society.*

27. Department of Trade and Industry, *Our Competitive Future*, n.p.

28. Leadbeater, *Living on Thin Air*, ix.

29. Graham Murdock, "Back to Work: Cultural Labor in Altered Times," in Beck, *Cultural Work*, 15, drawing on information from Smith, *Creative Britain*, 31.

30. Department of Trade and Industry, *Achieving Best Practice in Your Business: Capitalising on Convergence*, 25.

31. Smith, *Creative Britain*, 26.

32. Smith, *Creative Britain*, 83.

33. Florida, *The Rise of the Creative Class*, 8–9.

34. Florida, *The Rise of the Creative Class*, xiv.

35. Peters and Cantor, "Screen Acting as Work," 53–67.

36. Peters and Cantor, "Screen Acting as Work," 65.

37. It is also fascinating to note the extent to which so many of the theorists who tackle these dynamics have come from the Jewish diaspora.

38. Anderson, "Swept Away," n.p.

39. La Salle, "*Swept Away* Goes Way Off Course," n.p.

40. Godlovitch, *Musical Performance*, 52.

41. Bauman, *Modernity and Ambivalence*, 1, 7–8.

42. Kermode and Johnston, "Freejack," 66.

43. As promoted primarily by Piore and Sabel, *The Second Industrial Divide*.

44. Piore and Sabel, *The Second Industrial Divide*, 17.

45. Bradley et al., *Myths at Work*, 31–32, provides a fantastic summary of all of the repercussions and permutations of flexible specialization.

46. Dick Van Dyke's appallingly inaccurate cockney accent in *Mary Poppins* (Robert Stevenson, 1964) is consistently used as shorthand for someone unsuccessfully trying to pass him- or herself off as a Londoner—although this is hardly a realist acting performance.

47. Frith, *Performing Rites*, 225.

48. Scott, "No Madonna Is an Island," n.p.

49. La Salle, "*Swept Away* Goes Way Off Course," n.p.

50. Atkins, "Freejack," 68.

51. Jenny Cooney notes the impact of Jagger's insistent mouth upon the movie: "Jagger stalks his prey with a constant pout of those simian lips and proves yet again that he really does belong in rock and roll" (Cooney, "Freejack," 30).

52. Ben Thompson, "Pop and Film: The Charisma Crossover," in Romney and Wootton, *Celluloid Jukebox*, 34.

53. See Stahl, "Authentic Boy Bands on TV?" 313, for an in-depth analysis of how extratextual references and product placement can overlap when musicians appear on screen or, in his case, on television.

54. Madonna's reenactment and expansion of her self-sufficient bohemian persona in *Desperately Seeking Susan* harmed neither the film's story line nor her subsequent musical career, and Courtney Love's role in *The People vs. Larry Flint* (Milos Foreman, 1996) successfully merged her "out on a limb" public image with the part of a drug-using, free-speech-advocating pornographic pin-up.

55. For instance, James Berardinelli argues, "There's only one person who believes Madonna can truly act: Madonna" (Berardinelli, "Swept Away," n.p.). James Cameron-Wilson warns, "The trouble is that when you become as successful as Madonna Louise Ciccone, you begin to believe that you can do anything" (Cameron-Wilson, "Run for Your Wife," 56).

56. Atkinson, "Swept Away," n.p.

57. Jagger, for example, has fought the commercial release of the documentary *Cocksucker Blues* (Robert Frank, 1972), convinced that it will taint the aura of the Rolling Stones, while Madonna appeared somewhat overprotective of her image in *In Bed with Madonna/Madonna: Truth or Dare?* (Alek Keshishian, 1991) and *I'm Going to Tell You a Secret* (Jonas Åkerlund, 2005), despite the films' claims of "tell all" revelation.

58. In his investigation of displayed "authenticity" on screen, Stahl, "Authentic Boy Bands on TV?" 313–314, 320, historicizes this trait more fully within a particular 1960s moment of vocational and educational opportunities.

59. In addition to the arguments I put forward in chapter 3, Williams's *Culture and Society, 1780–1950* offers a lengthy and compelling definition of the Romantic tradition, one that situates the artist, the individual, and society (all concepts vital to this chapter) within their complex historical and economic settings. Although his emphasis is on British (and largely literary) examples and his study ends in 1950, the nucleus of the Romantic ideal he describes largely still holds true as a constantly regenerating fantasy.

60. Florida, *The Rise of the Creative Class,* 104, based on Department of Labor statistics.

61. Sennett, *The Corrosion of Character,* 22.

62. Peter Berger, "Some General Observations on the Problem of Work," in Berger, *The Human Shape of Work,* 213.

63. See Stahl, "Authentic Boy Bands on TV?" 324, for more ideas on how the acting and being balance is often maintained.

64. This sense that both music and film stars are strangely indeterminate figures and that it is tricky to separate out whether they are labor or capital, producers or commodities has a long history in cinema scholarship, including discussions in Dyer, *Stars;* King, "Articulating Stardom"; Gaines, *Contested Culture;* Clark, *Negotiating Hollywood;* and Marshall, *Celebrity and Power.* As Danae Clark observes of classical Hollywood movie actors, and the same could be said of popular musicians, stars embodied a profitably ambiguous relationship between "the real" and the fabricated or mass reproduced:

> [T]he fruits of labour produced a commodity that was particularly rich in surplus value. Even though the image or star icon was dislocated from the sphere of production, its representational form appeared to capture "the real thing" thus providing a strong source of fetishistic attachment with which to link the consumer to the actor's body in the sphere of circulation. (Clark, *Negotiating Hollywood,* 19)

65. For a further exploration of this topic, see Henwood, *After the New Economy,* 76–77.

66. Du Gay, *Consumption and Identity at Work,* 57–58.

67. Rose, *Governing the Soul,* 103. For a fuller historical account of this development in labor practices, please also refer to Rose, *Governing the Soul,* 102–118.

68. According to Neil Millward, "Between 1984 and 1990, full union recognition (i.e., where pay and conditions are jointly agreed by unions and management) in trade and industry fell from 52% to 40% of workplaces [in the United Kingdom]," and there has been "only 29% full union recognition by new workplaces created since 1984" (Millward, *The New Industrial Relations,* 15 and 21, based on Workplace Industrial Relations Surveys).

69. This topic is dealt with in more detail in Hochschild's *The Managed Heart.*

70. A more in-depth ethnography of these tactics, including their proximities to religious practices, is offered by Karen Lisa G. Salamon, "No Borders in Business: The Managerial Discourse of Organisational Holism," in Bewes and Gilbert, *Cultural Capitalism,* 134–157.

71. Dargis, "Swept Away," n.p.

72. La Salle, "*Swept Away* Goes Way Off Course," n.p.

73. In the director and producer's commentary on the DVD of *Swept Away,* Ritchie comments that he wanted to present a picture of Madonna that lived up to many people's negative impressions of her. This, however, does not seem to have sat well with many critics.

74. As John Anderson points out, "Her liberated if not actually feminist image remains, as it were, chaste. And we sit there grossly insulted" (Anderson, "Swept Away," n.p.).

75. Doug Henwood notes:

> A worker paid the average manufacturing wage would have to work sixty-two weeks to earn the median family's income in 1947. In 1973, it would have taken seventy-four weeks; in 2001, eighty-one weeks. So, despite the fact that productivity overall is up more than threefold over the last fifty years—and productivity in manufacturing [is] up more than fivefold—the average worker would have to toil six months longer to make the average income. And the increase in work effort came at a more punishing pace in the 1990s than it did in earlier decades. (Henwood, *After the New Economy,* 39–40)

76. *Labour Market Trends* (June 2006), 7, according to "Labour Market Trends and Globalization's Impact on Them."

77. Sylvère Lotringer, "Foreword: We the Multitude," in Virno, *A Grammar of the Multitude,* 12–13.

78. Angela McRobbie, "From Holloway to Hollywood: Happiness at Work in the New Cultural Economy," in du Gay and Pryke, *Cultural Economy,* 99.

79. Toynbee, *Making Popular Music,* 27.

80. After conducting an extensive multicountry survey, Hartley et al. found: "Employees who felt very insecure about their jobs had more psychosomatic complaints and were more depressed than employees who felt secure about their jobs. . . . feelings of job insecurity are accompanied by lower job satisfaction and a weaker commitment to the organization" (Hartley et al., *Job Insecurity,* 81–82). Bradley et al. argue that such a lifestyle is increasingly difficult to maintain with age:

[W]orkers whose efforts sustain the lean system may find that the sheer pace of their work excludes them from job security as they grow older, particularly where there is no effective union to negotiate an equitable solution. In this respect, lean production is a high-waste strategy: it wastes the wealth of workers and in many instances shortens their working lives. When the myths are exposed, managers may be left with the problem of managing very disappointed workers. (Bradley et al., *Myths at Work,* 50)

81. John Anderson uses this fact against her, joking that the film was a "remake of Lina Wertmuller's [*sic*] 1974 beach movie by wife-and-husband team of Madonna and Guy Ritchie, either of whom could cite it as grounds for divorce" (Anderson, "Swept Away," n.p.).

82. Cameron-Wilson, "Run for Your Wife," 56.

83. Marshall, *Celebrity and Power,* 91.

84. Angela McRobbie, "From Holloway to Hollywood: Happiness at Work in the New Cultural Economy," in du Gay and Pryke, *Cultural Economy,* 101.

85. Littler, "Celebrity and 'Meritocracy.'"

Conclusion

1. Rifkin, *The End of Work,* xxi.

2. Virno, *A Grammar of the Multitude,* 106.

3. Virno, *A Grammar of the Multitude,* 41.

4. Adorno, *Negative Dialectics,* 5.

5. I have not, for example, dealt with the pop compilation score, which would be fertile ground for such analysis as it is an offshoot of (or reason behind) horizontal integration, and its hermeneutic outcomes are often interpreted as happening "at the expense" of the film's cogency.

6. Virno, *A Grammar of the Multitude,* 52.

7. This is the kind of move that Tiziana Terranova notices in recent global protest movements which are

organised in a network mode. Advertised and organised through the internet . . . both as a way to escape the attention of the police and in terms of a more spontaneously aggregative model of political participation. . . . there is an ongoing attempt to engage with the network structure against its neo-Darwinist, vampiric grain. (Tiziana Terranova, "Of Systems and Networks: Digital Regeneration and the Pragmatics of Postmodern Knowledge," in Bewes and Gilbert, *Cultural Capitalism,* 130–131)

Bibliography

Adair, Gilbert, and Nick Roddick. *A Night at the Pictures: Ten Decades of British Film.* Bromley, UK: Columbus, 1985.

Adorno, Theodor W. *Essays on Music.* Ed. Richard Leppert. Berkeley: University of California Press, 2002.

———. *Negative Dialectics.* Trans. E. B. Ashton. London: Routledge, 2000.

Adorno, Theodor W., and Hanns Eisler. *Composing for the Films.* London: Athlone, 1994.

Adorno, Theodor W., and Max Horkheimer. *Dialectic of Enlightenment.* Trans. John Cumming. London: Verso, 1997.

Altman, Rick. *The American Film Musical.* Bloomington: Indiana University Press, 1987.

Altman, Rick, ed. *Sound Theory, Sound Practice.* New York: Routledge, 1992.

———, ed. "Cinema/Sound." Special issue, *Yale French Studies* 60 (1980).

American Film Institute. *American Film Institute Catalog: Within Our Gates: Ethnicity in American Feature Films, 1911–1960.* Berkeley: University of California Press, 1997.

Amin, Ash, ed. *Post-Fordism: A Reader.* Cambridge, Mass.: Basil Blackwell, 1995.

Anderson, John. "Swept Away." *Newsday,* 11 October 2002. Available: http://www.newsday.com/entertainment/movies/nyc-sweptaway,0,2874820.story.

Armes, Roy. *A Critical History of British Cinema.* London: Secker and Warburg, 1978.

Atkins, Ian. "Freejack." *Starburst* 284 (April 2002): 68.

Atkinson, Michael. "Swept Away." *Village Voice,* 9–15 October 2002. Available: http://www.villagevoice.com/film/0241,atkinson,39021,20.html.

Austin, Bruce A. "The Development and Decline of the Drive-In Movie Theater." In *Current Research in Film: Audiences, Economics, and Law,* ed. Bruce A. Austin (59–91). Norwood, UK: Ablex, 1985.

Badham, Richard J. *Theories of Industrial Society.* London: Croom Helm, 1986.

Baldwin, James. *The Devil Finds Work.* London: Michael Joseph, 1976.

Barker, Emma, Nick Webb, and Kim Woods, eds. *The Changing Status of the Artist.* New Haven, Conn.: Yale University Press, 1999.

Barker, Martin, ed. *The Video Nasties: Freedom and Censorship in the Media.* London: Pluto, 1984.

Barlow, Geoffrey, and Alison Hill, eds. *Video Violence and Children.* London: Hodder and Stoughton, 1985.

Barrell, Ray, ed. *The UK Labour Market: Comparative Aspects and Institutional Developments.* Cambridge: Cambridge University Press, 1994.

Barthes, Roland. *Mythologies.* St. Albans, UK: Paladin, 1972.

Baudry, Jean-Louis. "The Apparatus." *Camera Obscura* 1 (Fall 1976): 105–126.

———. "Ideological Effects of the Basic Cinematographic Apparatus." Trans. Alan Williams. *Film Quarterly* 28/2 (Winter 1974–1975): 39–47.

Bauman, Zygmunt. *The Individualized Society.* Oxford: Polity, 2001.

———. *Modernity and Ambivalence.* Oxford: Polity, 1991.

———. *Work, Consumerism and the New Poor.* Buckingham, UK: Open University Press, 1998.

Baxter, John. *An Appalling Talent: Ken Russell.* London: Michael Joseph, 1972.

Bazelon, Irwin. *Knowing the Score: Notes on Film Music.* New York: Van Nostrand Reinhold, 1975.

Beck, Andrew, ed. *Cultural Work: Understanding the Cultural Industries.* London: Routledge, 2003.

Bell, Daniel. *The Coming of Post-Industrial Society: A Venture in Social Forecasting.* New York: Basic, 1973.

———. *The End of Ideology: On the Exhaustion of Political Ideas in the Fifties.* Glencoe, Ill.: Free Press, 1960.

Berardinelli, James. "Swept Away." *Reelviews,* 28 June 2006. Available: http://movie-reviews.colossus.net/movies/s/swept_away2002.html.

Berger, Peter, ed. *The Human Shape of Work: Studies in the Sociology of Occupations.* South Bend, Ind.: Gateway, 1964.

Bernardi, Daniel, ed. *Classic Hollywood, Classic Whiteness.* Minneapolis: University of Minnesota Press, 2001.

Betrock, Alan. *The I Was a Teenage Juvenile Delinquent Rock 'n' Roll Horror Beach Party Movie Book: A Complete Guide to the Teen Exploitation Film: 1954–1969.* New York: St. Martin's, 1986.

Bewes, Timothy, and Jeremy Gilbert, eds. *Cultural Capitalism: Politics after New Labour.* London: Lawrence and Wishart, 2000.

Bilbow, Marjorie. "Lisztomania." *Screen International* 12/22 (November 1975): 14.

———. "Mahler." *Cinema TV Today* 1007813 (April 1974): 16.

Birchill, Frank. *Labour Relations.* Basingstoke, UK: Macmillan, 1992.

Blackburn, Phil, Rod Coombs, and Kenneth Green. *Technology, Economic Growth and the Labour Process.* Basingstoke, UK: Macmillan, 1985.

Bogle, Donald. *Toms, Coons, Mulattoes, Mammies and Bucks: An Interpretative History of Blacks in American Films.* New York: Continuum, 1992.

Bourdieu, Pierre. *Distinction: A Social Critique of the Judgement of Taste.* Trans. Richard Nice. London: Routledge, 1984.

Bradley, Harriet, Mark Erickson, Carol Stephenson, and Steve Williams. *Myths at Work.* Oxford: Polity, 2000.

Braverman, Harry. *Labor and Monopoly Capital: The Degradation of Work in the Twentieth Century.* New York: Monthly Review Press, 1974.

Bresson, Robert. *Notes on the Cinematographer.* Trans. Jonathan Griffin. London: Quartet, 1986.

Brophy, Philip. "Horrality: The Textuality of Contemporary Horror Films." In *The Horror Reader,* ed. Ken Gelder (275–285). London: Routledge, 2000.

———. *The Secret History of Film Music* (a selection of lectures along with articles originally published in *Wire,* 1997–1998). Available: http://media-arts.rmit.edu.ac/Phil_Brophy/soundtrackList.html.

Brophy, Philip, ed. *Cinesonic: Cinema and the Sound of Music.* North Ryde: Australian Film, Television and Radio School/Allen and Unwin Australia, 2000.

Brown, Mick. "War over Moog Sound of Music." *Sunday Times,* 6 June 1982, 4.

Brown, Richard K., ed. *The Changing Shape of Work.* Basingstoke, UK: Macmillan, 1997.

Brown, Royal S. *Overtones and Undertones: Reading Film Music.* Berkeley: University of California Press, 1994.

Brunette, Peter, and David Wills. *Screen/Play: Derrida and Film Theory.* Princeton, N.J.: Princeton University Press, 1989.

Brzezinski, Zbigniew. *Between Two Ages: America's Role in the Technetronic Era.* Harmondsworth, UK: Penguin, 1970.

Burnham, David. *The Rise of the Computer State.* New York: Random House, 1983.

Burt, George. *The Art of Film Music.* Boston: Northeastern University Press, 1994.

Cameron-Wilson, James. "Run for Your Wife." *Film Review,* December 2002, 56.

"Cannibal Apocalypse." *My Movie Journal Is Better Than Yours.* 11 September 2004. Available: http://mymovie.medialife.org/?action=movieDetails&movieID=914.

Castell, David. "Lisztomania." *Films Illustrated* 5/51 (November 1975): 100–101.

Castells, Manuel. *The Rise of the Network Society.* Cambridge, Mass., and Oxford: Blackwell, 1996.

Chadabe, Joel. *Electric Sound: The Past and Promise of Electronic Music.* Upper Saddle River, N.J.: Prentice-Hall, 1997.

Chapman, Alan. "Demographics Classifications." *Businessballs.* (2007) 18 Aug. 2007. Available: http://www.businessballs.com/demographicsclassifications.htm.

Chapple, Steve, and Reebee Garofalo. *Rock 'n' Roll Is Here to Pay.* Chicago: Nelson/Hall, 1978.

Chion, Michel. *Audio-Vision: Sound on Screen.* Ed. and trans. Claudia Gorbman. New York: Columbia University Press, 1994.

———. *The Voice in Cinema.* Trans. Claudia Gorbman. New York: Columbia University Press, 1999.

Clark, Danae. *Negotiating Hollywood: The Cultural Politics of Actors' Labor.* Minneapolis: University of Minnesota Press, 1995.

Clark, Randall. *At a Theater or Drive-In Near You: The History, Culture, and Politics of the American Exploitation Film.* New York: Garland, 1995.

Colerick, George. *Romanticism and Melody: Essays for Music Lovers.* London: Juventus, 1995.

Collins, Jim, ed. *High-Pop: Making Culture into Popular Entertainment.* Oxford: Blackwell, 2002.

Connolly, William. "Two More Departed." *Spaghetti Cinema* 65 (August 1996): 26–50.

Cook, Nicholas. *Analysing Musical Multimedia.* Oxford: Clarendon, 1998.

Cooney, Jenny. "Freejack." *Empire* 34 (April 1992): 30.

Courtney, Susan. *Hollywood Fantasies of Miscegenation: Spectacular Narratives of Gender and Race, 1903–1967.* Princeton, N.J.: Princeton University Press, 2005.

Cronin, James E. *Labour and Society in Britain, 1918–1979.* London: Batsford, 1984.

Curci, Loris, with Michael Gingold. "One Step Beyond." *Fangoria* 141 (April 1995): 62–68.

Custen, George F. *Bio/Pics: How Hollywood Constructed Public History.* New Brunswick, N.J.: Rutgers University Press, 1992.

———. "The Mechanical Life in the Age of Human Reproduction: American Biopics, 1961–1980." *Biography: An Interdisciplinary Quarterly* 23/1 (Winter 2000): 127–159.

Dargis, Manohla. "Swept Away." *Los Angeles Times,* 11 October 2002. Available: http://www.calendarlive.com/movies/reviews/cl-et-swept11oct11,0,63293.story.

Davis, Richard. *A Complete Guide to Film Scoring: The Art and Business of Writing Music for Movie and TV.* Boston: Berklee, 1999.

Davison, Annette. *Hollywood Theory, Non-Hollywood Practice: Cinema Soundtracks in the 1980s and 1990s.* Aldershot, UK: Ashgate, 2004.

Deleuze, Gilles, and Félix Guattari. *A Thousand Plateaus: Capitalism and Schizophrenia.* Trans. Brian Massumi. London: Athlone, 1996.

Dempsey, Michael. "Ken Russell, Again." *Film Quarterly* 31/2 (Winter 1977–1978): 19–24.

———. "The World of Ken Russell." *Film Quarterly* 25/3 (Spring 1972): 13–25.

Denisoff, R. Serge, and William Romanowski. "Katzman's *Rock Around the Clock:* A Pseudo-Event?" *Journal of Popular Culture* 24/1 (Summer 1990): 65–78.

———. *Risky Business: Rock in Film.* New Brunswick, N.J.: Transaction, 1991.

Department of Trade and Industry. *Achieving Best Practice in Your Business: Capitalising on Convergence: Case Studies.* London: HM Stationery Office, 2004.

———. *Our Competitive Future: Building the Knowledge Driven Economy.* London: HM Stationery Office, 1998.

Derrida, Jacques. *Dissemination.* Trans. Barbara Johnson. Chicago: University of Chicago Press, 1981.

———. *Positions*. Rev. ed. Trans. Alan Bass. London: Continuum, 2002.

Dickinson, Kay. "'The Very New Can Only Come from the Very Old': Ken Russell, National Culture and the Possibility of Experimental Television at the BBC in the 1960s." In *Experimental British Television,* ed. Laura Mulvey and Jamie Sexton (70–88). Manchester, UK: Manchester University Press, 2007.

Doherty, Thomas. "The Exploitation Film as History: *Wild in the Streets.*" *Literature/Film Quarterly* 12/3 (1984): 186–194.

———. *Pre-Code Hollywood: Sex, Immorality, and Insurrection in American Cinema, 1930–1934.* New York: Columbia University Press, 1999.

———. *Teenagers and Teenpics: The Juvenilization of American Movies in the 1950s.* Rev. ed. Philadelphia: Temple University Press, 2002.

Donnelly, Kevin, ed. *Film Music: Critical Approaches.* Edinburgh: Edinburgh University Press, 2001.

du Gay, Paul. *Consumption and Identity at Work.* London: Sage, 1996.

du Gay, Paul, ed. *Production of Culture/Cultures of Production.* London: Sage, 1997.

du Gay, Paul, and Michael Pryke, eds. *Cultural Economy.* London: Sage, 2002.

Dyer, Richard. "Entertainment and Utopia." In *Genre: The Musical,* ed. Rick Altman (176–189). London: BFI, 1981.

———. *Stars.* London: BFI, 1979.

Eames, John Douglas. *The MGM Story: The Complete History of Over Fifty Roaring Years.* London: Octopus, 1977.

Egan, Kate. *Trash or Treasure? Censorship and the Changing Meanings of the Video Nasties.* Manchester, UK: Manchester University Press, 2007.

Eisenstein, Sergei. *Film Form: Essays in Film Theory.* Ed. and trans. Jay Leyda. San Diego, Calif.: Harcourt Brace, 1977.

———. *S. M. Eisenstein: Selected Works.* Vol. 1: *Writings, 1922–34.* Ed. and trans. Richard Taylor. London: BFI, 1988.

———. *S. M. Eisenstein: Selected Works.* Vol. 2: *Towards a Theory of Montage.* Ed. Michael Glenny and Richard Taylor. Trans. Michael Glenny. London: BFI, 1991.

Equal Opportunities Commission. *Equal Pay for Work of Equal Value: A Guide to the Amended Equal Pay Act.* Manchester, UK: Equal Opportunities Commission, 1984.

Erikson, Erik H. *Childhood and Society.* London: Imago, 1951.

Evans, Mark. *Soundtrack: The Music of the Movies.* New York: Hopkins and Blake, 1975.

Evans, Mary. *Missing Persons: The Impossibility of Auto/Biography.* London: Routledge, 1999.

Fano, Michel. "Vers une dialectique du film sonore." *Cahiers du cinema* 152 (February 1964): 30–41.

Farber, Stephen. "Russellmania." *Film Comment* 11/6 (November–December 1975): 40–47.

Fenton, Harvey, Julian Grainger, and Gian Luca Castoldi. *Cannibal Holocaust and the Savage Cinema of Ruggero Deodato.* Guildford, UK: FAB Press, 1999.

Feuer, Jane. *The Hollywood Musical.* 2nd ed. Bloomington: Indiana University Press, 1993.

Fischer, Lucy. "The Image of Woman as Image: The Optical Politics of *Dames.*" In *Genre: The Musical,* ed. Rick Altman (70–84). London: BFI, 1981.

Flinn, Caryl. "The Legacy of Modernism: Peer Raben, Film Music and Political After Shock." In *The World of Sound in Film,* ed. Philip Brophy (171–188). North Ryde: Australian Film, Television and Radio School/Allen and Unwin Australia, 1999.

———. *The New German Cinema: Music, History, and the Matter of Style.* Berkeley: University of California Press, 2004.

———. *Strains of Utopia: Gender, Nostalgia, and Hollywood Film Music.* Princeton, N.J.: Princeton University Press, 1992.

Florida, Richard. *The Rise of the Creative Class . . . and How It's Transforming Work, Leisure, Community, and Everyday Life.* New York: Basic, 2002.

Fogarty, Michael, with Douglas Brooks. *Trade Unions and British Industrial Development.* London: Policy Studies Institute Press, 1986.

Fox, Alan. *History and Heritage: The Social Origins of the British Industrial Relations System.* London: Allen and Unwin, 1985.

"Freejack." *Ziggy's Video Realm.* Available: http://www.reelcriticism.com/ziggyrealm/reviews/freejack.html.

Friedman, Lester, ed. *British Cinema and Thatcherism: Fires Were Started.* London: UCL Press, 1993.

Frith, Simon. *Performing Rites: Evaluating Popular Music.* Oxford: Oxford University Press, 1998.

Fröbel, Folker, Jürgen Heinrichs, and Otto Kreye. *The New International Division of Labour.* Trans. Pete Burgess. Cambridge: Cambridge University, 1980.

Gabbard, Krin. *Jammin' at the Margins: Jazz and the American Cinema.* Chicago and London: University of Chicago Press, 1996.

Gaines, Jane. *Contested Culture: The Image, the Voice and the Law.* London: BFI, 1992.

Gallant, Chris, ed. *Art of Darkness: The Cinema of Dario Argento.* Guildford, UK: FAB Press, 2000.

Gardiner, John. "Variations on a Theme of Elgar: Ken Russell, the Great War, and the Television 'Life' of a Composer." *Historical Journal of Film, Radio and Television* 23/3 (August 2003): 195–209.

Gillett, Charlie. *The Sound of the City: The Classic History of Rock.* London: Souvenir, 1983.

Gillett, John. "The Music Lovers." *Sight and Sound* 40/2 (Spring 1971): 108–109.

Godlovitch, Stan. *Musical Performance: A Philosophical Study.* London: Routledge, 1998.

Gomery, Douglas. *Shared Pleasures: A History of Movie Presentation in the United States.* London: British Film Institute, 1992.

Gomez, Joseph. *Ken Russell: The Adaptor as Creator.* London: Muller, 1976.

Gomez, Joseph A. "*Mahler* and the Methods of Ken Russell's Films on Composers." *Velvet Light Trap* 14 (Winter 1975): 45–50.

Goodwin, Andrew. "Sample and Hold: Pop Music in the Digital Age of Production." *Critical Quarterly* 30/3 (Autumn 1988): 34–49.

Gorbman, Claudia. "Hanns Eisler in Hollywood." *Screen* 32/3 (Autumn 1991): 272–285.

———. *Unheard Melodies: Narrative Film Music.* London: BFI, 1987.

Graham, Allison. *Framing the South: Hollywood, Television, and Race during the Civil Rights Struggle.* Baltimore, Md.: Johns Hopkins University Press, 2001.

Gray, Ann. *Video Playtime: The Gendering of a Leisure Technology.* London: Routledge, 1992.

Gregory, James N. *The Southern Diaspora: How the Great Migrations of Black and White Southerners Transformed America.* Chapel Hill: University of North Carolina Press, 2005.

Grint, Keith. *The Sociology of Work.* 2nd ed. Oxford: Polity, 1997.

Guerrero, Ed. *Framing Blackness: The African American Image in Film.* Philadelphia: Temple University Press, 1993.

Guralnick, Peter. *Careless Love: The Unmaking of Elvis Presley.* Boston: Little, Brown, 1999.

Hagen, Earle. *Scoring for Films: A Complete Text.* New York: Criterion Music, 1971.

Harrod, Jeffrey. *Power, Production, and the Unprotected Worker.* New York: Columbia University Press, 1987.

Hartley, Jean, Dan Jacobson, Bert Klandermans, and Tinka van Vuuren. *Job Insecurity: Coping with Jobs at Risk.* London: Sage, 1991.

"Harum Scarum." *Recex Films.* Available: http://video.ils.unc.edu/recex/prototypes/reel/details.php?filmid=8232.

Hawkins, Gay. *The Ethics of Waste: How We Relate to Rubbish.* Lanham, Md.: Rowman and Littlefield, 2006.

Hawkins, Joan. *Cutting Edge: Art-Horror and the Horrific Avant-Garde.* Minneapolis: University of Minnesota Press, 2000.

Hay, James. "Rethinking the Intersection of Cinema, Genre, and Youth." *Scope* 7 (June 2002). Available: http://www.nottingham.ac.uk/film/scopearchive/articles/cinema-genre-youth.htm.

Heath, Edward. *Music: A Joy for Life.* London: Pavilion, 1997.

Hegel, Georg. *Phenomenology of Spirit.* Trans. A. V. Miller. Oxford: Clarendon, 1979.

———. *Science of Logic.* Trans. W. H. Johnston and L. G. Struthers. London: Allen and Unwin, 1951.

Henwood, Doug. *After the New Economy: The Binge . . . and the Hangover That Won't Go Away.* New York: New Press, 2003.

Hewison, Robert. *Culture and Consensus: England, Art and Politics since 1940.* London: Methuen, 1995.

Hill, Clifford, ed. *Video Violence and Children. Part 1: Children's Viewing Patterns in England and Wales (Report of a Parliamentary Group Video Enquiry).* London: Oasis Projects, 1983.

Hills, Matt. *Fan Cultures.* London: Routledge, 2002.

Hine, Thomas. *The Rise and Fall of the American Teenager.* New York: Perennial, 2000.

Hinson, Hal. "Freejack." *Washington Post,* 18 January 1992. Available: http://www.washingtonpost.com/wp-srv/style/longterm/movies/videos/freejackrhinson_a0a734.htm.

Hinton, James. *Labour and Socialism: A History of the British Labour Movement, 1867–1974.* Brighton, UK: Wheatsheaf, 1983.

Hochschild, Arlie. *The Managed Heart: The Commercialization of Human Feeling.* Berkeley: University of California Press, 2003.

Hogan, Lloyd. *Principles of Black Political Economy.* London: Routledge and Kegan Paul, 1984.

Hoggart, Richard. *The Uses of Literacy: Aspects of Working Class Life.* London: Chatto and Windus, 1957.

Holbrook, David. "Opinion: The Seduction of the Innocent: Why Are We So Indifferent?" *Sunday Times,* 2 January 1983, 14.

Holmes, Thom. *Electronic and Experimental Music.* 2nd ed. London and New York: Routledge, 2002.

Honey, Michael K. *Southern Labor and Black Civil Rights: Organizing Memphis Workers.* Urbana: University of Illinois Press, 1993.

Honeycutt, Kirk. "Swept Away." *Hollywood Reporter,* 11 October 2002. Available: http://www.hollywoodreporter.com/thr/article_display.jsp?vnu_content_id=1740948.

Hoover, Edgar M., and Raymond Vernon. *Anatomy of a Metropolis: The Changing Distribution of People and Jobs within the New York Metropolitan Region.* Cambridge, Mass.: Harvard University Press, 1959.

Hughes, Gordon, and Ross Fergusson, eds. *Ordering Lives: Family, Work and Welfare.* London: Routledge with Open University Press, 2000.

Hunt, Leon. "A (Sadistic) Night at the *Opera.*" In *The Horror Reader,* ed. Ken Gelder (324–336). London: Routledge, 2000.

Inglis, Ian, ed. *Popular Music and Film.* London: Wallflower, 2003.

Intellect. *Progress Towards a Knowledge Driven Economy: Intellect Response to the Trade and Industry Select Committee.* London: Intellect, 2003.

Jackson, John A. *Big Beat Heat: Alan Freed and the Early Years of Rock & Roll.* New York: Schirmer/Macmillan, 1991.

Jackson, Kenneth T. *Crabgrass Frontier: The Suburbanization of the United States.* New York: Oxford University Press, 1985.

Jackson, Timothy L. *Tchaikovsky: Symphony No. 6 (Pathétique).* Cambridge: Cambridge University Press, 1999.

Jaehne, Karen. "Wormania: Ken Russell's Best Laid Planaria." *Film Comment* 24/6 (November–December 1988): 51–54.

Jancovich, Mark, et al., eds. *Defining Cult Movies: The Cultural Politics of Oppositional Taste.* Manchester, UK: Manchester University Press, 2003.

Jenkins, Henry. *Textual Poachers: Television Fans and Participatory Culture.* London: Routledge, 1992.

Jenson, Jane, Elisabeth Hagen, and Ceallaigh Reddy, eds. *Feminization of the Labour Force: Paradoxes and Promises.* Cambridge: Polity, 1988.

Johnston, Claire, and Paul Willemen, eds. *Frank Tashlin.* Colchester, UK: Vineyard, 1973.

Jones, Alan. "Freejack." *Starburst* 165 (May 1992): 31.

———. "Inferno." *Cine Fantastique* 11/2 (Autumn 1981): 45.

Jones, LeRoi. *Blues People: The Negro Experience in White America and the Music That Developed from It.* Edinburgh: Payback, 1995.

"Just One Mistake." 2001. Available: http://honorelvis.com/e_library.htm.

Kalinak, Kathryn. *Settling the Score: Music and the Classical Hollywood Film.* Madison: University of Wisconsin Press, 1992.

Kassabian, Anahid. *Hearing Film: Tracking Identifications in Contemporary Hollywood Film Music.* London: Routledge, 2001.

Keay, Douglas. "Aids, Education and the Year 2000!" *Woman's Own* (31 Oct 1987), 8–10.

Keightley, Keir. "Manufacturing Authenticity: Imagining the Music Industry in Anglo-American Cinema, 1956–62." In *Movie Music: The Film Reader,* ed. Kay Dickinson (165–180). London: Routledge, 2003.

Kennedy, Michael. *Portrait of Elgar.* Oxford: Oxford University Press, 1968.

Kermode, Mark, and Trevor Johnston. "Freejack." *Sight and Sound* 2/6 (October 1992): 66.

King, Barry. "Articulating Stardom." *Screen* 26/5 (1985): 27–50.

Kolker, Robert. "Ken Russell's Biopics: Grander and Gaudier." *Film Comment* 9/3 (May–June 1973): 42–45.

Knight, Arthur. *Disintegrating the Musical: Black Performance and American Musical Film.* Durham, N.C.: Duke University Press, 2002.

Kumar, Krishan. *Prophecy and Progress: The Sociology of Industrial and Post-Industrial Society.* London: Penguin, 1978.

"Labour Market Trends and Globalization's Impact on Them." *International Labour Organization: Bureau for Workers' Activities.* 2006. Available: http://www.itcilo.it/english/actrav/telearn/global/ilo/seura/mains.htm.

Lack, Russell. *Twenty Four Frames Under: A Buried History of Film Music.* London: Quartet, 1997.

Landis, Paul H. *Understanding Teen-Agers.* New York: Appleton-Century-Crofts, 1955.

Larson, Randall. "Riz Ortolani: *Cannibal Holocaust.*" *Music from the Movies* 47 (2005): 71–72.

Larson, Randall D. *Musique Fantastique: A Survey of Film Music in the Fantastic Cinema.* London: Scarecrow, 1985.

La Salle, Mick. "*Swept Away* Goes Way Off Course." *San Francisco Chronicle,* 11 October 2002. Available: http://www.sfgate.com/cgi-bin/article.cgi?f=/c/a/2002/10/11/DD88484.DTL.

Lash, Scott, and John Urry. *Economies of Signs and Space.* London: Sage, 1994.

———. *The End of Organized Capitalism.* Cambridge: Polity, 1987.

Latham, Robert. *Consuming Youth: Vampires, Cyborgs, and the Culture of Consumption.* Chicago: University of Chicago Press, 2002.

Lawson, Steven F. *Civil Rights Crossroads: Nation, Community, and the Black Freedom Struggle.* Lexington: University Press of Kentucky, 2003.

Leadbeater, Charles. *Living on Thin Air: The New Economy—with a New Blueprint for the 21st Century.* London: Penguin, 2000.

Lee-Potter, Linda. "Switch Off the Nasties." *Daily Mail,* 29 June 1983, 7.

Lhamon, W. T. *Deliberate Speed: The Origins of a Cultural Style in the American 1950s.* Cambridge, Mass.: Harvard University Press, 2002.

Link, Stan. "Sympathy with the Devil? Music of the Psycho Post-*Psycho.*" *Screen* 45/1 (Spring 2004): 1–20.

Lipsitz, George. *The Possessive Investment in Whiteness.* Philadelphia: Temple University Press, 1998.

———. *Time Passages: Collective Memory and American Popular Culture.* Minneapolis: University of Minnesota Press, 1990.

"Lisztomania." *The Creative Fire of Ken Russell.* Available: http://members.aol.com/ streettb/krussell/liszt.htm.

Littler, Jo. "Celebrity and 'Meritocracy.'" *Soundings: A Journal of Politics and Culture* 26 (Spring 2004): 118–130.

———. "Making Fame Ordinary: Intimacy, Reflexivity and 'Keeping It Real.'" *Mediactive* 2 (January 2004): 8–25.

Longstreth, Richard. *City Center to Regional Mall: Architecture, the Automobile, and Retailing in Los Angeles, 1920–1950.* Cambridge: MIT Press, 1997.

Lowry, Brian. "Freejack." *Variety,* 27 January 1992, 18.

Lull, James. *Inside Family Viewing.* London: Comedia Routledge, 1990.

Lyotard, Jean-François. *The Inhuman: Reflections on Time.* Trans. Geoffrey Bennington and Rachel Bowlby. Cambridge: Polity, 1991.

MacCabe, Colin. *The Eloquence of the Vulgar.* London: BFI, 1999.

MacCormack, Patricia. "Masochistic Cinesexuality: The Many Deaths of Giovanni Lombardo Radice." In *Alternative Europe: Eurotrash and Exploitation Cinema since 1945,* ed. Ernest Mathijs and Xavier Mendik (106–116). London: Wallflower, 2004.

MacDonald, Laurence E. *The Invisible Art of Film Music.* New York: Ardsley House, 1998.

Mangum, Garth L., and Stephen F. Seninger. *Coming of Age in the Ghetto: A Dilemma of Youth Unemployment: A Report to the Ford Foundation.* Baltimore, Md.: Johns Hopkins University Press, 1978.

Marable, Manning. *Race, Reform and Rebellion: The Second Reconstruction in Black America, 1945–1982.* London: Macmillan, 1984.

Marcus, Greil. *Dead Elvis.* Garden City, N.Y.: Doubleday, 1989.

Marshall, P. David. *Celebrity and Power: Fame in Contemporary Culture.* Minneapolis: University of Minnesota Press, 1997.

Martin, John. *The Seduction of the Gullible: The Curious History of the British "Video Nasties" Phenomenon.* Nottingham, UK: Procrustes, 1997.

Martin, Linda, and Kerry Segrave. *Anti-Rock: The Opposition to Rock 'n' Roll.* Hamden, Conn.: Archon, 1988.

Marx, Karl. *Capital.* Vol. 1. Trans. Ben Fowkes. London: Penguin with *New Left Review,* 1990.

———. *Economic and Philosophic Manuscripts of 1844.* London: Lawrence and Wishart, 1959.

———. *The Poverty of Philosophy.* Trans. Harry Quelch. London: Twentieth Century, 1900.

Marx, Karl, and Friedrich Engels. *The Marx-Engels Reader.* 2nd ed. Ed. Robert C.
   Tucker. New York: Norton , 1978.

Maslin, Janet. "Scurrying Back in Time in Search of a Healthy Body." *New York Times,*
   18 January 1992. Available: http://movies.nytimes.com/movie/review?_
   r=1&res=9E0CE7DC1E38F93BA25752C0A964958260&oref=slogin.

Massey, Douglas S., and Nancy A. Denton. *American Apartheid: Segregation and the Making
   of the Underclass.* Cambridge, Mass.: Harvard University Press, 1993.

May, Trevor. *An Economic and Social History of Britain, 1790–1990.* 2nd ed. Harlow, UK:
   Longman, 1996.

McCarthy, Todd, and Charles Flynn, eds. *King of the Bs: Working within the Hollywood
   System: An Anthology of Film and History Criticism.* New York: Dutton, 1975.

McDonagh, Maitland. *Broken Mirrors/Broken Minds: The Dark Dreams of Dario Argento.*
   London: Sun Tavern Fields, 1991.

McDonald, Paul. "Film Acting." In *The Oxford Guide to Film Studies,* ed. John Hill and
   Pamela Church Gibson (30–35). Oxford: Oxford University Press, 1998.

McGuigan, Jim. *Culture and the Public Sphere.* London: Routledge, 1996.

McKercher, Catherine. *Newsworkers Unite: Labor, Convergence, and Northern American
   Newspapers.* Lanham, Md.: Rowman and Littlefield, 2002.

McRobbie, Angela. "Clubs to Companies: Notes on the Decline of Political Culture in
   the Speeded Up Creative Worlds." *Cultural Studies* 16/4 (1 July 2002): 515–531.

Medovoi, Leerom. *Rebels: Youth and the Cold War Origins of Identity.* Durham, N.C.: Duke
   University Press, 2005.

Mellencamp, Patricia. *A Fine Romance: Five Ages of Film Feminism.* Philadelphia: Temple
   University Press, 1995.

Messenger, Cory. "Act Naturally: Elvis Presley, the Beatles and 'Rocksploitation.'"
   Screening the Past 18 (29 July 2005). Available: http://www.latrobe.edu.au/
   screeningthepast/firstrelease/fr_18/CMfr18a.html.

Metz, Christian. "The Imaginary Signifier." Trans. Ben Brewster. *Screen* 16/2 (Summer
   1975): 14–76.

Miles, Tim. "Fury over the Video Rapist." *Daily Mail,* 28 June 1983, 1–2.

———. "The Men Who Grow Rich on Bloodlust." *Daily Mail,* 4 August 1983, 18–19.

———. "Rape of Young Minds." *Daily Mail,* 24 November 1983, 11.

Millward, Neil. *The New Industrial Relations.* London: PSI, 1994.

Modell, John. *Into One's Own: From Youth to Adulthood in the United States, 1920–1975.*
   Berkeley: University of California Press, 1989.

Moore-Gilbert, Bart, ed. *The Arts in the 1970s: Cultural Closure.* London: Routledge, 1994.

More, Charles. *The Industrial Age: Economy and Society in Britain, 1750–1995.* 2nd ed.
   London: Longon, 1997.

Morley, David. *Family Television: Cultural Power and Domestic Leisure.* London: Comedia,
   1986.

Mulvey, Laura. "Visual Pleasure and Narrative Cinema." *Screen* 16/3 (1975): 6–18.

Mundy, John. *Popular Music on Screen: From Hollywood Musical to Music Video.* Manchester,
   UK: Manchester University Press, 1999.

Murphy, A. D. "Lisztomania." *Variety,* 15 October 1975, 26.

Myerscough, John. *Facts about the Arts 2.* London: Policy Studies Institute, 1986.

Naremore, James. *Acting in the Cinema.* Berkeley: University of California Press, 1988.

Needham, Gary. "Progressive Shock! An Introduction to the Sound of Goblin." Unpublished manuscript.

Negus, Keith, and Michael Pickering. *Creativity, Communication and Cultural Value.* London: Sage, 2004.

Neighbour, Richard. "Hooking of the Video Junkies." *Daily Mail,* 13 August 1983, 6.

Newman, Kim. "Freejack." *Sight and Sound* 2/1 (May 1992): 49–50.

———. *Nightmare Movies: The New Edition.* London: Bloomsbury, 1988.

Office of National Statistics. *Labour Force Survey: Employment Rates by Age (1971–2007).* (2007) 18 Aug. 2007. http://www.statistics.gov.uk/STATBASE/expodata/files/862046511.csv.

Olson, Mancur. *The Rise and Decline of Nations: Economic Growth, Stagflation, and Social Rigidities.* New Haven, Conn.: Yale University Press, 1982.

Palladino, Grace. *Teenagers: An American History.* New York: Basic, 1996.

Park, James. *British Cinema: The Lights That Failed.* London: Batsford, 1990.

Parliamentary Debates: Commons 48 (7–18 November 1983): 521–580.

Parliamentary Debates: Commons 56 (12–23 March 1984): 610–674.

Pattison, Robert. *The Triumph of Vulgarity: Rock Music in the Mirror of Romanticism.* Oxford: Oxford University Press, 1987.

Paul, G. A. "Letter." *Film and Filming* 22 (December 1975): 4.

Payne, Stewart, and Bryan Carter. "Video Shares Shock: Miners' Pension Fund Bought into Film Supplying Nasties." *Daily Mail,* 4 July 1983, 2.

Peters, Ann K., and Muriel G. Cantor. "Screen Acting as Work." In *Individuals in Mass Communication Organisations,* ed. James S. Ettema and D. Charles Whitney (53–67). Beverly Hills, Calif.: Sage, 1982.

Petley, Julian. "The Beyond." *Films and Filming* 328 (January 1982): 37–38.

Phillips, Gene D. "Fact, Fantasy, and the Films of Ken Russell." *Journal of Popular Film* 5/3–4 (1976): 200–210.

———. *Ken Russell.* Boston: Twayne, 1979.

Pinch, Trevor, and Frank Trocco. *Analog Days: The Invention and Impact of the Moog Synthesizer.* Cambridge, Mass.: Harvard University Press, 2002.

Piore, Michael, and Charles Sabel. *The Second Industrial Divide: Possibilities for Prosperity.* New York: Basic, 1984.

Pollock, Griselda. "Artists, Mythologies and Media Genius, Madness and Art History." In *Picture This: Media Representations of Visual Art and Artists,* ed. Philip Hayward (75–114). London: John Libbey, 1988.

Pomerance, Murray, ed. *American Cinema of the 1950s.* Oxford: Berg, 2006.

Prendergast, Roy M. *Film Music: A Neglected Art.* New York: Norton, 1992.

Presley, Priscilla, with Sandra Harmon. *Elvis and Me.* London: Century, 1985.

Previn, André. "André Previn Meets Ken Russell." *Listener* 19 (September 1974): 367.

Rabinowitz, Paula. "Commodity Fetishism: Women in *Gold Diggers of 1933*," *Film Reader* 5 (1982): 141–149.

"Rape of Our Children's Minds." *Daily Mail,* 30 June 1983, 6.

Reay, Pauline. *Music in Film: Soundtracks and Synergy.* London: Wallflower, 2004.

Renowden, Gareth. "The Secret Video Show." *Daily Mail,* 12 May 1982, 12.

Rhines, Jesse Algernon. *Black Film / White Money.* New Brunswick, N.J.: Rutgers University Press, 1996.

Rifkin, Jeremy. *The End of Work: The Decline of the Global Work-Force and the Dawn of the Post-Market Era.* London: Penguin, 2000.

Roberts, Ken. *The Leisure Industries.* Basingstoke, UK: Palgrave Macmillan, 2004.

Robertson, D. J., and L. C. Hunter, eds. *Labour Market Issues in the 1970s.* Edinburgh: Oliver and Boyd, 1970.

Romney, Jonathan, and Adrian Wootton, eds. *Celluloid Jukebox: Popular Music and the Movies since the 50s.* London: BFI, 1995.

Rose, Nikolas. *Governing the Soul: The Shaping of the Private Self.* London: Routledge, 1991.

Rose, Tony. "Other Peoples [*sic*] Pictures." *Movie Maker* 5/5 (May 1971): 300–303.

Rosen, Charles. *The Romantic Generation.* London: HarperCollins, 1995.

Rosenfeldt, Diane. *Ken Russell: A Guide to Reference Sources.* Boston: Hall, 1978.

Rosenstone, Robert A. *Visions of the Past: The Challenge of Film to Our Idea of History.* Cambridge, Mass.: Harvard University Press, 1995.

Rosolato, Guy. "La voix: Entre corps et langage." *Revue française de psychanalyse* 38/1 (1974): 75.

Royle, Nicholas, ed. *Deconstruction: A User's Guide.* Basingstoke, UK: Palgrave, 2000.

Russell, Ken. *A British Picture: An Autobiography.* London: Heinemann, 1989.

Sabel, Charles F. *Work and Politics: The Division of Labor in Industry.* Cambridge: Cambridge University Press, 1982.

Sandahl, Linda J. *Encyclopedia of Rock Music on Film: A Viewer's Guide to Three Decades of Musicals, Concerts, Documentaries and Soundtracks, 1955–1986.* Poole, UK: Blandford, 1987.

Sanders, Don, and Susan M. Sanders. *The American Drive-In Movie Theater.* Sparkford, UK: Hanes, 2003.

Schaefer, Eric. *"Bold! Daring! Shocking! True!" A History of Exploitation Films, 1919–1959.* Durham, N.C.: Duke University Press, 1999.

Scheib, Richard. "Freejack." *Fortune City.* 1997. Available: http://members.fortunecity.com/roogulator/sf/freejack.htm.

Schopenhauer, Arthur. *The World as Will and Representation.* Trans. E. F. G. Payne. New York: Dover, 1969.

Schwichtenberg, Cathy, ed. *The Madonna Connection: Representational Politics, Subcultural Identities, and Cultural Theory.* Boulder, Colo.: Westview, 1993.

Sconce, Jeffrey. *Haunted Media: Electronic Presence from Telegraphy to Television.* Durham, N.C.: Duke University Press, 2000.

———. "Spectacles of Death: Identification, Reflexivity and Contemporary Horror." In *Film Theory Goes to the Movies,* ed. Jim Collins, Hilary Radner, and Ava Preacher Collings (103–119). London: Routledge, 1993.

———. "'Trashing' the Academy: Taste, Excess, and an Emerging Politics of Cinematic Style." *Screen* 36/4 (1995): 371–393.

Scott, A. O. "No Madonna Is an Island." *New York Times,* 11 October 2002. Available: http://movies.nytimes.com/movie/review?res=9D05E7DA173AF932A25753C1 A9649C8B63

Segal, David. "Elvis: One for the Money." *Washington Post,* 30 December 2004, C1.

Segrave, Kerry. *Drive-In Theaters: A History from Their Inception in 1933.* Jefferson, N.C.: McFarland, 1992.

———. *Jukeboxes: An American Social History.* Jefferson, N.C.: McFarland, 2002.

Sennett, Richard. *The Corrosion of Character: The Personal Consequences of Work in the New Capitalism.* New York: Norton, 1998.

Shapiro, Peter, ed. *Modulations: A History of Electronic Music: Throbbing Words in Sound.* New York: Caipirinha, 2000.

Sheldrake, John. *Industrial Relations and Politics in Britain, 1880–1989.* London: Pinter, 1991.

Shives, William. "Jumping Freejack Flash, It's a Gas, Gas, Gas . . . ," 23 July 2000. Available: http://www.epinions.com/mvie-review-79C7–1F30EDBA-397ACA09-prod5.

Showler, Brian, and Adrian Sinfield, eds. *The Workless State.* Oxford: Martin Robertson, 1981.

Silverman, Kaja. *The Acoustic Mirror: The Female Voice in Psychoanalysis and Cinema.* Bloomington and Indianapolis: Indiana University Press, 1988.

Silverstone, Roger. *Television and Everyday Life.* London: Routledge, 1994.

Simpson, Paul. "What Was Elvis' Worst Film?" *Elvis Information Network.* Available: http://www.elvisinfonet.com/worstfilm.html.

Smith, Chris. *Creative Britain.* London: Faber and Faber, 1998.

Smith, Jeff. "Movie Music as Moving Music: Emotion, Cognition, and the Film Score." In *Passionate Views: Film, Cognition, and Emotion,* ed. Carl Plantinga and Greg M. Smith (146–167). Baltimore, Md., and London: Johns Hopkins University Press, 1999.

———. *The Sounds of Commerce: Marketing Popular Film Music.* New York: Columbia University Press, 1998.

Smith, Tony. *Dialectical Social Theory and Its Critics: From Hegel to Analytical Marxism and Postmodernism.* Albany: State University of New York Press, 1993.

Snead, James. *White Screen, Black Images: Hollywood from the Dark Side.* London: Routledge, 1994.

Squier, Susan Merrill, ed. *Communities of the Air: Radio Century, Radio Culture.* Durham, N.C.: Duke University Press, 2003.

Stahl, Matthew. "Authentic Boy Bands on TV? Performers and Impresarios in *The Monkees* and *Making the Band*." *Popular Music* 21/3 (October 2002): 307–329.

Stewart, Jacqueline Najuma. *Migrations to the Movies: Cinema and Black Urban Modernity.* Berkeley: California University Press, 2005.

Storper, Michael, and Susan Christopherson. *The Changing Organization and Location of the Motion Picture Industry.* Los Angeles: Graduate School of Architecture and Urban Planning, University of California, 1985.

Street, Sarah. *British National Cinema.* London: Routledge, 1997.

Strinati, Dominic. *Capitalism, the State and Industrial Relations.* London: Croom Helm, 1982.

Tasker, Yvonne. *Working Girls: Gender and Sexuality in Popular Cinema.* London: Routledge, 1998.

Teitelbaum, Matthew, ed. *Montage and Modern Life, 1919–1942.* Cambridge, Mass., and London: MIT Press, 1992.

Théberge, Paul. *Any Sound You Can Imagine: Making Music/Consuming Technology.* Hanover, Conn.: Wesleyan University Press, 1997.

Therborn, Göran. *Why Some Peoples Are More Unemployed than Others: The Strange Paradox of Growth and Unemployment.* London: Verso, 1986.

Thomas, Tony. *Music for the Movies.* New York: Barnes, 1973.

Thomas, Tony, ed. *Film Score: The View from the Podium.* New York: Barnes, 1979.

Thompson, E. P. *The Making of the English Working Class.* New York: Pantheon, 1963.

Thompson, Kenneth, ed. *Work, Employment and Unemployment: Perspectives on Work and Society.* Milton Keynes, UK: Open University Press, 1984.

Thornton, Sarah. *Club Cultures: Music, Media and Subcultural Capital.* London: Routledge, 1996.

Throsby, David. *Economics and Culture.* Cambridge: Cambridge University Press, 2001.

Tibbetts, John C. *Composers in the Movies: Studies in Musical Biography.* New Haven, Conn.: Yale University Press, 2005.

Tilly, Charles. "Race and Migration to the American City." In *The Metropolitan Enigma: Inquiries into the Nature and Dimensions of America's "Urban Crisis,"* ed. James Q. Wilson (135–157). Cambridge, Mass.: Harvard University Press, 1968.

Timm, Larry M. *The Soul of Cinema: An Appreciation of Film Music.* Needham Heights, Mass.: Simon and Schuster, 1998.

Tinkcom, Matthew. *Working Like a Homosexual: Camp, Capital, Cinema.* Durham, N.C.: Duke University Press, 2002.

Tohill, Cathal, and Pete Tombs. *Immoral Tales: Sex and Horror Cinema in Europe, 1956–1984.* New York: St. Martin's, 1995.

Toynbee, Jason. *Making Popular Music: Musicians, Creativity and Institutions.* London: Hodder Headline Group, 2000.

Trade Union Research Unit. *Labour Market Issues. No. 5: The Flexible Firm and the Shape of Jobs to Come.* Oxford: Trade Union Research Unit, 1984.

Tunstall, Jeremy, ed. *Media Occupations and Professions.* Oxford: Oxford University Press, 2001.

Valentine, Maggie. *The Show Starts on the Sidewalk: An Architectural History of the Movie Theatre, Starring S. Charles Lee.* New Haven, Conn.: Yale University Press, 1994.

Vellenga, Dirk, with Mick Farren. *Elvis and the Colonel.* London: Grafton, 1989.

Vidal, Belén. "Feminist Historiographies and the Woman Artist's Biopic: The Case of *Artemisia*." *Screen* 48/1 (Spring 2007): 69–90.

"Video Sadists and Respectable Dupes." *Daily Mail*, 4 July 1983, 6.

"Video Violence." *Times*, 5 November 1983, 9.

Virno, Paolo. *A Grammar of the Multitude: For an Analysis of Contemporary Forms of Life.* Trans. Isabella Bertoletti, James Cascaito, and Andrea Casson. New York: Semiotext(e), 2004.

Waddell, Calum. "*Cannibal Holocaust:* Surviving the Jungle." *Fangoria* 248 (November 2005): 16.

Walker, Alexander. *National Heroes: British Cinema in the Seventies and Eighties.* London: Harrap, 1985.

Waller, Gregory A., ed. *Moviegoing in America: A Sourcebook in the History of Film Exhibition.* Oxford: Blackwell, 2002.

Ward, Brian. *Just My Soul Responding: Rhythm and Blues, Black Consciousness and Race Relations.* London: UCL Press, 1998.

————. *Radio and the Struggle for Civil Rights in the South.* Gainesville: University Press of Florida, 2004.

Watson, Tony J. *Sociology, Work and Industry.* London: Routledge, 1995.

Weber, Max. *The Protestant Ethic and the Spirit of Capitalism.* Trans. Stephen Kalberg. Oxford: Blackwell, 2002.

Weems, Robert E. *Desegregating the Dollar: African American Consumerism in the Twentieth Century.* New York: New York University Press, 1998.

Weis, Elisabeth, and John Belton, eds. *Film Sound: Theory and Practice.* New York: Columbia University Press, 1985.

Wiegman, Robyn. *American Anatomies: Theorizing Race and Gender.* Durham, N.C.: Duke University Press, 1995.

Williams, Howard. *Hegel, Heraclitus and Marx's Dialectic.* New York: Harvester Wheatsheaf, 1989.

Williams, Justin. "Ken Russell and the Romantic Artist: Studies in Musical Biography and 'Absolute Music'/Image Interaction in Film." Master's thesis, King's College, University of London, 2005.

Williams, Raymond. *Culture and Society, 1780–1950.* Harmondsworth, UK: Penguin, 1958.

Wilsher, Peter. "The Wasting Generation." *Sunday Times*, 5 September 1982, 14–15.

Wojcik, Pamela Robertson, and Arthur Knight, eds. *Soundtrack Available: Essays on Film and Popular Music.* Durham, N.C.: Duke University Press, 2001.

Young, Jock. *The Exclusive Society.* London: Sage, 1999.

Young, Lola. *Fear of the Dark: "Race," Gender and Sexuality in the Cinema.* London: Routledge, 1996.

Zabalza, A., and Z. Tzannatos. *The Effect of Britain's Anti-Discriminatory Legislation on Relative Pay and Employment.* London: Centre for Labour Economics, London School of Economics, 1983.

Zmijewsky, Steven, and Boris Zmijewsky. *Elvis: The Films and Career of Elvis Presley.* New York: Citadel, 1991.

Index

Adorno, Theodor, 18–20, 72–73, 103, 164, 166
African American musicians
    and rock 'n' roll, 34–35, 38, 45
    and rock 'n' roll movies, 46, 57–58, 71–72
    as workers, 47
AIP (American International Pictures), 58, 59
Altman, Rick, 28
Amadeus (Forman), 99, 101
Anzieu, Didier, 16
Argento, Dario, 151
    Inferno, 119, 127, 150
    Tenebrae, 119, 128, 150
Arts Council, The (UK), 112, 113, 114, 142
ASCAP (American Society of Composers,
    Authors and Publishers), 51, 53
Avila, Eric, 48

Badham, Richard J., 160
Baldwin, James, 75
Baraka, Amiri. *See* Jones, LeRoi
Bauman, Zygmunt, 166–70, 173, 187, 188, 194
Belafonte, Harry, 77
Bell, David, 98

Berry, Chuck, 9, 66
    "You Can't Catch Me" (*Rock, Rock, Rock*),
    69–70
Beynon, Huw, 25, 162
Beyond, The (Fulci), 119, 125, 146, 150
Blackboard Jungle, The (Brooks), 45
Blonksteiner, Alexander, 127
BMI (Broadcast Music, Inc.), 51
Bogel, Donald, 45
Boone, Pat, 58
Bourdieu, Pierre, 98, 110
Brzezinski, Zbigniew, 86

Cabin in the Sky (Minnelli), 46
Callaghan, James, 93
Calloway, Cab, 46
camp, 14, 193
    and Russell, 103, 116–17, 153, 167
Cannibal Apocalypse (Margheriti), 119, 127, 139,
    146, 150
Cannibal Ferox (Lenzi), 119, 126, 146
Cannibal Holocaust (Deodato), 119, 126, 128,
    149, 150

Index